The Sexual Contract

The Sexual Contract

Carole Pateman

Stanford University Press
Stanford, California
1988

Stanford University Press
Stanford, California
© 1988 Carole Pateman
Originating publisher: Polity Press, Cambridge
  in association with Basil Blackwell, Oxford
First published in the U.S.A. by
  Stanford University Press, 1988
Printed in Great Britain
Cloth ISBN 0-8047-1476-2
Paper ISBN 0-8047-1477-0
LC 87-63007

In memory of my father
Ronald Bennett

A ring of gold with the sun in it?
Lies, lies and a grief

      Sylvia Plath *The Couriers*

. . . the man remains
Sceptreless, free, uncircumscribed, but man
Equal, unclassed, tribeless, and nationless,
Exempt from awe, worship, degree, the king
Over himself;

      Percy Bysshe Shelley *Prometheus Unbound*

Contents

Preface

There has been a major revival of interest in contract theory since the early 1970s that shows no immediate signs of abating. New, sophisticated formulations of the idea of a social contract are accompanied by some highly technical and, in many cases, very elegant developments of contract argument, some of which are presented by Marxists, once firm opponents of the theoretical assumptions and practical implications of contract doctrine. My reason for adding a very different contribution to the literature is that something vital is missing from the current discussion. The sexual contract is never mentioned. The sexual contract is a repressed dimension of contract theory, an integral part of the rational choice of the familiar, original agreement. The original contract as typically understood today is only part of the act of political genesis depicted in the pages of the classic contract theorists of the seventeenth and eighteenth centuries. The aim of my study is to begin to break through the layers of theoretical self-censorship.

In one sense, this is an auspicious moment to write about the sexual contract. The extraordinarily widespread influence of contract doctrine means that the full ramifications of contract can now be glimpsed. In another sense, the moment is inauspicious; the very influence of contract theory threatens to bury the sexual contract more deeply than before and further to marginalize feminist argument critical of contract. That contract theory now has a new lease of life is not merely a consequence of the internal evolution of political theory but bound up with wider political developments centred on an interpretation of democracy as individual initiative (or choice), which can be summed up succinctly in the slogans of private enterprise and privatization. The whole political package is marketed under the name of freedom. Sales (at least until late 1987) have been spectacularly successful, with buyers coming from regions once resistant to such political advertisements. The old socialist arguments against contract have lost much of their cogency in the present political context and, if new forms of criticism are to be developed, a new look at contract theory is required. Contract theory is concerned with more than fictions of original agreements; contract theorists claim to show how major political institutions should properly be understood. Citizenship, employment and marriage are all contractual, but since they are seen through the lens of a drastically truncated contract theory – indeed, a theory that has literally been emasculated – the social contract and the employment contract are systematically misrepresented and the marriage contract is usually ignored.

I became aware that the social contract presupposed the sexual contract, and that civil freedom presupposed patriarchal right, only after several years' work on classical contract theory and associated theoretical and practical problems of consent. I was interested initially in political obligation and although my conclusions on that subject (published in _The Problem of Political Obligation_) diverged from many accounts, my argument largely remained within conventional boundaries. My discussion began to push against the confines of social contract theory by noting that the classic theorists had left a legacy of problems about women's incorporation into, and obligation within, civil society that contemporary arguments failed to acknowledge. I began to appreciate the depth and character of the failure only when I asked specifically feminist questions about the texts and about actual examples of contractual relations, instead of trying to deal with the problem of women's incorporation from within mainstream political theory. Conventional approaches cannot show why the problem is so persistent and intractable, or why the critics as well as the advocates of contract cannot take feminism seriously without undermining their construction of the 'political' and 'political' relations.

Some of my arguments have been prompted by writers customarily labelled radical feminists, but the classification of feminists into radicals, liberals and socialists suggests that feminism is always secondary, a supplement to other doctrines. Feminism, like socialism, is implicated to some degree in contract and, despite controversy for more than a decade among feminists about the concept of patriarchy, remarkably little attention has been paid to the contractual character of modern patriarchy. Nonetheless, my deepest intellectual debt is to the arguments and activities of the feminist movement, which has transformed my view both of political theory and of political life.

This book has been some years in the making and has benefited from many conversations, often on apparently unrelated topics, and discussions of papers and lectures in Australia and the United States, and I am grateful to all the participants. The writing was less protracted. I decided to attempt to draw together one strand of my work, and I wrote drafts of some of the material, while I was a Fellow at the Center for Advanced Study in the Behavioral Sciences at Stanford in 1984–5. I was fortunate to have such exceptionally congenial intellectual and physical surroundings and the assistance of the friendly, efficient staff while I was trying to get my thoughts in order. I was just as fortunate during 1986–7 when I was a Member of the School of Social Science at the Institute for Advanced Study at Princeton. At the Institute, I was in a very different but exceptionally tranquil yet stimulating intellectual environment. The whole of the present text was written in the private affluence of the Institute for Advanced Study, except for the final chapter, which was completed amid the public stringency of the University of Sydney.

I am especially grateful to Joan Scott for reading and commenting on chapters 1 to 4, to Itsie Hull for detailed comments on chapter 5 and to both of them and Giovanna Procacci for our lunch-time discussions of my work. I also owe thanks to Sandy Levinson for assistance with legal questions. I owe a different kind of debt to Maria Vigilante for relieving me of many of the tedious tasks associated with writing a book and for her critical enthusiasm, and to Peg Clarke and Lucille Allsen without whom, in this case, the book could not have been written. Their skills, acts of supererogation and cheerfulness in the face of a mess of sinister longhand and ill-typed pages rescued me and the book from a recurrence of repetitive strain injury. My husband transferred chapter 8 and this Preface to the computer and, once again, has given support to my academic work and has been an acute critic. I should also like to thank David Held for his encouragement and exemplary editorial efficiency.

1

Contracting In

Telling stories of all kinds is the major way that human beings have endeavoured to make sense of themselves and their social world. The most famous and influential political story of modern times is found in the writings of the social contract theorists. The story, or conjectural history, tells how a new civil society and a new form of political right is created through an original contract. An explanation for the binding authority of the state and civil law, and for the legitimacy of modern civil government is to be found by treating our society as if it had originated in a contract. The attraction of the idea of an original contract and of contract theory in a more general sense, a theory that claims that free social relations take a contractual form, is probably greater now than at any time since the seventeenth and eighteenth centuries when the classic writers told their tales. But today, invariably, only half the story is told. We hear an enormous amount about the *social* contract; a deep silence is maintained about the *sexual* contract.

The original contract is a sexual-social pact, but the story of the sexual contract has been repressed. Standard accounts of social contract theory do not discuss the whole story and contemporary contract theorists give no indication that half the agreement is missing. The story of the sexual contract is also about the genesis of political right, and explains why exercise of the right is legitimate – but this story is about political right as *patriarchal right* or sex-right, the power that men exercise over women. The missing half of the story tells how a specifically modern form of patriarchy is established. The new civil society created through the original contract is a patriarchal social order.

Social contract theory is conventionally presented as a story about freedom. One interpretation of the original contract is that the inhabitants of the state of nature exchange the insecurities of natural freedom for equal, civil freedom which is protected by the state. In civil society freedom is universal; all adults enjoy the same civil standing and can exercise their freedom by, as it were, replicating the original contract when, for example, they enter into the employment contract or the marriage contract. Another inter-pretation, which takes into account conjectural histories of the state of nature in the classic texts, is that freedom is won by sons who cast off their natural subjection to their fathers and replace paternal rule by civil government. Political right as paternal right is inconsistent with modern civil society. In this version of the story, civil society is created through the original contract after paternal rule – or patriarchy – is overthrown. The new civil order, therefore, appears to be anti-patriarchal or post-patriarchal. Civil society is created through contract so that contract and patriarchy appear to be irrevocably opposed.

These familiar readings of the classic stories fail to mention that a good deal more than freedom is at stake. Men's domination over women, and the right of men to enjoy equal sexual access to women, is at issue in the making of the original pact. The social contract is a story of freedom; the sexual contract is a story of subjection. The original contract constitutes both freedom and domination. Men's freedom and women's subjection are created through the original contract – and the character of civil freedom cannot be understood without the missing half of the story that reveals how men's patri-archal right over women is established through contract. Civil freedom is not universal. Civil freedom is a masculine attribute and depends upon patriarchal right. The sons overturn paternal rule not merely to gain their liberty but to secure women for themselves. Their success in this endeavour is chronicled in the story of the sexual contract. The original pact is a sexual as well as a social contract: it is sexual in the sense of patriarchal – that is, the contract establishes men's political right over women – and also sexual in the sense of establishing orderly access by men to women's bodies. The original contract creates what I shall call, following Adrienne Rich, 'the law of male sex-right'.[1] Contract is far from being opposed to patriarchy; contract is the means through which modern patriarchy is constituted.

One reason why political theorists so rarely notice that half the story of the original contract is missing, or that civil society is patriarchal, is that 'patriarchy' is usually interpreted patriarchally as paternal rule (the literal meaning of the term). So, for example, in the standard reading of the theoretical battle in the seventeenth century between the patriarchalists and social contract theorists, patriarchy is assumed to refer only to paternal right. Sir Robert Filmer claimed that political power was paternal power and that the procreative power of the father was the origin of political right. Locke and his fellow contract theorists insisted that paternal and political power were not the same and that contract was the genesis of political right. The contract theorists were victorious on this point; the standard interpretation is on firm ground – as far as it goes. Once more, a crucial portion of the story is missing. The true origin of political right is overlooked in this interpretation; no stories are told about its genesis (I attempt to remedy the omission in chapter 4). Political right originates in sex-right or conjugal right. Paternal right is only one, and not the original, dimension of patriarchal power. A man's power as a father comes after he has exercised the patriarchal right of a man (a husband) over a woman (wife). The contract theorists had no wish to challenge the original patriarchal right in their onslaught on paternal right. Instead, they incorporated conjugal right into their theories and, in so doing, transformed the law of male sex-right into its modern contractual form. Patriarchy ceased to be paternal long ago. Modern civil society is not structured by kinship and the power of fathers; in the modern world, women are subordinated to men *as men*, or to men as a fraternity. The original contract takes place after the political defeat of the father and creates modern *fraternal patriarchy*.

Another reason for the omission of the story of the sexual contract is that conventional approaches to the classic texts, whether those of mainstream political theorists or their socialist critics, give a misleading picture of a distinctive feature of the civil society created through the original pact. Patriarchal civil society is divided into two spheres, but attention is directed to one sphere only. The story of the social contract is treated as an account of the creation of the public sphere of civil freedom. The other, private, sphere is not seen as politically relevant. Marriage and the marriage contract are, therefore, also deemed politically irrelevant. To ignore the marriage contract is to ignore half the original contract. In the classic texts,

as I shall show in some detail, the sexual contract is displaced
onto the marriage contract. The displacement creates a difficulty
in retrieving and recounting the lost story. All too easily, the
impression can be given that the sexual contract and the social
contract are two separate, albeit related, contracts, and that the
sexual contract concerns the private sphere. Patriarchy then appears
to have no relevance to the public world. On the contrary, patriarchal right extends throughout civil society. The employment
contract and (what I shall call) the prostitution contract, both of
which are entered into in the public, capitalist market, uphold men's
right as firmly as the marriage contract. The two spheres of civil
society are at once separate and inseparable. The public realm
cannot be fully understood in the absence of the private sphere, and,
similarly, the meaning of the original contract is misinterpreted
without both, mutually dependent, halves of the story. Civil freedom
depends on patriarchal right.

My interest in the sexual contract is not primarily in interpreting
texts, although the classic works of social contract theory figure
largely in my discussion. I am resurrecting the story in order to
throw light onto the present-day structure of major social institutions
in Britain, Australia and the United States – societies which, we are
told, can properly be seen as if they had originated in a social
contract. The sense in which these societies are patriarchal can be
elucidated through the full story of the original contract; they have
enough in common historically and culturally to enable the same
story to be told (and many of my general arguments will also be
relevant to other developed Western countries). The manner in
which patriarchal domination differs from other forms of domination
in the late twentieth century becomes much clearer once the sexual
contract has been retrieved from oblivion. The connection between
patriarchy and contract has been little explored, even by feminists,
despite the fact that, in modern civil society, crucially important
institutions are constituted and maintained through contract.

The relationship between employer and worker is contractual,
and for many contract theorists the employment contract is the
exemplary contract. Marriage also begins in a contract. Feminists
have been greatly concerned with the marriage contract but their
writings and activities have been ignored for the most part, even by
most socialist critics of contract theory and the employment contract
who might have been expected to be keenly interested in feminist

arguments. (Except where specified, I shall use 'socialist' very broadly to include Marxists, social democrats, anarchists and so on.) In addition to the marriage and employment contracts, I shall also examine the contract between prostitute and client and have something to say about the slave contract (or, more precisely, as I shall discuss in chapter 3, what should be called the civil slave contract). At the end of chapter 7, I shall look at a more recent development, the contract entered by the so-called surrogate mother. These contracts are either regulated or prohibited by law and I shall touch upon the legal standing of parties to the contracts at various points in my discussion. I am not, however, writing about contract law. My concern is with contract as a principle of social association and one of the most important means of creating social relationships, such as the relation between husband and wife or capitalist and worker. Nor is my argument about property in the sense in which 'property' commonly enters into discussions of contract theory. Proponents and critics of contract theory tend to concentrate on property either as material goods, land and capital, or as the interest (the property) that individuals can be said to have in civil freedom. The subject of all the contracts with which I am concerned is a very special kind of property, the property that individuals are held to own in their persons.

Some knowledge of the story of the sexual contract helps explain why singular problems arise about contracts to which women are a party. The problems are never mentioned in most discussions of the classic texts or by contemporary contract theorists. Feminists have been pointing out the peculiarities of the marriage contract for at least a century and a half, but to no avail. The standard commentaries on the classic stories of the original contract do not usually mention that women are *excluded* from the original pact. Men make the original contract. The device of the state of nature is used to explain why, given the characteristics of the inhabitants of the natural condition, entry into the original contract is a rational act. The crucial point that is omitted is that the inhabitants are sexually differentiated and, for all the classic writers (except Hobbes), a difference in rationality follows from natural sexual difference. Commentaries on the texts gloss over the fact that the classic theorists construct a patriarchal account of masculinity and femininity, of what it is to be men and women. Only masculine beings are endowed with the attributes and capacities necessary to enter into contracts, the most important of which is ownership of property in the person; only men, that is to say, are 'individuals'.

In the natural condition 'all men are born free' and are equal to each other; they are 'individuals'. This presupposition of contract doctrine generates a profound problem: how in such a condition can the government of one man by another ever be legitimate; how can political right exist? Only one answer is possible without denying the initial assumption of freedom and equality. The relationship must arise through agreement and, for reasons which I shall explore in chapter 3, contract is seen as the paradigm of free agreement. But women are not born free; women have no natural freedom. The classic pictures of the state of nature also contain an order of subjection – between men and women. With the exception of Hobbes, the classic theorists claim that women naturally lack the attributes and capacities of 'individuals'. Sexual difference is political difference; sexual difference is the difference between freedom and subjection. Women are not party to the original contract through which men transform their natural freedom into the security of civil freedom. Women are the subject of the contract. The (sexual) contract is the vehicle through which men transform their natural right over women into the security of civil patriarchal right. But if women have no part in the original contract, if they can have no part, why do the classic social contract theorists (again with the exception of Hobbes) make marriage and the marriage contract part of the natural condition? How can beings who lack the capacities to make contracts nevertheless be supposed always to enter into this contract? Why, moreover, do all the classic theorists (including Hobbes) insist that, in civil society, women not only can but must enter into the marriage contract?

The construction of the difference between the sexes as the difference between freedom and subjection is not merely central to a famous political story. The structure of our society and our everyday lives incorporates the patriarchal conception of sexual difference. I shall show how the exclusion of women from the central category of the 'individual' has been given social and legal expression and how the exclusion has structured the contracts with which I am concerned. Despite many recent legal reforms and wider changes in the social position of women, we still do not have the same civil standing as men, yet this central political fact about our societies has rarely entered into contemporary discussions of contract theory and the practice of contract. Husbands no longer enjoy the extensive right over their wives that they possessed in the mid-nineteenth century when wives had the legal standing of property. But, in the 1980s, this aspect of conjugal subjection lingers on in legal jurisdictions that still refuse to admit any limitation to a husband's access to his wife's body and so deny that rape is possible within marriage. A common response is to dismiss this matter as of no relevance to *political* theorists and *political* activists. The possibility that women's standing in marriage may reflect much deeper problems about women and contract, or that the structure of the marriage contract may be very similar to other contracts, is thereby also dismissed from consideration. The refusal to admit that marital domination is politically significant obviates the need to consider whether there is any connection between the marriage contract and other contracts involving women.

Surprisingly little attention has been given to the connection between the original contract – which is generally agreed to be a political fiction – and actual contracts. The social contract, so the story goes, creates a society in which individuals can make contracts secure in the knowledge that their actions are regulated by civil law and that, if necessary, the state will enforce their agreements. Actual contracts thus appear to exemplify the freedom that individuals exercise when they make the original pact. According to contemporary contract theorists, social conditions are such that it is always reasonable for individuals to exercise their freedom and enter into the marriage contract or employment contract or even, according to some classic and contemporary writers, a (civil) slave contract. Another way of reading the story (as Rousseau saw) is that the social contract enables individuals voluntarily to subject themselves to the state and civil law; freedom becomes obedience and, in exchange, protection is provided. On this reading, the actual contracts of everyday life also mirror the original contract, but now they involve an exchange of obedience for protection; they create what I shall call *civil mastery* and *civil subordination*.

One reason why patriarchal domination and subordination has seldom received the attention it deserves is that *subordination* has all too often been a minor theme among critics of contract. A great deal of attention has been paid to the conditions under which contracts are entered into and to the question of exploitation once a contract has been made. Proponents of contract doctrine claim that contracts in everyday life match up well enough to the model of the original contract in which equal parties freely agree to the terms; actual contracts thus provide examples of individual freedom. Their critics, whether socialists concerned with the employment contract, or feminists concerned with the marriage contract or prostitution contract, have countered this claim by pointing to the often grossly unequal position of the relevant parties and to the economic and other constraints facing workers, wives and women in general. But concentration on coerced entry into contracts, important though this is, can obscure an important question; does contract immediately become attractive to feminists or socialists if entry is truly voluntary, without coercion?

Criticism has also been directed at exploitation, both in the technical Marxist sense of the extraction of surplus value and in the more popular sense that workers are not paid a fair wage for their labour and endure harsh working conditions, or that wives are not paid at all for their labour in the home, or that prostitutes are reviled and subject to physical violence. Again, exploitation is important, but the conjectural history of the origins of patriarchy contained in classic contract theory also directs attention to the creation of relations of domination and subordination. Since the seventeenth century, feminists have been well aware that wives are subordinate to their husbands but their criticism of (conjugal) domination is much less well known than socialist arguments that subsume subordination under exploitation. However, exploitation is possible precisely because, as I shall show, contracts about property in the person place right of command in the hands of one party to the contract. Capitalists can exploit workers and husbands can exploit wives because workers and wives are constituted as subordinates through the employment contract and the marriage contract. The genius of contract theorists has been to present both the original contract and actual contracts as exemplifying and securing individual freedom. On the contrary, in contract theory universal freedom is always an hypothesis, a story, a political fiction. Contract always generates political right in the form of relations of domination and subordination.

In 1919, G. D. H. Cole proclaimed that the wrong reply was usually given when people tried to answer the question of what was wrong with the capitalist organization of production; 'they would answer poverty [inequality], when they ought to answer slavery'.[2]

Cole exaggerated for polemical purposes. When individuals are juridically free and civil equals, the problem is not literally one of slavery; no one can, simultaneously, be human property and a citizen. However, Cole's point is that critics of capitalism – and contract – focus on exploitation (inequality) and thus overlook subordination, or the extent to which institutions held to be constituted by free relationships resemble that of master and slave. Rousseau criticized earlier contract theorists for advocating an original agreement that was tantamount to a slave contract. (I examined the question of the alienation of political power to representatives and the state, a matter central to the social contract, in *The Problem of Political Obligation*.) Rousseau is the only classic contract theorist who flatly rejects slavery and any contract – save the sexual contract – that bears a family resemblance to a slave contract. Differences between the classic writers become less important than their collective endorsement of patriarchy only from outside the confines of mainstream political theory. Patriarchal subordination is central to the theories of all the classic writers but has been almost entirely neglected by radical political theorists and activists (whether liberal or socialist, like G. D. H. Cole); feminist voices have gone unheeded.

The revival of the organized feminist movement from the late 1960s has also revived the term 'patriarchy'. There is no consensus about its meaning, and I shall examine the current feminist controversies in the next chapter. Debates about patriarchy are dogged by patriarchal interpretations, among the most important and persistent being two related arguments: that 'patriarchy' must be interpreted literally, and that patriarchy is a relic of the old world of status, or a natural order of subjection; in short, a remnant of the old world of paternal right that preceded the new civil world of contract. Patriarchy, that is, is seen as synonymous with the 'status' in Sir Henry Maine's famous characterization of the transformation of the old world into the new as a 'movement *from Status to Contract*'.[3] Contract thus gains its meaning as freedom in contrast to, and in opposition to, the order of subjection of status or patriarchy. The name of Sir Henry Maine and his famous aphorism are more often evoked in discussions of contract than closely examined. Maine's argument was concerned with the replacement of status, in the sense of absolute paternal jurisdiction in the patriarchal family, by contractual relations, and the replacement of the family by the individual as the fundamental 'unit' of society. 'Status' in Maine's sense overlaps with one of two other senses in which the term is often used today.

'Status' is sometimes used to refer more generally to ascription; human beings are born into certain social positions by virtue of their ascribed characteristics, such as sex, colour, age and so on. John Stuart Mill's criticism in *The Subjection of Women* of the insufficiently contractual marriage contract, which presupposed that one party, the wife, is born into a certain condition, rests on an implicit contrast between contract and status in this broad sense. Contemporary legal writers also use 'status' in a quite different fashion. For legal writers, 'contract' refers to a *laissez-faire* economic order, an order 'of freedom of contract', in which substantive individual characteristics and the specific subject of an agreement are irrelevant. Contract in this sense stands opposed to 'status' as legal (state) regulation. The regulation hedges contract about with limitations and special conditions that take into account precisely *who* is making a contract about *what* and under what *circumstances*. The development of a vast system of such regulation has led Patrick Atiyah to declare, in *The Rise and Fall of Freedom of Contract*, that it has 'become a cliché to say that there has been a reversion from "contract" to "status", a movement contrary to that perceived and described by Maine in 1861'.[4] However, Maine's and Atiyah's movements are located in very different historical contexts. 'Status' in the 1980s is far removed from Maine's status. I shall come back to the meaning of status and its connection to patriarchy and contract at various points in my argument.

The perception of civil society as a post-patriarchal social order also depends on the inherent ambiguity of the term 'civil society'. From one perspective, civil society is the contractual order that follows the pre-modern order of status, or the civil order of constitutional, limited government replaces political absolutism. From another perspective, civil society replaces the state of nature; and, yet again, 'civil' also refers to one of the spheres, the public sphere, of 'civil society'. Most advocates and opponents of contract theory trade on the ambiguity of 'civil'. 'Civil society' is distinguished from other forms of social order by the separation of the private from the public sphere; civil society is divided into two opposing realms, each with a distinctive and contrasting mode of association. Yet attention is focused on one sphere, which is treated as the only realm of political interest. Questions are rarely asked about the political significance of the existence of two spheres, or about how both spheres are brought into being. The origin of the public sphere is no mystery. The social contract brings the public world of civil law, civil freedom and equality, contract and the individual into being. What is the (conjectural) history of the origin of the private sphere?

To understand any classic theorist's picture of either the natural condition or the civil state, both must be considered together. 'Natural' and 'civil' are at once opposed to each other and mutually dependent. The two terms gain their meaning from their relationship to each other; what is 'natural' excludes what is 'civil' and vice versa. To draw attention to the mutual dependence of the state of nature/civil society does not explain why, after the original pact, the term 'civil' shifts and is used to refer not to the whole of 'civil society' but to one of its parts. To explain the shift, a double opposition and dependence between 'natural' and 'civil' must be taken into account. Once the original contract is entered into, the relevant dichotomy is between the private sphere and the civil, public sphere – a dichotomy that reflects the order of sexual difference in the natural condition, which is also a political difference. Women have no part in the original contract, but they are not left behind in the state of nature – that would defeat the purpose of the sexual contract! Women are incorporated into a sphere that both is and is not in civil society. The private sphere is part of civil society but is separated from the 'civil' sphere. The antinomy private/public is another expression of natural/civil and women/men. The private, womanly sphere (natural) and the public, masculine sphere (civil) are opposed but gain their meaning from each other, and the meaning of the civil freedom of public life is thrown into relief when counterposed to the natural subjection that characterizes the private realm (Locke misleads by presenting the contrast in partriarchal terms as between paternal and political power). What it means to be an 'individual', a maker of contracts and civilly free, is revealed by the subjection of women within the private sphere.

The private sphere is typically presupposed as a necessary, natural foundation for civil, i.e., public life, but treated as irrelevant to the concerns of political theorists and political activists. Since at least 1792 when Mary Wollstonecraft's *A Vindication of the Rights of Woman* appeared, feminists have persistently pointed to the complex interdependence between the two spheres, but, nearly two centuries later, 'civil' society is still usually treated as a realm that subsists independently. The origin of the private sphere thus remains shrouded in mystery. The mystery is deepened because discussions of social contract theory almost always pass directly from the eighteenth century to the present day and John Rawls' contemporary reformulation of the (social) contract story. Yet Sigmund Freud also (re)wrote more than one version of the story of the original contract. He is rarely mentioned, but perhaps there is good reason for the absence of Freud's name. Freud's stories make explicit that power over women and not only freedom is at issue before the original agreement is made, and he also makes clear that two realms are created through the original pact. In the classic texts (except for those of Hobbes) it can easily seem at first sight that there is no need to create the private sphere, since sexual relations between men and women, marriage and the family already exist in the state of nature. But the original contract brings 'civil society' into being, and the story of the sexual contract must be told in order to elucidate how the private realm (is held to be) established and why the separation from the public sphere is necessary.

The sexual contract, it must be emphasized, is not associated only with the private sphere. Patriarchy is not merely familial or located in the private sphere. The original contract creates the modern social whole of patriarchal civil society. Men pass back and forth between the private and public spheres and the writ of the law of male sex-right runs in both realms. Civil society is bifurcated but the unity of the social order is maintained, in large part, through the structure of patriarchal relations. In chapters 5 and 7 I shall examine some aspects of the public face of patriarchy and explore some of the connections between patriarchal domination in the two spheres. The dichotomy private/public, like natural/civil, takes a double form and so systematically obscures these connections.

Most contemporary controversy between liberals and socialists about the private and the public is not about the *patriarchal* division between natural and civil. The private sphere is 'forgotten' so that the 'private' shifts to the civil world and the *class* division between private and public. The division is then made within the 'civil' realm itself, between the private, capitalist economy or private enterprise and the public or political state, and the familiar debates ensue. Indeed, the general public now recognizes the term 'social contract' because it has been used to refer to relations between government, labour and capital in the 'civil' realm. In the 1970s in Britain, Labour governments made much of their social contract with the trades union movement, and the Accord between the state, capital and labour in Australia, forged in 1983, is often called a social contract. In the 1980s, books about the Reagan administration's economic policy have also been appearing in the United States with 'social contract' in the title.[5] Thus the liberal defence and socialist criticism of this variant of the private/public antinomy either defend or attack class domination and the employment contract. Patriarchal domination lies outside their frame of reference, along with questions about the relation between the marriage contract and employment contract and any hint that the employment contract, too, is part of the structure of patriarchy.

Over the past decade, the familiar terms of debate between liberals and socialists and among socialists themselves have become increasingly problematic. The inadequacy has been revealed in the face of a range of political, economic and intellectual developments, only one of which I want to touch on here. Feminists have shown how the proponents in these long-standing debates, often bitterly opposed to each other, share some important assumptions in common. The fundamental assumption is that the patriarchal separation of the private/natural sphere from the public/civil realm is irrelevant to political life. But the common ground extends further still. The complex relation between patriarchy, contract, socialism and feminism is relatively little explored. An examination of this area through the story of the sexual contract shows how certain current trends in socialism and feminism join hands with the most radical contract theory. The intersection is at the idea that, in Locke's famous formulation, 'every Man has a *Property* in his own *Person*';[6] all individuals are owners, everyone owns the property in their capacities and attributes.

The idea that individuals own property in their persons has been central to the struggle against class and patriarchal domination. Marx could not have written *Capital* and formulated the concept of labour power without it; but nor could he have called for the abolition of wage labour and capitalism, or what, in older socialist terminology, is called wage slavery, if he had not also rejected this view of individuals and the corollary that freedom is contract and ownership. That Marx, necessarily, had to use the idea of property ownership in the person in order to reject both this conception and the form of social order to which it contributed, is now in danger of being forgotten in the current popularity of market socialism and, in academic circles, rational choice or analytic Marxism. Similarly, the claim that women own the property in their persons has animated many feminist campaigns past and present, from attempts to reform marriage law and to win citizenship to demands for abortion rights. The appeal of the idea for feminists is easy to see when the common law doctrine of coverture laid down that wives were the property of their husbands and men still eagerly press for the enforcement of the law of male sex-right and demand that women's bodies, in the flesh and in representation, should be publicly available to them. To win acknowledgment that women own the property in their persons thus seems to strike a decisive blow against patriarchy, but, historically, while the feminist movement campaigned around issues that could easily be formulated in the language of ownership of the person, the predominant feminist argument was that women required civil freedom *as women*, not as pale reflections of men. The argument thus rested on an implicit rejection of the patriarchal construction of the individual as a masculine owner.

Today, however, many feminists appear to see only the advantages in the current political climate in making feminist demands in contractual terms, and to be unaware that the 'individual' as owner is the fulcrum on which modern patriarchy turns. This is especially true in the United States, where socialist arguments are now rarely heard and where the most radical form of contract doctrine is influential. I shall refer to the latter, which has its classical expression in Hobbes' theory, as *contractarian* theory or *contractarianism* (in the United States it is usually called libertarianism, but in Europe and Australia 'libertarian' refers to the anarchist wing of the socialist movement; since my discussion owes something to that source I shall maintain un-American usage). The 'individual' is the bedrock from which contractarian doctrine is constructed, and to the extent that socialism and feminism now look to the 'individual' they have joined hands with contractarians. When socialists forget that both acceptance *and* rejection of the individual as owner is necessary for their arguments, subordination (wage slavery) disappears and only exploitation is visible. When feminists forget that, though acceptance of the 'individual' may be politically necessary, so also is rejection, they acquiesce in the patriarchal construction of woman-hood.

For contemporary contractarians, or, following Hegel, from what I shall call 'the standpoint of contract',[7] social life and relationships not only originate from a social contract but, properly, are seen as an endless series of discrete contracts. The implication of this view can be seen by considering an old philosophical conundrum. An ancient belief is that the universe rests on an elephant, which, in turn, stands on the back of a turtle; but what supports the turtle? One uncompromising answer is that there are turtles all the way down. From the standpoint of contract, in social life there are contracts all the way down. Moreover, no limits can be placed on contract and contractual relations; even the ultimate form of civil subordination, the slave contract, is legitimate. A civil slave contract is not significantly different from any other contract. That individual freedom, through contract, can be exemplified in slavery should give socialists and feminists pause when they make use of the idea of contract and the individual as owner.

Familiar arguments against contract, whether from the Left or those of Hegel, the greatest theoretical critic of contract, are all thrown into a different light once the story of the sexual contract is retrieved. Ironically, the critics, too, operate within parameters set by the original patriarchal contract and thus their criticisms are always partial. For example, marital subjection is either endorsed or ignored, the patriarchal construction of the 'worker' never recognized and the implications of the civil slave contract are never pursued. This is not to say that an examination of patriarchy from the perspective of the sexual contract is a straightforward task; misunderstandings can easily arise. For instance, some feminists have justifiably become concerned at the widespread portrayal of women as merely the subjects of men's power, as passive victims, and to focus on patriarchal subordination might appear to reinforce this portrayal. However, to emphasize that patriarchal subordi-nation originates in contract entails no assumption that women have merely accepted their position. On the contrary, an understanding of the way in which contract is presented as freedom and as anti-patriarchal, while being a major mechanism through which sex-right is renewed and maintained, is only possible because women (and some men) have resisted and criticized patriarchal relations since the seventeenth century. This study depends on their resistance, and I shall refer to some of their neglected criticisms of contract.

Attention to the subordination constituted by original contract, and by contract more generally, is itself another possible source of misunderstanding. Michel Foucault's influential studies might suggest that the story of the sexual contract will generate a view of power and domination that remains stuck in an old juridical formulation 'centered on nothing more than the statement of the law and the operation of taboos'.[8] Certainly, law and contract, and obedience and contract, go hand in hand, but it does not follow that contract is concerned only with law and not also, in Foucault's terminology, with discipline, normalization and control. In the *History of Sexuality* Foucault remarks that 'beginning in the eighteenth century, [new power mechanisms] took charge of men's existence, men as living bodies'.[9] But beginning in the seventeenth century, when stories of the original contract were first told, a new mechanism of subordination and discipline enabled men to take charge of women's bodies and women's lives. The original contract (is said to have) brought a modern form of law into existence, and the actual contracts entered into in everyday life form a specifically modern method of creating local power relations within sexuality, marriage and employment. The civil state and law and (patriarchical) discipline are not two forms of power but dimensions of the complex, multifaceted structure of domination in modern patriarchy.

To tell the story of the sexual contract is to show how sexual difference, what it is to be a 'man' or 'woman', and the construction of sexual difference as political difference, is central to civil society. Feminism has always been vitally concerned with sexual difference and feminists now face a very complex problem. In modern patriarchy the difference between the sexes is presented as the quintessentially natural difference. Men's patriarchal right over women is presented as reflecting the proper order of nature. How then should feminists deal with sexual difference? The problem is that, in a period when contract has a wide appeal, the patriarchal insistence that sexual difference is politically relevant all too easily suggests that arguments that refer to women *as women* reinforce the patriarchal appeal to nature. The appropriate feminist response then seems to be to work for the elimination of all reference to the difference between men and women in political life; so, for example, all laws and policies should be 'gender neutral'. I shall say something about the now ubiquitous terminology of 'gender' in the final chapter. Such a response assumes that 'individuals' can be separated from sexually differentiated bodies. Contract doctrine relies on the same assumption in order to claim that all examples of contract involving property in the person establish free relations. The problem is that the assumption relies on a political fiction (an argument I shall present in some detail in chapters 5 and 7).

When feminism uncritically occupies the same terrain as contract, a response to patriarchy that appears to confront the subjection of women head-on also serves to consolidate the peculiarly modern form of patriarchal right. To argue that patriarchy is best confronted by endeavouring to render sexual difference politically irrelevant is to accept the view that the civil (public) realm and the 'individual' are uncontaminated by patriarchal subordination. Patriarchy is then seen as a private familial problem that can be overcome if public laws and policies treat women as if they were exactly the same as men. However, modern patriarchy is not, first and foremost, about women's familial subjection. Women engage in sexual relations with men and are wives before they become mothers in families. The story of the sexual contract is about (hetero)sexual relations and women as embodied sexual beings. The story helps us understand the mechanisms through which men claim right of sexual access to women's bodies and claim right of command over the use of women's bodies. Moreover, heterosexual relations are not confined to private life. The most dramatic example of the public aspect of patriarchal right is that men demand that women's bodies are for sale as commodities in the capitalist market; prostitution is a major capitalist industry.

Some feminists fear that references to 'men' and 'women' merely reinforce the patriarchal claim that 'Woman' is a natural and timeless category, defined by certain innate, biological characteristics. To talk about Woman, however, is not at all the same thing as talking about women. 'The eternal Woman' is a figment of the patriarchal imagination. The constructions of the classical contract theorists no doubt are influenced by the figure of Woman and they have a good deal to say about natural capacities. Nonetheless, they develop a social and political, albeit patriarchal, construction of what it means to be masculine or feminine in modern civil society. To draw out the way in which the meaning of 'men' and 'women' has helped structure major social institutions is not to fall back on purely natural categories. Nor is it to deny that there are many important differences between women and that, for example, the life of a young Aboriginal woman in inner Sydney will be markedly different from the life of the wife of a wealthy white banker in Princeton. At various points in my argument I shall make specific reference, say, to working-class women, but, in an exploration of contract and patriarchal right, the fact that women are *women* is more relevant than the differences between them. For example, the social and legal meaning of what it is to be a 'wife' stretches across class and racial differences. Of course, not all married couples behave in the same way as 'wives' and 'husbands', but the story of the sexual contract throws light onto the *institution* of marriage; however hard any couple may try to avoid replicating patriarchal marital relations, none of us can entirely escape the social and legal consequences of entering into the marriage contract.

Finally, let me make clear that although I shall be (re)telling conjectural histories of the origins of political right and repairing some omissions in the stories, I am not advocating the replacement of patriarchal tales with feminist stories of origins.

2

Patriarchal Confusions

The story of the original contract provides a conjectural history of the origins of modern patriarchy. Before I can retrieve the lost story of the sexual contract, something has to be said about 'patriarchy'. The term is very controversial and its meaning is a vexed question. 'Patriarchy' refers to a form of political power, but although political theorists spend a great deal of time arguing about the legitimacy and justification of forms of political power, the patriarchal form has been largely ignored in the twentieth century. The standard interpretation of the history of modern political thought is that patriarchal theory and patriarchal right were dead and buried three hundred years ago. Since the late seventeenth century, feminists have been pointing out that almost all political theorists have in fact, explicitly or tacitly, upheld patriarchal right. Feminists have also waged some long, and often very bitter, political campaigns against patriarchal subordination. However, none of this has been sufficient to convince all but the smallest minority of male political theorists or activists that patriarchal right still exists, demands theoretical scrutiny and is as worthy an opponent as aristocratic, class or other forms of power.

The revival of the organized feminist movement since the late 1960s has brought 'patriarchy' back into popular and academic currency. There has been a wide-ranging debate among feminists about the meaning of 'patriarchy' and such questions as whether, in our own society, the term should be used in its literal meaning of rule by fathers; whether patriarchy is a universal feature of human society or is historically and culturally variable; whether matriarchy or sexual equality has ever existed and, if so, how the 'world historical defeat of the female sex' (to use Engels' dramatic formulation) came about;[1] whether patriarchal relations are found primarily in the family or whether social life as a whole is structured by patriarchal power; and what relationship exists between patriarchy or sexual domination and capitalism or class domination. There is no consensus on any of these questions and contemporary feminists use 'patriarchy' in a variety of senses. Some have argued that the problems with the concept are so great that it should be abandoned. To follow such a course would mean that, to the best of my knowledge, feminist political theory would then be without the only concept that refers specifically to the subjection of women, that singles out the form of political right that all men exercise by virtue of being men. If the problem has no name, patriarchy can all too easily slide back into obscurity beneath the conventional categories of political analysis.

Of course, a term can always be made up to serve the same purpose as 'patriarchy', and there are several candidates available, such as phallocracy and related terms like androcentric and genderic. However, apart from the awkwardness of many such concoctions, there is no good reason to abandon patriarchy, patriarchal or patriarchalism. Most of the confusion arises because 'patriarchy' has yet to be disentangled from patriarchal interpretations of its meaning. Even feminist discussions tend to remain within the confines of patriarchal debates about patriarchy. A feminist history of the concept of patriarchy is badly needed. To abandon the concept would mean the loss of a political history that is still to be charted. Reference may be made to Virginia Woolf's use of 'patriarchy' in *Three Guineas* and Weber has received an acknowledgment,[2] but feminist arguments rarely give an indication of the length or complexity of the modern controversies about patriarchy. Over the last decade or so feminists have often, apparently unknowingly, recapitulated some of the central features of major controversies of the past three hundred years. There have been three great periods of debate about patriarchy. The first occurred in the seventeeth century and resulted in the development of a specifically modern theory of patriarchy. The second debate took place from 1861 and continued into the twentieth century; Rosalind Coward has recently provided a valuable account of the participants and issues in this debate in *Patriarchal Precedents*. The third debate began with the current revival of the organized feminist movement and is still under way.

Perhaps the most remarkable feature of present feminist discussions is that so few of the participants even mention the great theoretical battle between the patriarchalists and the social contract theorists and their political allies during the seventeenth century. The received view, that there was a 'rapid decline after 1690 of patriarchalism as a viable political ideology',[3] is a measure of the greatness of the achievement of the social contract theorists. A few feminist political theorists have recently discussed the argument between Locke and Sir Robert Filmer but their discussions tend to owe more to political theory, and thus to patriarchal theory, than to feminism. The exclusion of women from participation in the act that creates civil society does not figure very largely in these discussions. Melissa Butler asks why Locke said nothing about women's part in the original social contract, but her discussion is an almost perfect example of an uncritical liberal interpretation of Locke and tells us more about the repression of the story of the sexual contract than about the way which Locke and Filmer dealt with sexual relations. Butler suggests that Locke's silence on women and the social contract was because he did not want to risk alienating his (male) audience. She also suggests that Locke's arguments leave open the possibility that women could have been party to the social contract; 'Locke's views on women', according to Butler, 'exemplified his individualism.'[4] In a way this is right – but not, as Butler assumes, because his individualism is genuinely universal and able to incorporate women, but because, as I shall show in the next chapter, Locke's 'individual' is masculine.

Locke's position has recently also been claimed to have 'less to do with his specific stances on women and more to do with the nature of his articulation of the separation of the familial and the political'.[5] However, these two aspects of Locke's argument cannot be separated from each other; it is not possible to appreciate the character of modern patriarchy, or the key theoretical contribution that Locke made to its construction, without also appreciating that the separation of the family from political life had everything to do with Locke's view of women. The meaning of the separation of family and politics or private and public (civil) only becomes clear when put into the context of the sexual contract. When feminists follow standard readings of Locke and Filmer, modern society can be pictured as post-patriarchal and patriarchy seen as a pre-modern and/or familial social form. Patriarchy can then be reduced merely to the displacement of early familial relationships onto the political realm. Thus, Jean Elshtain states that, to call contemporary society 'patriarchal', is to 'muddle and distort reality . . . patriarchy as a social form no longer holds, at least not for advanced industrial societies'. Patriarchy, rather, is symbol, metaphor, language; 'our political vocabulary resonates with terms whose meanings are drawn from our earliest social relationships within families.'[6] This may well be true, but to single out this aspect of our political language reinforces patriarchal interpretations of late twentieth-century society. The continuing domination of adult men over adult women disappears from view when patriarchy is reduced to the language and symbols of paternal (or perhaps parental) power over infants and children.

Zillah Eisenstein presents a rare challenge to the patriarchal account of the argument between Locke and Filmer. Unusually, Eisenstein does not take the defeat of paternal power and the separation of political from paternal power at face value, and so she sees Locke as a 'patriarchal anti-patriarchalist'. She argues that, although 'the model of father and son has been displaced by a model of liberal equality',[7] equal status is not therefore accorded to men and women. Eisenstein points out that Locke's stress on the fact that the Fifth Commandment ('honour thy father and thy mother') enjoins parental, not merely paternal, authority over children, does not mean that he questions the power of men as husbands. Locke, she argues, 'uses the equality between men and women in parenting to debunk only the despotic absolutist nature of paternal power between husband and wife'. The husband still exercises power over his wife, but the power is less than absolute. Eisenstein is nevertheless misled by Locke's category of 'paternal power' into referring to the 'paternal power between husband and wife'. Conjugal power is not paternal, but part of masculine sex-right, the power that men exercise as men, not as fathers.

To gain an understanding of the political significance of the status accorded to women in the formulation of a modern conception of patriarchy, the term 'patriarchy' has to be untangled from several overlapping and mutually reinforcing patriarchal assumptions and interpretations, some of which can be seen at work in the discussions of Locke and Filmer to which I have just referred. The most powerful assumption is that 'patriarchy' is properly understood in its literal meaning of rule by the father or as father-right. The

difficulties and misunderstandings to which this assumption leads
are compounded when almost everyone in the present debate about
patriarchy assumes that the father can simply be seen in a common-
sense manner as one of two parents. Very oddly, little attention has
been paid to the political meaning of patriarchal fatherhood. The
literal interpretation is related to and encourages another common
assumption; that patriarchal relations are familial relations. The
familial view of patriarchy is also linked to the widely heard claim
that patriarchy is a universal feature of human society. In all three
periods of debate over patriarchy many of the competing arguments
turned on different conjectural histories of social and political
origins. The genesis of the (patriarchal) family is frequently seen as
synonymous with the origin of social life itself, and the origin of
patriarchy and the origin of society are treated as the same process.

The story of an original contract that creates civil society is also
bound up with controversies over the origins of liberalism and
capitalism. In the twentieth century, conjectural histories of political
origins have formed part of arguments about the relation between
capitalism and patriarchy, although, curiously, reference is rarely
made in current socialist-feminist discussions to the story of the
original contract. The paternal and familial interpretation of patriarchy is also influential here. If patriarchy is universal, it must pre-
date capitalism; patriarchy can then appear as a feudal relic or a
remnant of the old world of status that sets the familial, paternal,
natural, private sphere apart from the conventional, civil, public
world of contract and capitalism.

In order to cut through some of the intricacies of the debates and
to dispel some of the confusions, it is useful to distinguish three
forms of patriarchal argument, that are not mutually exclusive. I
shall call the first *traditional* patriarchal thought. For centuries, the
family, and the authority of the father at its head, provided the
model or the metaphor for power and authority relations of all kinds.
Traditional patriarchal argument assimilates all power relations to
paternal rule. In seventeenth-century England, the obedience of
subjects to the state was taught from the pulpit using this analogy.
In the Catechism, the Fifth Commandment was interpreted to
mean, in one influential statement, that 'the Civil Parent is he
whom God hath established the Supreme Magistrate, . . . This is
the common father of all those that are under his authority'.[8]
Traditional patriarchal thought is also full of stories, of speculative

or conjectural histories, about the way in which political society emerged from the patriarchal family or the coming together of many such families, and similar stories are told by many of the classic contract theorists. In his invaluable (if patriarchal) account of the seventeenth-century controversies, *Patriarchalism in Political Thought*, Gordon Schochet remarks that political argument that looks to origins (what he calls genetic argument) died at the end of the seventeenth century: 'after 1690, genetic justification and the identification of familial and political power were becoming dead issues'.[9] The perception that familial and, more importantly, conjugal, power was political power faded after the defeat of Sir Robert Filmer at the hands of Locke, but that is not to say that genetic justification died too. The controversy over patriarchy that began in the 1860s was over the question whether father-right or mother-right was the 'original' social form. Many echoes of traditional patriarchal argument can be heard in these debates and they can be heard again, too, in recent feminist stories about the end of matriarchy and the origins of patriarchy. Moreover, although Schochet emphasizes that classic contract theory is a genetic argument, so is contemporary contract theory. For contract theorists, contractual relations are legitimate precisely because of the manner in which they originate.

Schochet emphasizes that Sir Robert Filmer broke with traditional patriarchal argument by claiming that paternal and political power were not merely analogous but *identical*. Filmer justified absolute monarchy with the argument that kings were fathers and fathers were kings, and in the 1680s and 1690s 'the Filmerian position very nearly became the official state ideology.'[10] I shall call Filmer's argument *classic* patriarchalism. The classic theory – the second of the three forms of patriarchal argument – was a fully developed theory of political right and political obedience and it was the first of its kind – 'there was no patriarchal theory of obligation prior to 1603'[11] – but it was very short-lived. The patriarchal theory that died at the end of the seventeenth century was Filmer's classic form. Filmer wrote, as Schochet has shown, in response to the challenge thrown down by the claim of the contract theorists that all men were naturally free. The classic patriarchal argument was that sons were born into subjection to their fathers and, therefore, into political subjection. Political right was natural and not conventional, no consent or contract was involved and political power was paternal, having its origin in the procreative power of the father. I shall look at Sir Robert Filmer's argument and the battle between classic patriarchalism and social contract theory in chapter 4, and show how the classic theory was transformed by the contract theorists into a third form, into *modern* patriarchy. Modern patriarchy is fraternal, contractual and structures capitalist civil society.

A major source of confusion in debates over patriarchy is that conjectural histories of the development of the patriarchal family or civil society, including those of the classic contract theorists, are presented as stories of the origin of human society or civilization. Freud, for example, writes his accounts of the original pact as (stories) about the genesis of civilization and, in an influential feminist interpretation of Freud, Juliet Mitchell takes his argument at face value. But 'civilization' is not synonymous with human society. The term 'civilization' came into general use toward the end of the eighteenth century, being preceded by 'civility', and it expressed 'a particular stage of European history, sometimes the final or ultimate stage'.[12] The idea of civilization 'celebrated the associated sense of modernity: an achieved condition of refinement and order'.[13] In short, 'civilization' refers to an historically and culturally specific form of social life, and the concept is closely bound up with the emergence of the idea of 'civil society' (the society created through the original contract). I emphasized in chapter 1, that the meaning of 'civil society' is ambiguous and gains its meaning from a series of contrasts and opposition to other social forms. One contrast is between civil society and the state of nature but to picture the state of nature as a pre-social or asocial state is to claim that civil society represents social life – civilization – itself. To add to the confusion, other contract theorists picture the patriarchal family as the original and natural social form, and civil or political society then develops, in the traditional patriarchal fashion, out of the family or families.

The second wave of controversy about patriarchy that began in 1861 with the publication of Sir Henry Maine's *Ancient Law* and Johann Bachofen's *Mother Right* centred on accounts of the origin of the patriarchal family or civilization. But how are these nineteenth- and early twentieth-century debates to be interpreted? The first battle over patriarchy, as I have already noted, is typically read as an engagement over paternal power or father-right, not as about patriarchal right as sex-right. Rosalind Coward offers a similar view of the second battle. She argues that, from the 1860s, 'sexual relations, in the sense that they are interrogated by contemporary feminism, were not the real subject of these debates. The real subject was that of the nature of political and social alliances.' The debates were about the relation 'between familial forms and the political organisation of society'.[14] But because legal historians, anthropologists and psychoanalytic theorists argued about the patriarchal family and civilization, it does not follow that the 'real subject' of their argument was not *also* sexual and conjugal relations. Coward discusses Freud's conjectural history of the origin of 'civilization', but (like Juliet Mitchell some years earlier) she reads Freud's stories through the patriarchal lens of Lévi-Strauss and Lacan so she interprets their subject as social classification, as kinship, exogamy and the incest taboo, and not sexual domination.

Coward states in the first chapter of *Patriarchal Precedents* that Maine's *Ancient Law* 'marked the summation of ideas about the patriarchal family which had dominated political theory throughout the seventeenth and eighteenth centuries. But it also represented a methodological and theoretical approach which would ultimately overturn the last lingering traces of this political theory'.[15] Coward's statement is misleading on two counts. First, Maine's discussion of the patriarchal family and the power of the father, the *patria potestas*, is very different from those of earlier writers, although it bears some resemblance to Hobbes' view of the family. Filmer's patriarchal father enjoys the absolute power of the *patria potestas* who, under Roman law, had power of life and death over his sons. The politically defeated fathers of the social contract theorists have been stripped of this ancient power; they become modern fathers in modern, private families. Moreover, most of the classic contract theorists, in the fashion of traditional patriarchal argument, claimed that the family was a natural institution and that the power of the father over family members arose naturally from the father's paternal capacities and care, even though his power might also be based on consent. Hobbes, in contrast, argues that the family is an 'artificial' institution and that the father's right is purely conventional or contractual, which, for Hobbes, means based on force. Sir Henry Maine also argued that the patriarchal family – the original social form – was conventional not natural. Maine emphasizes that 'the history of political ideas begins, . . . with the assumption that kinship in blood is the sole possible ground of community in political functions.'[16] The assumption is false. The patriarchal family was not based on natural ties of blood but on what Maine calls a 'Legal Fiction'. The earliest families and societies (which were associations of families) absorbed many strangers, but the fiction was maintained that all sprang from the same blood line or descended from the same ancestor (father). The fiction was so powerful that no distinction was drawn between 'the fiction of adoption' and 'the reality of kinship'.[17] These families were held together through obedience to the patriarchal head. Paternal political right constituted the ancient family. *Patria potestas* might have been seen as arising from the natural power of fatherhood, but Maine's argument that absolute paternal right was based on a fiction, not nature, means that his account of the patriarchal family is very different from that found in most other traditional, classic or modern patriarchal writings.

The second point is that Maine's book does not, as Coward suggests, overturn earlier political theory; rather, Maine is writing firmly within the parameters set by the classic contract theorists. Bachofen argued that mother-right or matriarchy was the original social form and a long debate about origins began, but Maine's *Ancient Law* is about a different origin. To be sure, he insists that the ancient or original family is patriarchal, but Maine's focus is not the 'beginning' in the sense of social life or civilization, but the 'beginning' of modern civil society. He is concerned with what comes *after* the patriarchal family – or the traditional world of status – not whether matriarchy came *before* paternal right. In 'progressive societies', that is, those about which the social contract theorists wrote, the patriarchal family is ceasing to be the unit from which society is constituted. Instead, the individual is becoming primary and relations among individuals are formed through free agreement; 'the tie between man and man which replaces by degrees those forms of reciprocity in rights and duties which have their origin in the Family . . . is Contract.'[18] However, Maine also remarks that, although the old forms of tutelage have almost disappeared, a wife still remains under the tutelage of her husband.

The patriarchal interpretation of 'patriarchy' as paternal right has had the paradoxical consequence of obscuring the origin of the family in the relation between husband and wife. The fact that men and women enter into a marriage contract – an 'original' contract that constitutes marriage and the family – and are husbands and wives *before* they are fathers and mothers is forgotten. Conjugal right

then becomes subsumed under father-right and, as the stories of
contemporary feminists who have revived the idea of an original
matriarchy illustrate, argument about patriarchy revolves around
the (familial) powers of mothers and fathers, so obscuring the wider
social question of the character of relations between men and women
and the scope of masculine sex-right. Coward refers to Malinowski's
comment that the swan-song of the earlier examples of the mother-
right hypothesis was Robert Briffault's *The Mothers*, published in
1927,[19] but the contemporary women's movement has produced a
proliferation of conjectural histories of the origins of patriarchy and
the events that led to the world historical defeat of the female sex,
using much the same mixture of anthropology, history, religion and
myth as a century ago.

There is, however, an interesting difference between the two
waves of speculation about origins. 'In the beginning', the earlier
stories run, social life was governed by mother-right, descent was
matrilineal and sexual promiscuity prevented understanding of
paternity. The stories give different accounts of how it came about
that mother-right was overturned, but the process depended upon
the certain knowledge of paternity. What was the meaning of the
triumph of father-right? Coward notes that 'socialist imagery of the
period was full of democratic "maternal" communism in opposition
to individualistic patriarchal capitalism.'[20] Nevertheless, most of the
conjectural histories identified the victory of the father with the
origin of civilization. Patriarchy was a cultural and social triumph.
The acknowledgement of paternity was interpreted as an exercise of
reason, an advance that was necessary for, and laid the basis for, the
emergence of civilization – all of which was the work of men. I shall
come back to this point shortly. Coward also notes that many of the
proponents in the controversy over mother-right found it almost
impossible to believe in matriarchy as the inverse of patriarchy;
'virtually no one followed Bachofen's vision of all-powerful women,
his Amazons, struggling to defend mother-right.' At best it was
argued that early society was matrilineal (i.e., descent was traced
through the mother).[21] Women were believed incapable of having
ruled over men. This is where many contemporary feminist conjectural histories differ. An original matriarchy is postulated which is
the opposite of patriarchy; mothers, not fathers, exercise political
right.

The question that is immediately suggested by all such stories is
whether conjectures about remote origins have any relevance to

social and political institutions in the 1980s. The latest feminist conjectural history is Gerda Lerner's *The Creation of Patriarchy*, a very sophisticated example of the genre. Lerner carefully distances her work from arguments postulating a single cause of patriarchy, or myths of an original matriarchy; both men and women, she stresses, participated in creating patriarchy. Lerner argues that patriarchy arose in the West in ancient Mesopotamia from 6,000–3,000 BC. She offers some fascinating speculations about the mechanisms involved, including several alternatives that might account for the 'exchange of women' (an idea derived from Claude Lévi-Strauss on which I shall comment in chapter 4) which, she suggests, was a crucial development. Lerner states that she is tracing 'the development of the leading ideas, symbols and metaphors by which patriarchal gender relations were incorporated into Western civilization'.[22] In gaining an understanding of this development women can change their consciousness of themselves and their position. But how useful is it to go back to remote origins in Mesopotamia when there are stories available of a much closer origin? Moreover, this more recent 'beginning' of patriarchy is coincident with the emergence of the modern civil social order in which we still live.

To talk of a universal (Western) 'umbrella of patriarchy' makes sense only in that, in Lerner's words, 'there is not a single society known where women-as-a-group have decision-making power *over* men or where they define the rules of sexual conduct or control marriage exchanges.'[23] That is not to say, however, as Lerner recognizes, that women's position has always been the same – that, as some feminists have claimed, women stand outside history[24] – or that women have never exercised any kind of self-determination or social power. Women's social and economic position and the range of their activities have varied enormously in different cultures and in different historical epochs. If 'patriarchy' really did entail a denial of the existence of such variety, then we should relinquish the term without further ado. Most feminists who want to see 'patriarchy' abandoned advocate this course because they see the concept as timeless and ahistorical. Patriarchy, Michele Barrett declares, 'is redolent of a universal and trans-historical oppression';[25] and Sheila Rowbotham argues that it 'implies a universal and ahistorical form of oppression which returns us to biology . . . [it] implies a structure which is fixed,. . . [and] suggests a fatalistic submission'.[26]

Such interpretations are hard to avoid when 'patriarchy' is linked to conjectural histories of origins that tell of the beginning of history, social life or civilization. When 'patriarchy' is used in this sense the historical distinctiveness of the modern civil order disappears and pre-modern forms appear to have been maintained until the present day. For example, following Freud's presentation of the original pact as the story of the creation of civilization or social life itself, Juliet Mitchell not only argues in *Psychoanalysis and Feminism* that patriarchy is the 'law of the father', but that women's social location is within the kinship structure. She argues further that the kinship structure has now become 'archaic' so that, for the first time, there is a possibility that patriarchy might be overthrown.[27] The story of the original contract, including the versions found in Freud's writings, confirms that 'kinship' became archaic a long time ago. The victory of contract theory over classic patriarchalism signalled the end of a social order structured by kinship and the rule of the father. Modern society is structured by universal, conventional bonds of contract, not the particular, ascriptive bonds of kinship. In the modern world, 'kinship' is transformed into the 'family', which has its own principle of association and its own social location in the private sphere, separate from public 'civil' society.

Other feminists, aware that the traditional order of kinship and father-right is not a modern order, yet interpreting 'patriarchy' literally, have argued that the concept has no application in our society. Gayle Rubin argues that 'patriarchy' should be confined to societies of 'Old Testament-type pastoral nomads'.[28] Similarly, though a little less drastically, Michele Barrett argues that 'patriarchy' is useful in 'contexts where male domination is expressed through the power of the father over women and over younger men. Clearly some societies have been organized around this principle, although not capitalist ones'.[29] Capitalist societies thus appear to be post-patriarchal, the societies of contract.

To compound the confusion, contract, like patriarchy, can be seen as a universal phenomenon as well as distinctive to a modern world that has moved away from patriarchy (the movement 'from status to contract'). Classic social contract theory marks a decisive shift in the use of the idea of contract in political argument. The original contract creates (tells the story of the creation of) a new social order constituted by the conventional bonds of contract. Contract as the general basis for social order is very different from examples of contract in earlier times. *The Creation of Patriarchy* includes a fascinating discussion of Yahweh's covenant with

Abraham, the story of which is told in the book of *Genesis*. Yahweh demands a spectacular symbol of patriarchal power as a token of the covenant; namely the circumcised flesh of the penis. Lerner points out that little interest has been displayed in the choice of the token (although she notes that Calvin urged that 'we must inquire, whether any analogy is here apparent between the visible sign, and the thing signified') and she pointedly asks why, if a bodily mark was needed to distinguish His chosen people, *this* mark was demanded.[30] Women clearly lack the means to participate in Abraham's covenant, but their exclusion from participation in the original contract in the texts of classic social contract theory is secured in a much less obviously patriarchal fashion. The distinctiveness of the original contract is precisely that it appears to be universal, to include everyone who is to be incorporated into the new civil order.

Lerner also refers to another 'unwritten contract' which is part of the 'umbrella of patriarchy'. She argues that for almost four thousand years the umbrella has covered 'paternalistic dominance', a form of domination mitigated by mutual rights and obligations. 'The dominated exchange submission for protection, unpaid labor for maintenance. . . . The basis of paternalism is an unwritten contract for exchange: economic support and protection given by the male for subordination in all matters, sexual service, and unpaid domestic service given by the female.'[31] On the face of it, paternalistic dominance looks like modern contract which, I shall be arguing, typically takes the form of the exchange of obedience for protection. But the similarity exists only if contract is taken out of its historical context. Lerner's language of paternalism is a very misleading way to talk of modern contractual patriarchy. 'Paternalist' may well be an appropriate term to describe examples of contract in the pre-modern world, where social relations were structured by kinship or Sir Henry Maine's status. Contract, too, could then be seen in the light of the familial and paternal model of social relations and social hierarchy, and assimilated to status, which carried its own duties, incumbent on the individual irrespective of agreement. Thus, Gordon Schochet remarks of seventeenth-century England, that ordinary people were aware of 'a contractual tradition' but that it was part of 'the patriarchal explanation of social rank'. Contract was not understood by them in the same way that we understand it today; 'contract seems to have been used more as a formal explanation of how people entered relationships than as a definition of the nature and content of those stations.'[32] In the same century, however, in the hands of the social contract theorists, contract was being turned into its modern form and into an anti-paternalist doctrine.

Strangely enough, although the paternal and familial interpretation of patriarchy is so popular, feminist arguments about patriarchy have had little or nothing to say about paternalism and its relation to patriarchy. However, among philosophers, including contractarians, a debate over paternalism has been going on for some time. The argument is over the question whether certain activities, including entry into contracts, can legitimately be prohibited or controlled by law to prevent harm to individuals, even though the activities are undertaken voluntarily. The philosophers' debate about paternalism overlaps with the argument among legal writers about contract and status, to which I referred in chapter 1; should the law be used to limit and regulate freedom of contract and so hedge contract about with status? Both controversies overlap again with the political battle over the welfare state waged between socialists and the New Right over the past several years. Indeed, in the 1940s, in a famous essay on citizenship and the welfare state, T. H. Marshall wrote that 'social [welfare] rights in their modern form imply an invasion of contract by status.'[33] Use of 'paternalism' to refer to these issues is not without interest for any consideration of modern patriarchy; why *this* term?

The straightforward answer is that the relationship of the loving father to his son provides the model for the relation of the citizen to the state. Just as a father forbids his son to act in certain ways because he knows that the son will thereby harm himself, and the father has a duty to protect his son, so the state protects citizens through legal paternalism. Contractarians are the most consistent opponents of paternalism and the story of the social contract shows why. The language of paternalism harks back to the traditional patriarchal model of the political order; all rulers are like fathers – but this model was destroyed by contract theory. In the story of the social contract the father is (metaphorically) killed by his sons, who transform (the paternal dimension of) the father's patriarchal right into civil government. The sons alienate this aspect of political power into the hands of representatives, the state. (Rousseau tells a different story.) When the state places unwarranted restrictions on freedom of contract, the term 'paternalism' illustrates that the citizen's (the son's) freedom is compromised. The state is acting like a father and treating individuals like sons who cannot yet act for their own good. Anti-paternalism can thus appear to be the final round in the battle between contract and patriarchy.

Such a view of the relation between paternalism, contract, patriarchy and status once again depends on a patriarchal interpretation of patriarchy as paternal power, as an aspect of the old world of status intruding into and distorting the new world of contract. This view also depends on continued repression of the story of the sexual contract. The simultaneous seizure by the sons of *both* dimensions of the defeated father's political right, his sex-right as well as his paternal right, is not mentioned. The anti-paternalism of contractarians can therefore appear to be anti-patriarchal. Furthermore, to treat patriarchy as paternalism (or to see the state as like a father) also neatly glosses over the great difference between parent–child relations and patriarchal relations between adult men and women. I shall say more about the difference in the next chapter; here, the pertinent point is that paternalism is controversial precisely because the legally prohibited or controlled acts are between 'consenting adults'. The label 'paternalism' directs attention to familial relations and helps ensure that critical questions about contractual relations between men and women are then deflected.

One does not have to worry about the significance of paternalism, or to read stories about the origins of society, to associate the family with patriarchy. Loud voices still assert that women's proper social place is the private world of the family, and the multitude of social and legal sanctions that have been applied to keep us there tend to concentrate the mind on familial relations. To identify patriarchy with the family can have unexpected consequences, one of which is that the mother and not the father has recently been singled out as the powerful parent! If the writ of paternal right has long since run its course – and the legally and socially sanctioned powers available to fathers in their families are now a shadow of what they once were – what upholds patriarchy? The answer offered by some feminist writers influenced by the sociologized psychoanalytic theory popular in the United States is that it is upheld by mothers; or, more generally, the answer is that patriarchy is maintained through the (universal) fact that mothering, almost exclusively, is undertaken by women. In her influential *The Reproduction of Mothering*, Nancy Chodorow argues that 'certain broad universal sexual asymmetries in the social organization of gender [are] generated by women's mothering'.[34] More strongly, Isaac Balbus has claimed that 'mother-monopolized child rearing' is 'the psychological basis of male domination', and that the pre-Oedipal power of the mother is at the heart of patriarchy; 'it is the experience of maternal, rather than paternal, authority that is the ultimate source of acquiescence in and support for authoritarian politics.'[35]

Both writers suggest that 'shared parenting' is the solution to patriarchy. Echoing stories of the overthrow of matriarchy – only this time with the paradoxical twist that patriarchy is to be brought to an end – the 'patriarchal mother' must be dethroned in favour of what can be called 'parental-right'. To call such a suggestion absurd is not to argue that fathers should not care for their children; the absurdity lies in the argument that patriarchal right derives from womens' position as mothers. The meaning and value accorded to motherhood in civil society is, rather, a consequence of the patriarchal construction of sexual difference as political difference. The argument that maternal power is central to patriarchy can be put forward only because so little attention has been paid to the social and political meaning of the patriarchal father and the power of his fatherhood. This is perhaps the most surprising omission in feminist arguments about patriarchy. The implicit assumption is usually made that 'father' means that a man has a natural, physiological relation to a child. The assumption is that there is a definitive relation between sexual intercourse and fatherhood so that 'paternity is . . . the semantic equivalent of maternity.'[36] A (patriarchal) father is merely one of two parents.

The fact that the relation of father to child is more difficult to establish than the relation of mother to child has not, of course, been overlooked. Fatherhood never quite escapes from uncertainty. At one level, questions can arise about which man has actually fathered a particular child. Doubt about who is the father of a child can be politically important when property is at stake and men have gone to great lengths to devise means to ensure that women do not mislead them on this matter. Rousseau, for example, declared that an unfaithful wife 'dissolves the family and breaks all the bonds of nature. In giving the man children which are not his, she betrays both. She joins perfidy to infidelity. I have difficulty in seeing what disorders and crimes do not flow from this one'.[37] More fundamentally, questions have been raised about knowledge of paternity itself.

No uncertainty can exist about knowledge of maternity. A woman who gives birth is a mother and a woman cannot help but know that she has given birth; maternity is a natural and a social fact. But a considerable gap in time separates any act of coitus from the birth of a child; what then is the connection between the role of the man in sexual intercourse and childbirth? Paternity has to be discovered or invented. Unlike maternity, paternity is merely a social fact, a human invention.

Mary O'Brien has argued that patriarchal political life is a result of men's need to overcome the uncertainty surrounding paternity. The discontinuity between men's alienation of their seed during coitus and the birth of a child has led men to create political theory and political organization; 'man the procreator, by virtue of his need to mediate his alienation from procreation, is essentially man the creator. What he has created are the institutional forms of the social relations of reproduction.'[38] In order for men as fathers to appropriate children elaborate institutional mechanisms are required, including marriage and the separation of the private from the public sphere. Nevertheless, to see the power of fatherhood as *the* creative political force there is no need to resort to ontological arguments about masculine reproductive being (and, as I shall indicate in chapter 7, the contract of so-called surrogate motherhood relies on the fact that men's sperm is quite literally alienable and thus differs from other property in the person). O'Brien's argument assumes that men have tried to make the meaning of paternity socially equivalent to maternity by eliminating uncertainty. On the contrary, the power of patriarchal fatherhood has always depended on paternity and maternity having different social meanings.

In the 1960s and 1970s anthropologists once again engaged in a dispute over the knowledge or ignorance about the natural facts of paternity of certain Pacific peoples. Carol Delaney has recently pointed out that the anthropologists' arguments are based on neglect of the social meaning of paternity. Accounts that apparently show ignorance of the natural facts of insemination and pregnancy accurately reflect the social construction of fatherhood. The physiological facts of motherhood and fatherhood have never been seen socially in the same way; 'maternity has meant giving nurture and giving birth. Paternity has meant begetting. *Paternity has meant the primary, essential and creative role.*'[39] Socially, to use Delaney's term, procreation has been seen in 'monogenetic' fashion as a consequence of the creative force of the father's seed. The monogenetic view was central to classic patriarchalism, as Sir Robert Filmer's writings reveal, but it is still current. While I was writing this chapter, the Primate of the Netherlands was reported as having stated that a women waits for the man's sperm which is the 'dynamic, active, masculine vector of new life'.[40]

My interest is in the political implications of the creative, masculine capacity, which, in its modern form, is not paternal. The patriarchal claim is that men are not only the prime movers in the genesis of new physical life but, as O'Brien has pointed out, *they also beget social and political life*. O'Brien argues that we lack a philosophy of birth. In one sense this is so, but in another sense this is far from the case. Political theory is full of stories of men giving political birth, of men creating new forms of political life or political life itself. The discovery of paternity is said to be the crucial turning-point in Bachofen's conjectural history of the overthrow of matriarchy and the creation of civilization. The power of women has to be defeated if civilization is to emerge; the discovery of paternity is the vital intellectual advance and creative force that enables men to achieve this momentous feat. At the turning-point between the old world of status and the modern world of contract another story of masculine political birth is told. The story of the original contract is perhaps the greatest tale of men's creation of new political life. But this time women are already defeated and declared procreatively and politically irrelevant. Now the father comes under attack. The original contract shows how his monopoly of politically creative power is seized and shared equally among men. In civil society all men, not just fathers, can generate political life and political right. Political creativity belongs not to paternity but masculinity.

But exactly how should the social order generated by men's creative capacity be characterized? Is civil society as a whole post-patriarchal? John Stuart Mill once wrote that 'the feudal family, the last historical form of patriarchal life, has long perished, and the unit of society is not now the family or clan, . . . but the individual; or at most a pair of individuals, with their unemancipated children.'[41] Similarly, if modern society is fatherless then all the old forms must have been left behind; 'the domination peculiar to this [civil] epoch expresses itself . . . as the transformation of all relationships and activity into objective, instrumental, depersonalized forms.'[42] Impersonal contractual relations have replaced the old, personal subjection of status or patriarchy. Or, to make the point slightly differently, patriarchy has been replaced by the civil contractual relations of capitalism; capitalist economic relations and patriarchal relations are mutually exclusive in form. Keith Tribe has recently interpreted the arguments of Hobbes and Locke in this fashion. He argues that in the 'discourse' of the seventeenth century, 'men', as political and economic agents, were patriarchal household heads, not the free individuals of capitalist discourse. The 'discursive demonstration' of capitalist relations was not possible within the framework within which Hobbes and Locke wrote. The patriarchal household included servants and slaves (it was not the 'family' of husband, wife and children) and the master of the household did not direct the activity of his servant as a capitalist. Nor did the relations between masters as economic agents take a capitalist form. [43]

However, Tribe's argument overlooks the significance of the original contract and the difference between modern and traditional or classic patriarchy. A master of a household is not a capitalist, but not all civil subordination takes a capitalist form, and nor is capitalist subordination post-patriarchal. As I shall explore in detail, the 'discourse' of Hobbes and Locke necessarily had room for both patriarchy and capitalism; the 'individuals' who entered the capitalist economy were heads of households (which later became 'families' like those we inhabit in the 1980s). To understand modern patriarchy, including capitalist economic relations, it is necessary to keep the contract between master and servant or master and slave firmly in mind, and to consider the connection between 'personalized' contract in the domestic sphere and contract in the 'impersonal', public world of capitalism. Unfortunately, few feminist discussions of patriarchy and capitalism draw the connections tightly enough.

One recent feminist argument is that the older family form of patriarchy has now given way to a public form, [44] but this leaves open the question of the character of extra-familial relations before patriarchy was transformed. Was the civil, i.e., public, realm outside patriarchy until this recent transformation? In feminist discussions of capitalism and patriarchy the typical assumption is that patriarchy is universal and/or paternal and familial. Patriarchy then seems to pre-date capitalism and now, in some way, exists alongside or within, or as an adjunct to, capitalist relations. The most influential feminist accounts of the connection between the two social forms rely on what has come to be called a dual-systems argument; patriarchy and capitalism are seen as two autonomous systems. Sometimes patriarchy is seen as an ideological and psychological structure, sometimes as another set of material social relations that is separate from the social relations of capitalism. The latter argument is best illustrated by Heidi Hartmann's much-discussed 'The Unhappy Marriage of Marxism and Feminism'. She presents the relationship as a 'partnership' between patriarchy and capitalism; 'patriarchy as a system of relations between men and women exists in capitalism' and the 'accumulation of capital both accommodates itself to patriarchal social structure and helps to perpetuate it.'[45] The assumption, as critics have noted, is that a more or less adequate account of capitalism and class domination is available and feminism is merely supplementing this account.[46]

The difficulties of breaking with this approach can be seen in Zillah Eisenstein's discussion, which is unusual in arguing that 'capitalism still is patriarchal', and that 'in the transition from feudalism to capitalism, patriarchy changed in relation to these economic changes, but it also set the limits and structure of this change.' Yet, she also states that we must recognize 'two systems, one economic, the other sexual, which are relatively autonomous from each other', but, she adds, 'they are completely intertwined.'[47] If capitalism is patriarchal, it is hard to see what is to be gained by insisting that there are two systems. One of the advantages of approaching the question of patriarchy through the story of the sexual contract is that it reveals that civil society, including the capitalist economy, has a patriarchal structure. The capacities that enable men but not women to be 'workers' are the same masculine capacities required to be an 'individual', a husband and head of a family. The story of the sexual contract thus begins with the construction of the individual. To tell the story in a way that illuminates capitalist relations in modern patriarchy, the theoretical route through which (civil) slavery comes to exemplify freedom also has to be considered.

3

Contract, the Individual and Slavery

Classic social contract theory and the broader argument that, ideally, all social relations should take a contractual form, derive from a revolutionary claim. The claim is that individuals are naturally free and equal to each other, or that individuals are born free and born equal. That such a notion can seem commonplace rather than revolutionary today is a tribute to the successful manner in which contract theorists have turned a subversive proposition into a defence of civil subjection. Contract theory is not the only example of a theoretical strategy that justifies subjection by presenting it as freedom, but contract theory is remarkable in reaching that conclusion from its particular starting-point. The doctrine of natural individual freedom and equality was revolutionary precisely because it swept away, in one fell swoop, all the grounds through which the subordination of some individuals, groups or categories of people to others had been justified; or, conversely, through which rule by one individual or group over others was justified. Contract theory was the emancipatory doctrine *par excellence*, promising that universal freedom was the principle of the modern era.

The assumption that individuals were born free and equal to each other meant that none of the old arguments for subordination could be accepted. Arguments that rulers and masters exercised their power through God's will had to be rejected; might or force could no longer be translated into political right; appeals to custom and tradition were no longer sufficient; nor were the various arguments from nature, whether they looked to the generative power of a father, or to superior birth, strength, ability or rationality. All these familiar arguments became unacceptable because the doctrine of individual freedom and equality entailed that there was only one justification for subordination. A naturally free and equal individual must, necessarily, *agree* to be ruled by another. The creation of civil mastery and civil subordination must be voluntary; such relationships can be brought into being in one way only, through free agreement. There are a variety of forms of free agreement but, for reasons which I shall explore below, contract has become paradigmatic of voluntary commitment.

When individuals must freely agree or contract to be governed, the corollary is that they may refuse to be bound. Since the seventeenth century, when doctrines of individual freedom and equality and of contract first became the basis for general theories of social life, conservatives of all kinds have feared that this possibility would become reality and that contract theory would therefore become destructive of social order. Children, servants, wives, peasants, workers and subjects and citizens in the state would, it was feared, cease to obey their superiors if the bond between them came to be understood as merely conventional or contractual, and thus open to the whim and caprice of voluntary commitment. Conservatives had both cause to be alarmed and very little cause at all. The cause for alarm was that, in principle, it is hard to see why a free and equal individual should have sufficiently good reason to subordinate herself to another. Moreover, in practice, political movements have arisen over the past three centuries that have attempted to replace institutions structured by subordination with institutions constituted by free relationships. However, the anxiety was misplaced, not only because these political movements have rarely been successful, but because the alarm about contract theory was groundless. Rather than undermining subordination, contract theorists justified modern civil subjection.

The classic social contract theorists assumed that individual attributes and social conditions always made it reasonable for an individual to give an affirmative answer to the fundamental question whether a relationship of subordination should be created through contract. The point of the story of the social contract is that, in the state of nature, freedom is so insecure that it is reasonable for individuals to subordinate themselves to the civil law of the state, or, in Rousseau's version, to be subject to themselves collectively, in a participatory political association. The pictures of the state of nature and the stories of the social contract found in the classic texts vary widely, but despite their differences on many important issues, the classic contract theorists have a crucial feature in common. They all tell patriarchal stories.

Contract doctrine entails that there is only one, conventional, origin of political right, yet, except in Hobbes' theory where both sexes are pictured as naturally free and equal, the contract theorists also insist that men's right over women has a natural basis. Men alone have the attributes of free and equal 'individuals'. Relations of subordination between *men* must, if they are to be legitimate, originate in contract. Women are born into subjection. The classic writers were well aware of the significance of the assumptions of contract doctrine for the relation between the sexes. They could take nothing for granted when the premise of their arguments was potentially so subversive of all authority relations, including conjugal relations. The classic pictures of the state of nature take into account that human beings are sexually differentiated. Even in Hobbes' radically individualist version of the natural condition the sexes are distinguished. In contemporary discussions of the state of nature, however, this feature of human life is usually disregarded. The fact that 'individuals' are all of the same sex is never mentioned; attention is focused instead on different conceptions of the masculine 'individual'.

The naturally free and equal (masculine) individuals who people the pages of the social contract theorists are a disparate collection indeed. They cover the spectrum from Rousseau's social beings to Hobbes' entities reduced to matter in motion, or, more recently, James Buchanan's reduction of individuals to preference and production functions; John Rawls manages to introduce both ends of the spectrum into his version of the contract story. Rousseau criticized his fellow social contract theorists for presenting individuals in the state of nature as lacking all social characteristics, and his criticism has been repeated many times. The attempt to set out the purely natural attributes of individuals is inevitably doomed to fail; all that is left if the attempt is consistent enough is a merely physiological, biological or reasoning entity, not a human being. In order to make their natural beings recognizable, social contract theorists smuggle social characteristics into the natural condition, or their readers supply what is missing. The form of the state or political association that a theorist wishes to justify also influences the 'natural' characteristics that he gives to individuals; as Rawls stated recently, the aim of arguing from an original position, Rawls' equivalent to the state of nature, 'is to get the desired solution'.[1] What is not often recognized, however, is that the 'desired solution' includes the sexual contract and men's patriarchal right over women.

Despite disagreement over what counts as a 'natural' characteristic, features so designated are held to be common to all human beings. Yet almost all the classic writers held that natural capacities and attributes were sexually differentiated. Contemporary contract theorists implicitly follow their example, but this goes unnoticed because they subsume feminine beings under the apparently universal, sexually neuter category of the 'individual'. In the most recent rewriting of the social contract story sexual relations have dropped from view because sexually differentiated individuals have disappeared. In *A Theory of Justice*, the parties in the original position are purely reasoning entities. Rawls follows Kant on this point, and Kant's view of the original contract differs from that of the other classic contract theorists, although (as I shall indicate in chapter 6) in some other respects his arguments resemble theirs. Kant does not offer a story about the origins of political right or suggest that, even hypothetically, an original agreement was once made. Kant is not dealing in this kind of political fiction. For Kant, the original contract is 'merely an *idea* of reason',[2] an idea necessary for an understanding of actual political institutions. Similarly, Rawls writes in his most recent discussion that his own argument 'tries to draw solely upon basic intuitive ideas that are embedded in the political institutions of a constitutional democratic regime and the public traditions of their interpretation'. As an idea of reason, rather than a political fiction, the original contract helps 'us work out what we now think'.[3] If Rawls is to show how free and equal parties, suitably situated, would agree to principles that are (pretty near to) those implicit in existing institutions, the appropriate idea of reason is required. The problem about political right faced by the classic contract theorists has disappeared. Rawls' task is to find a picture of an original position that will confirm 'our' intuitions about existing institutions, which include patriarchal relations of subordination.

Rawls claims that his parties in their original position are completely ignorant of any 'particular facts' about themselves.[4] The parties are free citizens, and Rawls states that their freedom is a 'moral power to form, to revise, and rationally to pursue a conception of the good', which involves a view of themselves as sources of valid claims and as responsible for their ends. If citizens change their idea of the good, this has no effect on their 'public identity', that is, their juridical standing as civil individuals or citizens. Rawls also states that the original position is a 'device of representation'.[5] But representation is hardly required. As reasoning entities (as Sandel has noticed), the parties are indistinguishable one from another. One party can 'represent' all the rest. In effect, there is only one individual in the original position behind Rawls' 'veil of ignorance'.[6] Rawls can, therefore, state that 'we can view the choice [contract] in the original position from the standpoint of one person selected at random.'[7]

Rawls' parties merely reason and make their choice – or the one party does this as the representative of them all – and so their bodies can be dispensed with. The representative is sexless. The disembodied party who makes the choice cannot know one vital 'particular fact', namely, its sex. Rawls' original position is a logical construction in the most complete sense; it is a realm of pure reason with nothing human in it – except that Rawls, of course, like Kant before him, inevitably introduces real, embodied male and female beings in the course of his argument. Before ignorance of 'particular facts' is postulated, Rawls has already claimed that parties have 'descendants' (for whom they are concerned), and Rawls states that he will generally view the parties as 'heads of families'.[8] He merely takes it for granted that he can, at one and the same time, postulate disembodied parties devoid of all substantive characteristics, and assume that sexual difference exists, sexual intercourse takes place, children are born and families formed. Rawls' participants in the original contract are, simultaneously, mere reasoning entities, and 'heads of families', or men who represent their wives.

Rawls' original position is a logical abstraction of such rigour that nothing happens there. In contrast, the various states of nature pictured by the classic social contract theorists are full of life. They portray the state of nature as a condition that extends over more than one generation. Men and women come together, engage in sexual relations and women give birth. The circumstances under which they do so, whether conjugal relations exist and whether families are formed, depends on the extent to which the state of nature is portrayed as a social condition. I shall begin with Hobbes, the first contractarian, and his picture of the asocial war of all against all. Hobbes stands at one theoretical pole of contract doctrine and his radical individualism exerts a powerful attraction for contemporary contract theorists. However, several of Hobbes' most important arguments had to be rejected before modern patriarchal theory could be constructed.

For Hobbes, all political power was absolute power, and there was no difference between conquest and contract. Subsequent contract theorists drew a sharp distinction between free agreement and enforced submission and argued that civil political power was limited, constrained by the terms of the original contract, even though the state retained the power of life and death over citizens. Hobbes also saw all contractual relations, including sexual relations, as political, but a fundamental assumption of modern political theory is that sexual relations are not political. Hobbes was too revealing about the civil order to become a founding father of modern patriarchy. As I have already mentioned, Hobbes differs from the other classic contract theorists in his assumption that there is no natural mastery in the state of nature, not even of men over women; natural individual attributes and capacities are distributed irrespective of sex. There is no difference between men and women in their strength or prudence, and all individuals are isolated and mutually wary of each other. It follows that sexual relations can take place only under two circumstances; either a man and woman mutually agree (contract) to have sexual intercourse, or a man, through some stratagem, is able to overpower a woman and take her by force, though she also has the capacity to retaliate and kill him.

Classic patriarchalism rested on the argument that political right originated naturally in fatherhood. Sons were born subject to their fathers, and political right was paternal right. Hobbes insists that all examples of political right are conventional and that, in the state of nature, political right is maternal not paternal. An infant, necessarily, has two parents ('as to the generation, God hath ordained to man a helper'),[9] but both parents cannot have dominion over the child because no one can obey two masters. In the natural condition the mother, not the father, has political right over the child; 'every woman that bears children, becomes both a *mother* and a *lord*.'[10] At birth, the infant is in the mother's power. She makes the decision whether to expose or to nourish the child. If she decides to 'breed him', the condition on which she does so is that, 'being grown to full age he become not her enemy';[11] that is to say, the infant must contract to obey her. The postulated agreement of the infant is one example of Hobbes' identification of enforced submission with voluntary agreement, one example of his assimilation of conquest and consent. Submission to overwhelming power in return for protection, whether the power is that of the conqueror's sword or the mother's power over her newly born infant, is always a valid sign of agreement for Hobbes: 'preservation of life being the end, for which one man becomes subject to another, every man [or infant] is supposed to promise obedience, to him [or her], in whose power it is to save, or destroy him.'[12] The mother's political right over her child thus originates in contract, and gives her the power of an absolute lord or monarch.

The mother's political power follows from the fact that in Hobbes' state of nature 'there are no matrimonial laws.'[13] Marriage does not exist because marriage is a long-term arrangement, and long-term sexual relationships, like other such relationships, are virtually impossible to establish and maintain in Hobbes' natural condition. His individuals are purely self-interested and, therefore, will always break an agreement, or refuse to play their part in a contract, if it appears in their interest to do so. To enter into a contract or to signify agreement to do so is to leave oneself open to betrayal. Hobbes' natural state suffers from an endemic problem of keeping contracts, of 'performing second'. The only contract that can be entered into safely is one in which agreement and performance take place at the same time. No problem arises if there is a simultaneous exchange of property, including property in the person, as in a single act of coitus. If a child is born as a consequence of the act, the birth occurs a long time later, so the child belongs to the mother. A woman can contract away her right over her child to the father, but there is no reason, given women's natural equality with men, why women should always do this, especially since there is no way of establishing paternity with any certainty. In the absence of matrimonial laws, as Hobbes notes, proof of fatherhood rests on the testimony of the mother.

Hobbes' criticism of the natural basis of father-right suggests that there is only one form of political right in the state of nature: mother-right. There can, it seems, be no dominion of one adult over another because individuals of both sexes are strong enough and have wit enough to kill each other. No one has sufficient reason to enter into a contract for protection. But is this so clear? Even if marriage does not exist, are there families in the natural state? Hobbes has been seen, by Hinton for example, as a patriarchalist not an anti-patriarchalist (on the question of paternal right). Hobbes' was 'the strongest patriarchalism because it was based on consent', and he took 'patriarchalism for granted and insert[ed] the act of consent'.[14] Hinton refers to Hobbes' mention of a 'patrimonial kingdom' and to some passages where Hobbes appears to fall back on the traditional patriarchal story of families growing into kingdoms ('cities and kingdoms . . . are but greater families.')[15] The criterion for a 'family–kingdom' is that the family becomes strong enough to protect itself against enemies. Hobbes writes that the family,

> if it grow by multiplication of children, either by generation, or adoption; or of servants, either by generation, conquest, or voluntary submission, to be so great and numerous, as in probability it may protect itself, then is that family called a *patrimonial kingdom*, or monarchy by acquisition, wherein the sovereignty is in one man, as it is in a monarch made by *political institution*. So that whatsoever rights be in the one, the same also be in the other.[16]

Hobbes also writes of 'an *hereditary kingdom*' which differs from a monarchy by institution – that is to say, one established by convention or contract – only in that it is 'acquired by force'.[17]

To see Hobbes as a patriarchalist is to ignore two questions: first, how have fathers gained their power in the state of nature when Hobbes has taken such pains to show that political right is mother-right?; second, why is political right in the family based on force? Certainly, Hobbes is not a patriarchalist in the same sense as Sir Robert Filmer, who claims that paternal right is natural, deriving from procreative capacity or generation, not conquest. Hobbes turns Filmer's social bonds into their opposite: Filmer saw families and kingdoms as homologous and bound together through the natural procreative power of the father; Hobbes saw families and kingdoms as homologous, but as bound together through contract (force). For Hobbes, the powers of a mother in the natural state were of exactly the same kind as those of family heads and sovereigns. Perhaps Hobbes is merely inconsistent when he introduces families into the state of nature. But since he is so ruthlessly consistent in everything else – which is why he is so instructive in a variety of ways about contract theory – this seems an odd lapse. The argument that Hobbes is a patriarchalist rests on the patriarchal view that patriarchy is paternal and familial. If we cease to read Hobbes patriarchally it becomes apparent that his patriarchalism is conjugal not paternal and that there is something very odd about Hobbes' 'family' in the natural condition.

The 'natural' characteristics with which Hobbes endows his individuals mean that long-term relationships are very unlikely in his state of nature. However, Hobbes states in *Leviathan* that in the war of all against all 'there is no man who can hope by his own strength, or wit, to defend himself from destruction, without the help of confederates.'[18] But how can such a protective confederation be formed in the natural condition when there is an acute problem of keeping agreements? The answer is that confederations are formed by conquest, and, once formed, are called 'families'. Hobbes' 'family' is very peculiar and has nothing in common with the families in Filmer's pages, the family as found in the writings of the other classic social contract theorists, or as conventionally understood today. Consider Hobbes' definition of a 'family'. In *Leviathan* he states that a family 'consists of a man and his children; or of a man and his servants; or of a man, and his children, and servants together; wherein the father or master is the sovereign'.[19] In *De Cive* we find, 'a *father* with his *sons* and *servants*, grown into a civil person by virtue of his paternal jurisdiction, is called a *family*.'[20] Only in *Elements of Law* does he write that 'the father or mother of the family is sovereign of the same.'[21] But the sovereign is very unlikely to be the mother, given Hobbes' references to 'man' and 'father' and the necessity of securing patriarchal right in civil society.

If one male individual manages to conquer another in the state of nature the conqueror will have obtained a servant. Hobbes assumes that no one would wilfully give up his life, so, with the conqueror's sword at his breast, the defeated man will make a (valid) contract to obey his victor. Hobbes defines dominion or political right acquired through force as 'the dominion of the master over his servant'.[22] Conqueror and conquered then constitute 'a little body politic, which consisteth of two persons, the one sovereign, which is called the *master*, or lord; the other subject, which is called the *servant*'.[23] Another way of putting the point is that the master and servant are a confederation against the rest, or, according to Hobbes' definition, they are a 'family'. Suppose, however, that a male individual manages to conquer a female individual. To protect her life she will enter into a contract of subjection – and so she, too, becomes the servant of a master, and a 'family' has again been formed, held together by the 'paternal jurisdiction' of the master, which is to say, his sword, now turned into contract. Hobbes' language is misleading here; the jurisdiction of the master is not 'paternal' in the case of either servant. In an earlier discussion, together with Teresa Brennan, of the disappearance of the wife and mother in Hobbes' definition of the family, we rejected the idea that her status was that of a servant.[24] I now think that we were too hasty. If a man is able to defeat a woman in the state of nature and form a little body politic or a 'family', and if that 'family' is able to defend itself and grow, the conquered woman is subsumed under the status of 'servant'. All servants are subject to the political right of the master. The master is then also master of the woman servant's children; he is master of everything that his servant owns. A master's power over all the members of his 'family' is an absolute power.

In the state of nature, free and equal individuals can become subordinates through conquest – which Hobbes calls contract. But in the state of nature there are no 'wives'. Marriage, and thus husbands and wives, appear only in civil society where the civil law includes the law of matrimony. Hobbes assumes that, in civil society, the subjection of women to men is secured through contract; not an enforced 'contract' this time, but a marriage contract. Men have no need forcibly to overpower women when the civil law upholds their patriarchal political right through the marriage contract. Hobbes states that in civil society the husband has dominion 'because for the most part commonwealths have been erected by the fathers, not by the mothers of families'.[25] Or again, 'in all cities, . . . constituted of *fathers*, not *mothers*, governing their families, the domestical command belongs to the man; and such a contract, if it be made according to the civil laws, is called matrimony.'[26]

There are two implicit assumptions at work here. First, that husbands are civil masters because men ('fathers') have made the original social contract that brings civil law into being. The men who make the original pact ensure that patriarchal political right is secured in civil society. Second, there is only one way in which women, who have the same status as free and equal individuals in the state of nature as men, can be excluded from participation in the social contract. And they must be excluded if the contract is to be sealed; rational, free and equal women would not agree to a pact that subordinated women to men in civil society. The assumption must necessarily be made that, by the time the social contract is made, all the women in the natural condition have been conquered by men and are now their subjects (servants). If any men have also been subjected and are in servitude, then they, too, will be excluded from the social contract. Only men who stand to each other as free and equal masters of 'families' will take part.

A story can be constructed that is (almost) consistent with Hobbes' general assumption about individuals, to show why it might come about that men are able to conquer women in the natural condition. In order to combat and turn upside-down the argument that political right followed naturally from the father's generative powers, Hobbes had to argue that mother-right, not paternal right, existed in the natural condition and that mother-right originated in contract. So the story might run that, at first, women are able to ensure that sexual relations are consensual. When a woman becomes a mother and decides to raise her child, her position changes; she is put at a slight disadvantage against men, since now she has her infant to defend too. A man is then able to defeat the woman he had initially to treat with as an equal (so he obtains a 'family'). The problem with the story is that, logically, given Hobbes' assumption that all individuals are completely self-interested, there seems no reason why any woman (or man) would contract to become a lord over an infant. Infants would endanger the person who had right over them by giving openings to their enemies in the war of all against all. Thus, all stories of original social contracts and civil society are nonsense because the individuals in the state of nature would be the last generation. The problem of accounting for the survival of infants is part of a general problem in contractarianism, and I shall return to the wider questions in chapter 6. One might speculate that a thinker of Hobbes' brilliance could have been aware of a difficulty here and was thus prompted to make his remark that, in the state of nature, we should think of individuals as springing up like mushrooms, a comment that Filmer dealt with scornfully and swiftly.

Hobbes is unusual in his openness about the character and scope of political domination or political right in civil society. For Hobbes, the distinction between a civil individual or citizen and an individual in subjection to a master is not that the former is free and the latter bound; 'the subjection of them who institute a commonwealth themselves, is no less absolute, than the subjection of servants.' Rather, the difference is that those who subject themselves to Leviathan (the state) do so because they judge that there is good reason for their action, and so they live in 'a state of better hope' than servants. Their 'hope' arises from the fact that an individual 'coming in freely, calleth himself, though in subjection, a *freeman*', and in civil society free men have 'the honour of equality of favour with other subjects', and 'may expect employments of honour, rather than a servant'.[27] Or, as Hobbes puts the point in another formulation, 'free subjects and sons of a family have above servants in every government and family where servants are; that they may both undergo the more honourable offices of the city or family.'[28] In civil society, Leviathan's sword upholds the civil laws that give individuals protection from forcible subjection, but individuals of their own volition can enter into contracts that constitute 'masters' and 'servants'. Or, more accurately, male individuals can.

In the natural state all women become servants, and all women are excluded from the original pact. That is to say, all women are also excluded from becoming civil individuals. No woman is a free subject. All are 'servants' of a peculiar kind in civil society, namely 'wives'. To be sure, women become wives by entering into a contract, and later I shall explore the puzzle of why beings who lack the status of (civil) individuals who can make contracts nonetheless are required to enter into the marriage contract. The relationship between a husband and wife differs from subjection between men, but it is important to emphasize that Hobbes insists that patriarchal subjection is also an example of *political* right. He stands alone in this. The other classic contract theorists all argue that conjugal right is not, or is not fully, political.

The latter is true even of Pufendorf, who begins, like Hobbes, by including women as 'individuals' in the natural state, but whose consistency soon lapses. Pufendorf argues that although, by nature, 'the male surpasses the female in strength of body and mind',[29] the inequality is not sufficient to give him natural mastery over her. Pufendorf, however, also argues that natural law shows us that marriage is the foundation of social life, and that marriage exists in the state of nature. Women do not have to get married in the natural condition. If a woman wishes merely to have a child and to retain power over it, then she can make a contract with a man 'to give each other the service of their bodies'. If the contract 'has no added convention on continued cohabitation, it will confer no authority of the one over the other, and neither will secure a right over the other'.[30] But marriage, Pufendorf declares, 'square[s] more precisely with the condition of human nature'.[31] The difference between the sexes is not sufficient to ensure men's natural mastery over women, but it turns out that it is enough to underwrite their conjugal mastery. Pufendorf writes that:

> Whatever right a man has over a woman, inasmuch as she is his equal, will have to be secured by her consent, or by a just war. Yet since it is the most natural thing for marriages to come about through good will, the first method is more suited to the securing of wives, the second to that of handmaids.[32]

The assumption is that a woman *always* agrees to subordinate herself as a wife, because of the man's degree of superior strength, and the fact that the man 'enjoys the superiority of his sex'.[33]

Pufendorf investigates the question whether marriage gives the husband 'sovereignty, or dominion, properly so called'; that is to say, whether he gains a political right. Marriage is like business where, once a business contract is concluded, the will of one party must prevail (although Pufendorf does not mention that there is presumably no fixed rule in business about which of the parties will exercise the right). A husband's power, however, is not that of a political sovereign. His right, like that of the ruling business partner, is limited, and extends only to the marriage itself; 'in matters peculiar to marriage the wife is obligated to adapt herself to the will of her husband, yet it does not at once follow that he necessarily has power over her in other acts as well.' Marriage is what Pufendorf calls 'an unequal league' in which the wife owes the husband obedience and, in return, he protects her.[34] A husband does not require the full sovereign power of life and death over his wife. The husband's right, then, is not properly political. But nor does it arise from nature. Conjugal right originates in 'an intervening pact and voluntary subjection on the part of the wife'.[35] Women's status as 'individuals' is thus immediately undercut in the state of nature. Beings who must always contract to subordinate themselves to others who enjoy a natural superiority cannot stand as free equals, and thus they cannot become civil individuals when the passage is made into civil society.

The matter is more straightforward in the state of nature pictured by Locke. Women are excluded from the status of 'individual' in the natural condition. Locke assumes that marriage and the family exist in the natural state and he also argues that the attributes of individuals are sexually differentiated; only men naturally have the characteristics of free and equal beings. Women are naturally subordinate to men and the order of nature is reflected in the structure of conjugal relations. At first sight, however, Locke can appear to be a true anti-patriarchalist – Hinton claims that he 'countered the patriarchalist case almost too effectively' – and he has even been seen as an embryonic feminist.[36] Locke points out more than once that the Fifth Commandment does not refer only to the father of a family. A mother, too, exercises authority over children; the authority is parental not paternal. More strikingly, Locke suggests that a wife can own property in her own right, and he even introduces the possibility of divorce, of a dissoluble marriage contract. When 'Procreation and Education are secured and Inheritance taken care for', then separation of husband and wife is a possibility; 'there being no necessity in the nature of the thing, nor to the ends of it, that it should always be for Life'. He goes on to say that the liberty that a wife has 'in many cases' to leave her husband illustrates that a husband does not have the power of an absolute monarch.[37]

In civil society, no one enjoys an *absolute* political right, unconstrained by the civil law. The question is not whether a husband is an absolute ruler, but whether he is a ruler at all, and, if he always has a limited (civil) right over his wife, how that comes about. Locke's answer is that conjugal power originates in nature. When arguing with Sir Robert Filmer about Adam and Eve, Locke disagrees about the character of Adam's power over Eve, not that his power exists. The battle is not over the legitimacy of a husband's conjugal right but over what to call it. Locke insists that Adam was not an absolute monarch, so that Eve's subjection was nothing more 'but that Subjection [wives] should ordinarily be in to their Husbands'. We know that wives should be subject, Locke writes, because 'generally the Laws of mankind and customs of Nations have ordered it so; *and there is, I grant, a Foundation in Nature for it.*'[38] The foundation in nature that ensures that the will of the husband

and not that of the wife prevails is that the husband is 'the abler and the stronger'.[39] Women, that is to say, are not free and equal 'individuals' but natural subjects. Once a man and a woman become husband and wife and decisions have to be made, the right to decide, or 'the last Determination, i.e., the Rule', has to be placed with one or the other (even though Locke's argument against Filmer and Hobbes is designed to show why the rule of one man is incompatible with 'civil' life). Locke states that 'it naturally falls to the Man's share' to govern over their 'common Interest and Property', although a husband's writ runs no further than that.[40]

None of this disturbs Locke's picture of the state of nature as a condition 'wherein all the Power and Jurisdiction is reciprocal, . . . without Subordination or Subjection'. When he states that he will consider 'what State all Men are naturally in', in order to arrive at a proper understanding of the character of (civil) political power, 'men' should be read literally.[41] The natural subjection of women, which entails their exclusion from the category of 'individual', is irrelevant to Locke's investigation. The subjection of women (wives) to men (husbands) is not an example of political domination and subordination. Locke has already made this clear, both in his argument with Filmer over Adam and Eve in the *First Treatise*, and in his opening statement in chapter I of the *Second Treatise* before he begins his discussion of the state of nature in chapter II. He writes that the power of a father, a master, a lord and a husband are all different from that of a magistrate, who is a properly political ruler with the power of life and death over his subjects. In the *First Treatise*, Locke claims that Eve's subjection

> can be no other Subjection than what every Wife owes her Husband . . . [Adam's] can be only a Conjugal Power, not Political, the Power that every Husband hath to order the things of private Concernment in his Family, as Proprietor of the Goods and Lands there, and to have his Will take place before that of his wife in all things of their common Concernment; but not a Political Power of Life and Death over her, much less over anybody else.[42]

Rousseau, who was critical of so much else in the theories of Hobbes, Pufendorf and Locke, has no difficulty with their arguments about conjugal right. He maintains that civil order depends on the right of husbands over their wives, which, he argues,

arises from nature, from the very different natural attributes of the sexes. Rousseau has much more to say than the other classic social contract theorists about what it is in women's natures that entails that they must be excluded from civil life. He elaborates at some length on the reasons why women 'never cease to be subjected either to a man or to the judgements of men', and why a husband must be a 'master for the whole of life'; I shall return to Rousseau's arguments in chapter 4. [43]

Several puzzles, anomalies and contradictions, which I shall take up in subsequent chapters, arise from the theoretical manoeuvering of the classic social contract theorists on the question of conjugal right and natural freedom and equality. Perhaps the most obvious puzzle concerns the status of conjugal or sex-right; why, since Hobbes, has it so rarely been seen as an example of political power? In civil society all absolute power is illegitimate (uncivil), so the fact that a husband's right over his wife is not absolute is not sufficient to render his role non-political. On the other hand, a distinguishing feature of civil society is that only the government of the state is held to provide an example of political right. Civil subordination in other 'private' social arenas, whether the economy or the domestic sphere, where subordination is constituted through contract, is declared to be non-political.

There are other difficulties about the origin of conjugal right. The classic contract theorists' arguments about the state of nature contrive to exclude women from participation in the original contract. But what about the marriage contract? If women have been forcibly subjugated by men, or if they naturally lack the capacities of 'individuals', they also lack the standing and capacities necessary to enter into the original contract. Yet the social contract theorists insist that women are capable of entering, indeed, must enter, into one contract, namely the marriage contract. Contract theorists simultaneously deny and presuppose that women can make contracts. Nor does Locke, for example, explain why the marriage contract is necessary when women are declared to be naturally subject to men. There are other ways in which a union between a man and his natural subordinate could be established, but, instead, Locke holds that it is brought into being through contract, which is an agreement between two equals.

Nor do the puzzles end once the marriage contract is concluded. Most of the classic social contract theorists present marriage as a natural relationship that is carried over into civil society. Marriage is not unique in this respect, other contractual relations are held to exist in the natural condition. The curious feature of marriage is that it retains a natural status even in civil society. Once the original contract has been made and civil society has been brought into being, the state of nature is left behind and contract should create civil, not natural, relations. Certainly, the relation between employer and worker is seen as civil, as purely contractual or conventional. But marriage must necessarily differ from other contractual relations because an 'individual' and a natural subordinate enter into the contract, not two 'individuals'. Moreover, when the state of nature is left behind, the meaning of 'civil' society is not independently given, but depends upon the contrast with the 'private' sphere, in which marriage is the central relationship. To put my later arguments about these issues into perspective, some further discussion is required about two matters; first, about the idea of 'contract' itself, and second, about contractual or civil slavery.

The first question that must be asked is why contract is seen as the paradigm of free agreement. The answer can best be ascertained by starting with the 'individual' as found in Hobbes' theory and in contemporary contractarianism, who is seen as naturally complete in himself. That is to say, the boundaries that separate one individual from another are so tightly drawn that an individual is pictured as existing without any relationships with others. The individual's capacities and attributes owe nothing to any other individual or to any social relationship; they are his alone. The contractarian individual necessarily is the proprietor of his person and his attributes, or, in C. B. Macpherson's famous description, he is a possessive individual. The individual owns his body and his capacities as pieces of property, just as he owns material property. According to this view, each individual can and must see the world and other individuals only from the perspective of his subjective assessment of how best to protect his property, or, as it is often put, from the perspective of his self-interest. Complete individual isolation disappears in the less radically individualist picture of the state of nature drawn by, say, Locke, but the crucial assumption remains; 'every Man', Locke writes, 'has a *Property* in his own *Person*. This no body has any Right to but himself.'[44] The individual's task is thus to ensure that his property right is not infringed. Individual self-protection is the problem that has to be solved in the state of nature – and the solution is contract. More precisely, since the problem has to be solved for every individual, it is the problem of social order (or to use the fashionable jargon of rational choice and game theory, a co-ordination problem), and the solution is the original contract. But why *contract*?

If the individual owns his capacities, he stands in the same external relation to this intimate property as to any other. To become the owner of the property in his person, the individual must create a relation between himself and his property, he must take possession of himself and put his will into his person and capacities to make them 'his'. Similarly, if the individual has no natural relation with any other, then all relationships must be conventional, the creation of individuals themselves; individuals must will their social relationships into existence. They do this if, and only if, they can protect their property by creating a relationship. A necessary condition of such protection is that each individual recognize the others as property owners like himself. Without this recognition others will appear to the individual as mere (potential) property, not owners of property, and so equality disappears. Mutual recognition by property owners is achieved through contract: 'contract presupposes that the parties entering it recognize each other as persons and property owners' – the words are Hegel's, the greatest critic of contract theory, who lays bare the presuppositions of contract. [45]

If property is to be protected, one individual can have access to the property of another only with the latter's agreement. An individual will allow the use of his property by another, or rent it out or sell it, only if his protection is not infringed, if it is to his advantage. If this is the case for two individuals they will make a contract with each other. Both parties to the contract enter on the same basis, as property owners who have the common purpose, or common will, to use each other's property to mutual advantage. Kant argued that the practice of contract could only be viable if such a common will was seen as a necessary part of contract and the parties transcended the standpoint of two self-interested individuals. They must, that is to say, bargain in good faith and recognize that contracts must be kept. A problem about contract arises unless the two parties declare their agreement simultaneously. Kant argued that, empirically, their declarations must be separated in time; one must follow the other, even though the time separating the two declarations might be very small indeed:

> If I have promised, and another person is now merely willing to accept, during the interval before actual Acceptance, however short it may be, I may retract my offer, because I am thus far still free; and, on the other side, the Acceptor, for the same reason, may likewise hold himself not to be bound, up till the moment of Acceptance, by his counter-declaration.

The solution to this problem is that the two declarations necessarily must be understood not as two (speech) acts that follow each other, but 'in the manner of a *pactum re initum*, as proceeding from a *common* Will'.[46]

Such a solution is not open to contractarians; if individuals necessarily act only from self-interest, the requisite 'idea of reason' of a common will cannot be generated. Contractarianism (as Hobbes' theory illustrates) gives rise to an acute problem about contract, and the problem preoccupies many contemporary philosophers. The only contract that can be made in a contractarian world is a simultaneous exchange. If there is a delay in the fulfillment of the contract then it is extremely unlikely ever to be completed, and if one individual performs first, it is always in the interest of the other to break the contract. The social contract and civil law provide security for contract by ensuring that individuals can trust each other. That the security is not complete, especially in times when contractarianism is socially influential, is illustrated by the current concern with problems of co-operation, 'performing second', free riding and the like.

Individuals recognize each other as property owners by making mutual use of, or *exchanging*, their property. Exchange is at the heart of contract; as Hobbes states, 'all contract is mutuall translation, or change of right.'[47] Each individual gains through the exchange – neither would alienate his property unless that were the case – so the exchange is therefore equal. Socialist critics of the employment contract and feminist critics of the marriage contract have attacked the claim that, if two individuals make a contract, the fact that the contract has been made is sufficient to show that the exchange must be equal. The critics point out that, if one party is in an inferior position (the worker or the woman), then he or she has no choice but to agree to disadvantageous terms offered by the superior party. However, socialist and feminist criticism of the inequality of the participants in the employment and marriage contracts takes for granted the character of the exchange itself. What does the 'exchange' in the contracts in which I am interested consist in? What exactly is exchanged?

In principle, the exchange could take a variety of forms and any kind of property could be exchanged, but the contracts that have a prominent place in classic social contract theory are not only about material goods, but property in the peculiar sense of property in the person, and they involve an exchange of obedience for protection. This exchange does not immediately have much connection with the pictures conjured up in stories of the state of nature, in which two individuals bargain over property in the woods and, for example, one exchanges some of the nuts he has gathered for part of a rabbit killed by the other. Talk of 'exchange' can be misleading in the context of property in the person. Contract theory is primarily about a way of creating social relationships constituted by subordination, not about exchange. To be sure, exchange is involved, but again, what is at issue is 'exchange' – or more accurately, two exchanges – in a special sense.

First, there is the exchange constitutive of contract and a social relationship. Unless certain signs of the commitment of the will are seen as property, this exchange does not involve property. Rather, the contract is concluded and the relationship is brought into being through the exchange of words, that is, through the performance of a speech act (or exchange of other signs, such as signatures). Once the words are said, the contract is sealed and individuals stand to each other in a new relationship. Thus, in the social contract, natural male individuals transform themselves into civil individuals (citizens); in the employment contract, men turn themselves into employer and worker; and, in the marriage contract, women become wives and men become husbands by virtue of saying 'I do'. (It should be noted, *contra* Kant, that the words could be said simultaneously, so that there is no problem about making such contracts in the state of nature; the problem is enforcement.) The second 'exchange' could not be more different from the first. The new relationship is structured through time by a permanent exchange between the two parties, the exchange of obedience for protection (and I shall say more about protection later). The peculiarity of this exchange is that one party to the contract, who provides protection, has the right to determine how the other party will act to fulfill their side of the exchange. In subsequent chapters, I will explore various ways in which the property in the person of the subordinate is used by the superior (a very odd exchange). But, as an initial illustration of this point, consider the employment contract.

I noted earlier that the contractarian conception of social life implies that there is contract 'all the way down'; social life is nothing more than contracts between individuals. Economic life should thus be structured accordingly. The fact that contractarians treat the employment contract as the exemplary contract suggests that economic institutions provide an example of their ideal. But in a capitalist firm, as Coase's neo-classical analysis makes clear, if a workman moves from one department to another, this is not because he has freely bargained with the employer and made a new contract; he moves 'because he is ordered to do so'. A firm is not, as it were, a contractarian society in miniature, constituted through a continual series of discrete contracts; as Coase writes, 'for this series of contracts is substituted one.' The employer contracts only once with each worker. In the employment contract, the worker 'for a certain remuneration (which may be fixed or fluctuating) agrees to obey the direction of an entrepreneur *within certain limits*. The essence of the contract is that it should only state the limits to the powers of the entrepreneur'.[48] Coase notes that if there were no limits the contract would be a contract of voluntary slavery. Coase also emphasizes that, the longer the period for which the employer contracts to use the services of the worker, the more desirable it is that the contract should not be specific about what the employer can command the worker to do; it is the employer's prerogative to direct the worker in his work, and, for Coase, this is the essence of the employment contract. Contract creates a relation of subordination.

In the marriage contract the 'exchange' between the parties is even more curious since only one 'individual' owner of property in the person is involved. I remarked in the previous chapter that some contemporary feminists have drawn on Lévi-Strauss, who, far from seeing the marriage contract and the exchange it incorporates as in any way curious or contradictory, proclaims that 'marriage is the archetype of exchange.'[49] And, according to Lévi-Strauss, what is exchanged during the making of the marriage contract is a singular form of property, 'that most precious category of goods, women'.[50]

Women are exchanged just as words are exchanged, and, like words, women are signs. In the penultimate paragraph of *The Elementary Forms of Kinship*, Lévi-Strauss comments that women are not merely signs (property), but also persons. The quandary whether certain human beings are nothing but property arises in another context too; for certain purposes, slave-masters could not but help recognize that their property was also human. The contradiction inherent in slavery, that the humanity of the slave must necessarily be simultaneously denied and affirmed, recurs in a variety of dramatic and less dramatic guises in modern patriarchy. Women are property, but also persons; women are held both to possess and to lack the capacities required for contract – and contract demands that their womanhood be both denied and affirmed.

Only the postulate of natural equality prevents the original social contract from being an explicit slave contract; or, to put this another way, only the postulate of natural equality prevents all the stories about social contracts from turning into a variety of coercive arrangements. The necessity of the assumption of equality in the state of nature has been illustrated (rather despite himself) by James Buchanan, a contemporary contractarian. Buchanan argues that, if contract theory is to be as general as possible, inequality rather than equality must characterize 'the original conceptual setting'.[51] He pictures two individuals in the unequal setting, where resources are scarce. One individual will discover that he can obtain goods not only by producing for himself, but by seizing them when needed from the stocks of the other. Both individuals will then have to devote resources to defending their property. Buchanan argues that, therefore, the original agreement, which must precede any social contract, is a contract, or 'bilateral behavioral exchange, of mutual disarmament.[52] However, there is no reason why such an agreement should occur in a condition of inequality.

Under the heading 'Conquest, Slavery and Contract', Buchanan also briefly mentions other possible outcomes in the original setting where 'personal differences are sufficiently great'.[53] Some individuals may be capable of killing others, and the disarmament pact will be made only after a proportion of the population has been eliminated. In this case, as in the two-person case, Buchanan's original setting looks very like Hobbes' state of nature; the inequalities between the two individuals or between the survivors are not sufficiently large to enable any individual or a group decisively to defeat the others. In effect, Buchanan has smuggled a rough natural equality back in. Individuals therefore have a reason and an incentive to contract to disarm: general security of property is secured. Buchanan's other example is quite different. Here the outcome of the assumption that some individuals have 'superior capacities' is that the strong seize the goods of the weak and less capable (instead of killing them). They then make a disarmament contract, but in this case, Buchanan states, it 'may be something similar to the slave contract'. Once the weak are conquered, a contract is made in which the weak agree to produce for the strong in exchange for 'something over and above bare subsistence'. Both sides gain from this slave contract because of the reduction in 'defense and predation effort'.

Buchanan remarks that his account may 'represent a somewhat tortuous interpretation of slavery', but that it is designed to make his analysis completely general. In fact, apart from the references to disarmament, his argument is in the tradition of the classic contract theorists' discussions of slave contracts. His argument also shows the necessity, not the redundancy, of the assumption about natural equality if the inherent problems of contract theory are not to become too obvious. If some individuals are assumed by nature to be significantly stronger or more capable than others, and if it is also assumed that individuals are always self-interested, then the social contract that creates equal civil individuals or citizens, governed by impartial laws, is impossible; the original pact will establish a society of masters and slaves. The strong – in their own interests – will conquer, forcibly disarm and seize the goods of the weak, and then make a contract in which the conquered agree henceforth to work in return for their subsistence, or protection. The strong can present the contract as being to the advantage of both; the strong no longer have to labour and the weak now can be assured that their basic needs will be provided for. Alternatively, both sides could be seen as bearing a burden; the slaves have to work (to obey), the masters bear responsibility for the slaves' welfare. The slave contract weighs equally heavily on, or is to the equal advantage of, them both.

To generalize Buchanan's argument raises some embarrassing questions about actual contracts in our society. When the strong coerce the weak into the slave contract, the obvious objection is that it is not really a 'contract'; the coercion invalidates the 'agreement'. Hobbes exemplifies one extreme in contract theory by drawing no distinction between free agreement and coerced submission. The formation of the 'family' in the state of nature illustrates Hobbes' assumption that, when individuals contract with one another, their reasons for doing so make no difference to the validity of the contract; the fact that the contract has been 'willed' into being is sufficient. Hobbes denies that there is any difference between, say, sitting alone in one's study and carefully weighing up whether to enter into a contract, and making the decision with a gun at one's head. But there is no need to go as far as the conqueror's sword. An 'incentive' is always available in conditions of substantial social inequality that will ensure that the 'weak' enter into contracts. When social inequality prevails, questions arise about what counts as voluntary entry into a contract. This is why socialists and feminists have focused on the conditions of entry into the employment contract and the marriage contract. Men and women in the Anglo–American countries are now juridically free and equal citizens, but, in unequal social conditions, the possibility cannot be ruled out that some or many contracts create relationships that bear uncomfortable resemblances to a slave contract.

Contract, one critic has commented recently, 'is a device for traders, entrepreneurs, and capitalists, not for children, servants, indentured wives, and slaves'.[54] But this is not quite so; contract is seen as a device entirely suitable for servants and wives – and some contract theorists have also seen contract as a device for slaves. The assumptions of contract theory would appear to rule out slavery, at least among men. The central claim of contract theory is that contract is the means to secure and enhance individual freedom. Slavery is the antithesis to freedom, exemplifying the total subjection of an individual to the arbitrary will of a master. Thus contract and slavery must be mutually exclusive. Why, then, do some contract theorists, past and present, include slave contracts, or contracts that closely resemble slave contracts, among legitimate agreements?

The idea of a slave contract, or what I am calling civil slavery, has a very fanciful air about it. Most people would not think of a slave making a contract to work for a master of his own free will, but rather (like the slaves in the American South) being forcibly transported from Africa, involuntarily bought and sold and then put to work under the threat of the lash. On this matter, if on few others concerning contract, Rawlsian intuitions are a reliable guide. Contractual slavery has only one element in common with slavery as it existed historically; real slavery is for life and so is the duration of the slave contract. Numerous examples can be found of people selling themselves into slavery,[55] but such self-enslavement is not the same as voluntary entry into civil slavery. The civil slave contract does not create a slave in the usual sense of 'slave'. Instead, the slave contract creates a 'slave' who is just like a worker or wage labourer, except for the duration of his contract. Contemporary contractarians, following some earlier precedents, assimilate the slave contract to the employment contract; the civil slave contract is merely an extended employment contract.

There is a nice historical irony here. In the American South, slaves were emancipated and turned into wage labourers, and now American contractarians argue that all workers should have the opportunity to turn themselves into civil slaves. But the slave society of the Old South stands apart from other societies, ancient and modern, where economic production was based on slavery (slaves have, of course, existed too in many societies where economic production depended on other forms of labour, including Britain; I shall say something about Britain in chapter 5). In North America a slave society formed part of a wider social order that proclaimed itself as civil, perhaps the prime example of a civil society, a society based on contract. Six states in the Old South passed legislation between 1856 and 1860 that enabled blacks voluntarily to enslave themselves.[56] The Founding Fathers of the United States – notably Thomas Jefferson, who owned slaves until the day he died – proclaimed the familiar tenets of the social contract theorists, especially as formulated by Locke; 'every body of men', Jefferson cried, possess 'the right of self-government. They receive it with their being from the hand of nature'.[57]

Slaves form a unique category of labourers, although in practice it may be hard in many cases to distinguish the conditions under which a slave exists from the conditions of other forms of unfree labour, such as serfdom, peonage, indentured, bonded or convict labour. A slave is different from other labourers because he is, legally, the property of a master. A slave ceases to be a person and becomes a thing, a *res*, a commodity that can be bought and sold like any other piece of property. The master owns not merely the labour, or services or labour power, of a slave but the slave himself. Thus one succinct definition of a slave states that 'his person is the property of another man, his will is subject to his owner's authority, and his labor or services are obtained through coercion.'[58] But slavery involves more than the transformation of humans into property. A slave, in Orlando Patterson's striking formulation, is 'a socially dead person'. The slave was forced into 'a secular excommunication' so that 'he ceased to belong in his own right to any legitimate social order.' The slave was also 'dishonored in a generalized way' because his social existence and worth was entirely reflected through the master.[59] Perhaps it hardly needs to be said that a person does not become a dishonoured, socially dead piece of property by entering a civil contract.

Historically, most authorities are agreed, slavery originated not in contract but in war and conquest:

> Archetypically, slavery was a substitute for death in war. . . . Slavery was not a pardon; it was, peculiarly, a conditional commutation. The execution was suspended only as long as the slave acquiesced in his powerlessness. The master was essentially a ransomer. What he brought or acquired was the slave's life, and restraints on the master's capacity wantonly to destroy his slave did not undermine his claim on that life.[60]

Slavery remained bound up with violence and conquest. Slaves died and were manumitted and, if the stock of slaves was to be maintained, the original acquisition had continually to be repeated (although in the American South slaves reproduced themselves at a high rate and manumissions were infrequent).[61] A conservative estimate is that at least *fifteen million* Africans were taken as slaves to the New World.[62] Slave-masters took pains to ensure that their slaves were marked as powerless through a variety of means, including naming, clothing, hair-styles, language and body marks,[63] and use of the emblematic master's instrument, the whip. Moses Finley recounts a (fictitious) tale from Herodotus about the manner in which the Scythians regained their mastery over their slaves in revolt: 'so long as they see us with arms, they think themselves our equals and of equal birth. But once they see us with whips instead of arms, they will understand that they are our slaves.'[64] Centuries later, Nietzsche has the little old woman say to Zarathustra, 'you are going to women? Do not forget the whip!'[65]

The idea that individuals or categories of human beings could be permanently subjugated is a human invention. Gerder Lerner speculates that slavery came about because an example of subordination and 'otherness' had already developed. Women were already subordinated to the men of their social groups. Men must have observed that women easily became socially marginal if they were deprived of the protection of their kinsmen or were no longer required for sexual use, and so men 'learned that differences can be used to separate and divide one group of humans from another'. They also developed the means to make such separation into permanent slavery.[66] Whatever its origins, Lerner emphasizes a feature of slavery that is often glossed over: the first slaves were *women*.[67] The question of why men were killed and women enslaved seems to admit of only one answer; women slaves could be put to more uses than men slaves. Women can be used sexually by men in addition to being used as a labour force, and, through sexual use, the slave labour force can be reproduced. One historian of slavery has written that 'free sexual access to slaves marks them off from all other persons as much as their juridical classification as property.'[68] Moreover, once women had been captured, used sexually and given birth, they might resign themselves to their captive state in an attempt to protect their children, and so give an incentive for other women, rather than men, to be enslaved.[69]

Be that as it may, the real historical slave, female or male, appears to stand at the opposite pole from the wage labourer. The slave is captured, turned into property and forced to labour. In return, the slave receives the subsistence that enables the slave-master to continue to enjoy his or her labour. In complete contrast, the worker is juridically free and a civil equal; he voluntarily enters into an employment contract and in exchange he receives a wage. The worker does not contract out himself or even his labour to a master. The worker is an 'individual' who offers the capitalist use of part of the property that he owns in his person; namely, his services or, in socialist terminology, his labour power. The employment contract exemplifies the individual's freedom to dispose of his property as he, and only he, sees fit. Contract is thus central to *free* labour.

But contract doctrine cuts both ways. On the one hand, the natural freedom and equality of men can be used to denounce the immorality, violence and injustice of slavery, an argument used extensively by the abolitionists. On the other hand, men as 'individuals' may legitimately contract out their services, the property they own in their persons. If the individual owns the property in his person then he, and he alone, must decide how that property is to be used. Only the individual owner can decide whether or not it is to his advantage to enter into a particular contract, and he may decide that his interests are best met by contracting out his services for life in return for the protection (subsistence) that such a contract affords. The assumption that the individual stands to the property in his person, to his capacities or services, as any owner stands to his material property, enables the opposition between freedom and slavery to be dissolved. Civil slavery becomes nothing more than one example of a legitimate contract. Individual freedom becomes exemplified in slavery. The opposition between autonomy and subjection can thus be maintained only by modifying or rejecting contract doctrine: limits can be placed on freedom of contract (a strategy that contractarians are now contesting); or the conception of the individual as owner can be rejected in favour of alternative conceptions.

Advocates of the slave contract, from the classic social contract theorists, through defenders of slavery in the Old South, to contemporary contractarians, argue that conventional definitions of a 'slave' are outmoded and inaccurate in civil society. For instance, the definition that I quoted above – that a slave is property, that his labour is coerced and that he is subject to the authority of his master – applies, it is held, only to earlier forms of slavery, not the modern contractual form. A civil slave is neither property nor subject to compulsion, although he is subject to the authority of his master. In the latter respect he is just like any other worker. As I have indicated, the employment contract constitutes the worker as the subordinate of his employer who has the right to direct him in his work. An employer, though, is not quite like a slave-master; the right of an employer is the limited right of a modern civil master, not the absolute right of the slave-master. Contractual slaves can thus take their place in civil society as member of families and workplaces.

One well-known defence of slavery in the American South, George Fitzhugh's *Cannibals All!*, argued that slaves were better off than ordinary workers, but his argument, though ingenious, is not modern in form. Fitzhugh looks back to Locke's patriarchalist antagonist Sir Robert Filmer. [70] Fitzhugh argues that men are born into subjection and that the family, which includes slaves, with its master at its head, is the model for political order. Fitzhugh's writings are intriguing because of his attack on wage labour, civil freedom, equality and consent (contract). He brands Locke as a 'presumptuous charlatan, who was as ignorant of the science or practice of government as any shoemaker or horse jockey'.[71] Fitzhugh accepted the arguments of critics of the horrors of capitalism in Britain in the nineteenth century. Workers were merely slaves without masters (the subtitle of his book) whose condition was far worse than that of the black slaves who had all their needs provided for. The slave-owner had to make complete provision for life for his slaves, unlike the capitalist who, 'living on his income, gives nothing to his subjects. He lives by mere exploitation'.[72] Fitzhugh defended slavery against capitalism by appealing to the old pre-capitalist and pre-contractual patriarchal order. But there were other, less well-known, defenders of slavery who claimed that slavery (as it actually existed in the Old South) was based on a contract between master and slave. Slavery could thus be incorporated into the new civil world.

Perhaps the most extraordinary such defence of slavery in the Old South is the Reverend Samuel Seabury's *American Slavery Distinguished from the Slavery of English Theorists and Justified by the Law of Nature*. According to Seabury, 'slavery in the United States rests on a different foundation' from slavery in earlier times.[73] A Roman slave-master, for example, had absolute, unlimited power over his slaves, who were his captives and his property. In America, a master exercised only a limited power and, therefore, could not be seen as the owner of his slave. Seabury states that there is 'no *proper* sense' in which the master is an owner; he 'has a *conditional* right to the *service* of the slave'. The slave is neither coerced nor property. Seabury writes, 'the truth is, so far as I can see, that the *obligation to service for life*, on condition of protection and support, is the *essence* of American slavery.'[74] Another American advocate of slavery agreed with Seabury on this point:

> Slavery is the duty and obligation of the slave to labor for the mutual benefit of both master and slave, under a warrant to the slave of protection, and a comfortable subsistence, under all circumstances. The person of the slave is not property, no matter what the fictions of the law may say; but the right to his labor is property, and may be transferred like any other property, or as the right to the services of a minor and apprentice may be transferred.[75]

Property in services can be made the subject of contract. The slave contract has no special features that differentiate it from other examples of free contract and the slave is merely one labourer among others.

The Reverend Seabury quotes from Pufendorf and Grotius, and, with the exception of Hobbes (and, for very different reasons, Rousseau), the classic social contract theorists give ample authority for a contractual defence of slavery. On this issue, as on many others, Hobbes lets contractual cats out of the bag. Hobbes' social contract brings Leviathan into being, whose absolute power is symbolized by the sword. A contractarian starting-point implies an absolutist conclusion. In the absence of all natural relations and all trust between individuals, the only way in which long-term associations can be sustained is through the force of the sword and through absolute obedience.[76] Hobbes renames conquest as 'contract' and this makes him unsuitable as a model for modern contract theorists. In addition, his account of slavery comes much too close to its historical origins. Hobbes defines a slave as an individual who is captured and kept in prison or chains until his master decides his fate. A slave is under no obligation to his master. Nor is such a captive of any use to his master (unless, one can add, the slave is female and the use is sexual, which is not inhibited by chains). If the captive is to be useful, he must be released from his chains and bound in another way. The conqueror thus has an incentive to offer his captive a contract which releases him from prison and spares his life – and, according to Hobbes, puts an end to his slavery. Once the individual has exchanged his life in return for a pledge of obedience to his master he becomes a 'servant'. To save his life, he indicates 'either in express words, or by other sufficient signs of the will' that his conqueror may have the use of his body, 'at his pleasure', for as long as his life is spared.[77] Hobbes holds that the contract transforms slavery into servitude, but Hobbes' description of the master's power over the servant looks like that of a slave-master: 'the Master of the Servant, is Master . . . of all he hath; and may exact the use thereof; that is to say, of his goods, of his labour, of his servants, and of his children, as often as he shall think fit.'[78]

Grotius clings to the idea that the master owns the slave, but he provides a more promising basis for civil slavery than Hobbes. Grotius states firmly that 'to every man it is permitted to enslave himself to any one he pleases for private ownership.'[79] However, a slave-owner does not have the absolute right of the power of life and death over his slave. Grotius distinguishes two forms of slavery. In 'complete slavery', the slave 'owes lifelong service in return for nourishment and other necessaries of life'. The second form is 'incomplete slavery' which includes 'men hired for pay'.[80] Grotius also emphasizes the advantage of complete slavery; 'the lasting obligation to labour is repaid with a lasting certainty of support, which often those do not have who work for hire by the day.'[81] Despite Grotius' endorsement of slavery, Pufendorf offers the most serviceable contractual story. In some passages quoted by the Reverend Seabury, Pufendorf presents a conjectural history of the origin of slavery that renders slavery compatible with a natural condition in which men 'have no common master, and one is not subject to the other'.[82]

There are two ways, Pufendorf conjectures, in which slavery was established by consensus. His first suggestion is that the development of households led to the discovery 'how conveniently the affairs of the household can be cared for by the services of others', namely slaves. Pufendorf suggests that the slaves probably freely offered their services, 'being compelled by want or a sense of their own incapacity'. The slaves received in exchange 'a perpetual supply of food and other necessaries'.[83] Alternatively, Pufendorf suggests that, once men in their natural condition turned their attention to increasing their possessions, some men accumulated more than others. The 'sagacious and more wealthy' then invited the 'more sluggish and the poorer sort' to hire themselves out to work. Both the rich and the poor came to see that there were mutual advantages in this arrangement. The poor gradually attached themselves permanently to wealthy families and worked as the rich commanded, and, in exchange, the wealthy masters 'provided sustenance and all other necessities of life'. Pufendorf concludes that, 'the first beginnings of slavery followed upon the willing consent of men of poorer condition, and a contract of the form of "goods for work": I will always provide for you, if you will always work for me.'[84]

The obvious question raised by Pufendorf's stories is why such a contract is a slave contract. Why is it not an employment contract? Why do not the 'poorer sort' turn themselves into servants or workers through the contract? (Perhaps a less obvious question, to which I shall return in later chapters, is why the marriage contract is not a slave contract; Pufendorf's slaves are incorporated into families and a wife, like a slave, is under the jurisdiction of the master of the family for her lifetime.) The question about slaves and workers is not so easy to answer as might be thought. Four criteria are usually held to separate an employer from a slave-master. First, an employer is a civil master and does not have the absolute power of the slave-owner; second, an employment contract runs for a short specified period, not for life (in the 1660s, in Virginia, for example, indentured servants were legally distinguished from slaves by the fact that 'all negroes and other slaves shall serve *durante vita*');[85] third, an employer does not obtain right over the person or labour of a worker but a right to his services or use of his labour power; fourth, an employer does not provide subsistence but pays wages to his workers. These four criteria are less robust than is usually assumed.

Pufendorf separates sovereignty over men from proprietorship over material things. A sovereign master can say of his subject as of his property, 'he is mine', but, Pufendorf argues, although he has the absolute right to do as he will with material property, which cannot be injured, a master's right over human subjects is limited. He has a duty to protect his slaves in return for their obedience to his commands.[86] Pufendorf's master begins to look rather like an employer, especially since there is no need for Pufendorf's masters to own their slaves as property. They need only enter into a contract with the slaves which gives them right of command for life over the use to which the slave's services are put.

Locke's arguments are instructive on the dividing-line between freedom, free labour and slavery. Locke, like Hobbes, argues that '*as soon as Compact enters, Slavery ceases.*'[87] The relationship between master and slave cannot be established through contract. A slave, for Locke, is an individual who is under the absolute domination of a master; a slave-master has the power of life and death over his slave. Locke argues that no individual has the right to dispose of his own life (a power that belongs to God), so he cannot give himself up into the absolute power of another. A master and slave are in a state of war. Thus, where a household includes slaves, the master's relation to them differs from the civil mastery that he exercises over his wife and children, which is limited in its scope and stops short of the power of life and death. The master and the slave are not in civil society even though the slave is included in the family.

The civil relationship, established through contract, is that of master and servant. The master and servant contract 'for a limited Power on the one side, and Obedience on the other'.[88] A free man, Locke tells us, turns himself into a servant by 'selling . . . for a certain time, the Service he undertakes to do, in exchange for wages he is to receive: . . . the Master [has] but a Temporary Power over him, and no greater, than what is contained in the Contract between 'em'.[89] But how long is a 'certain time'? Locke's individuals own the property in their persons, including their labour power. Only the property owner can decide how best to use his property, so there is no reason why Locke's servant should not judge that a lifetime's contract with the same master will afford him the maximum amount of protection. If he enters into such a contract what then is his status? Is he a servant or a slave? According to Locke, he cannot be a slave if the relationship is created through contract. But a (civil) slave contracts away the property in his labour power for life, and so is something more than a servant. Thus, the limitation on the duration of the contract appears to be the only thing that divides a slave from a servant or wage labourer.

Contemporary contractarians argue that any such dividing-line should be swept away. In *Anarchy, State and Utopia*, a book much applauded by political philosophers, Robert Nozick asks whether 'a free system would allow [the individual] to sell himself into slavery', and he answers 'I believe that it would.'[90] More strongly, Philmore, for example, argues for a '*civilized* form of contractual slavery'.[91] Philmore cites Locke, which may seem surprising given the conventional view of Locke as an unambiguous champion of freedom. Locke did not own slaves, but he held stock in the Royal Africa Company which had a monopoly in the slave trade and he also promoted the Company's trade to Virginia in the late 1690s from his position at the Board of Trade. According to Philmore, a slave contract is nothing more than a form of employment contract; 'contractual slavery [is] . . . the individual . . . extension of the employer–employee contract.' Philmore makes no bones about the fundamental role of the employment contract in contractarian argument. He asserts that 'any thorough and decisive critique of voluntary slavery . . . would carry over to the employment contract. . . . Such a critique would thus be a *reductio ad absurdum*'.[92] The difference between the conventional employment contract and a slave contract is merely the duration of the contract. Civilized slavery is a contract for life. Philmore calls this 'warranteeism' (taking the term from another defender of slavery in the American South in the nineteenth century). The master exchanges 'a lifetime guarantee of food, clothing, and shelter (or equivalent money income) in return for the lifetime right to [the slave's] labor services'.[93] In civilized slavery, however, the contract can be ended by the slave on payment of requisite damages.

Philmore's argument for contractual or civilized slavery depends on three unstated assumptions. First, the argument depends on the possibility of separating services or labour power from the person and labour of the slave. The difference between warranteeism and (historical) slavery hinges on the new conception of the individual as a naturally free and equal individual who owns property in his person. The individual's property can be contracted out without any injury to, detriment to, or diminishment of the individual self which owns the property. That an individual can contract out the property in his labour power, rather than his labour or person, is usually taken to distinguish free wage labour from unfree slavery. For a contractarian it is the feature that demonstrates that (civilized) slavery is nothing more than an extended wage-labour contract, and an exemplification, not the denial, of the individual's freedom!

Second, the contractarian argument appears to circumvent the great contradiction and paradox of slavery; that the master must at once deny and affirm the humanity of the slave. Finley notes that the contradiction did not worry slave-owners in the ancient world; only in modern times does it become a problem.[94] An explanation for the unease felt by American slave-masters is that, historically, only they owned slaves within a social order centred on an (ostensibly) universal doctrine of individual freedom and equality. By arguing that slavery was based on a contract and that the slave was not property, only his services were, defenders of slavery in the nineteenth century and contemporary advocates of the slave contract appear to have overcome the contradiction. The civil slave, too, is an 'individual' who has freely contracted to give a lifetime's labour to a master, and the latter must respect the same rights in the case of his slave as of any other employee who, juridically, is a free and equal citizen. However, the apparent dissolution of the paradox of slavery depends upon the claim that services, capacities, labour power can be separated from the person. The claim cannot be upheld; the idea of labour power or services (as I shall explore in some detail in chapter 5) is another political fiction.

Third, Philmore's argument also rests on the assumption that, in return for obedience, the civil slave receives not just subsistence or protection but an 'equivalent money income', that is, a wage. A distinguishing feature of a free worker is that he does not receive protection; he is not paid in kind or with truck but receives wages. In the case of the civil slave the wages are guaranteed for life by the employment contract, and this raises the question of what status the wage is assumed to have in arguments for contractual slavery. In Britain in the eighteenth century, the question of the meaning of a wage was considered by opponents of slavery. They argued that the dividing-line between a slave and a free worker was constituted by the existence of a sign that a true exchange had been made between worker and employer; the sign was payment of a wage in return for the worker's services. The context in which the question arose shows clearly how ambiguous the distinction is between protection and a wage. The matter at issue was the situation of colliers and salters in Scotland who were bound for life in their work (and who could be sold by mine and salt-work owners along with the rest of their means of production; some of them even wore collars bearing their owners' names). Their servitude was abolished in 1775 (as a result of *Knight v. Wedderburn*) but eminent opponents of slavery had argued that the colliers were distinct from slaves because they received (relatively high) wages. Their lifetime servitude was attributed to commercial necessity and the peculiar conditions of the industries. David Brion Davis comments that 'for antislavery advocates . . . it was not the slave's subordination or lack of mobility that ran contrary to nature. It was rather the lack of any token of exchange which would make the worker responsible, at least theoretically, for his own destiny.'[95]

Contemporary contractarianism rests on the claim that the 'individual' is sovereign master of his own destiny; only he has the right of disposition over the property in his person. By contracting out his property in an employment contract the individual becomes a worker and receives a wage. But is the wage, particularly if guaranteed for a lifetime, a token of freedom or subordination, a sign of free labour or wage slavery? A peculiar kind of freedom is invoked when it can be exemplified in subjection for life. The ease with which contractarians turn slavery into wage labour also raises questions about the connections and resemblances between slavery, civil slavery and other contracts involving property in the person. The issue of the relation between contracts of various kinds is, more often than not, glossed over, but it has received some attention recently in the controversy over paternalism. Philmore, for example, proclaims that it is a 'fundamental contradiction' in a modern liberal society for the state to prohibit slave contracts.[96] Philosophers have run into difficulties in finding a really convincing reason why slave contracts should not be upheld by law, or why, to put this a different way, slave contracts should not be brought under the protection of the original contract.

Contractarianism is anti-paternalist, but resolution of the problem of slave contracts is harder for less radical advocates of contract. Most participants in the debate over paternalism have no reservations about other contracts in which protection is offered in exchange for obedience, so they find it hard to give acceptable reasons to rule out state enforcement of a contract that provides the ultimate form of protection. Ruling out the civil slave contract becomes even more difficult if, as has happened in the case of the marriage contract, such a contract could be brought to an end before the lifelong term is completed. For many philosophers, the indissoluble character of the slave contract poses the major difficulty; 'the problem with voluntary slavery contracts is that the conditions for assuring oneself that there is a continuing affirmation [of the contract by the slave] do not exist.'[97] In a recent survey of the current controversy over paternalism, the conclusion is reached that the only reason for prohibiting indissoluble slave contracts is that individuals change their minds. Moreover, the claim is made that, in contemporary Western societies, the only reason why dissoluble slave contracts cannot be admitted is that society does not have an interest in such contracts, whereas it does have an interest in enforcing dissoluble marriage contracts and employment contracts. Such an argument leaves open the possibility that, in some circumstances, slave contracts are in the interest of society. The claim is duly made that, in conditions of great scarcity, dissoluble slavery contracts may serve a societal interest if they reduce welfare costs and enable progress to be made to a condition of moderate rather than extreme scarcity.[98]

The best-known statement of the case against state enforcement of slave contracts was made by John Stuart Mill in his famous essay *On Liberty*, in which Mill insisted that freedom and slavery were incompatible. He states that a slave contract would be 'null and void'. An individual may voluntarily choose to enter such a contract if he sees it to his advantage, but, in so doing,

he abdicates his liberty; he foregoes any future use of it beyond that single act. He therefore defeats, in his own case, the very purpose

which is the justification of allowing him to dispose of himself. . . .
The principle of freedom cannot require that he should be free not to
be free. It is not freedom, to be allowed to alienate his freedom.

Mill adds that 'these reasons, the force of which is so conspicuous in
this peculiar case, are evidently of far wider application.'[99] Mill was
very unusual in going on to apply these reasons to the marriage
contract and the subjection of women, and so to question patriarchal
right. Mill was also sympathetic to the arguments of the co-operative
socialists and willing to question the employment contract, but he
did not bring these two wider applications of his criticism together.

Mill's argument against slavery had been foreshadowed a century
before by one of the classic contract theorists. Rousseau, too,
rejected slave contracts and any relationship that arose because one
man, from economic necessity, had to sell himself to another; but he
supported the sexual contract wholeheartedly. Rousseau is an exception to the consensus among the classic contract theorists that
slavery, or something divided from it by the most permeable of lines,
can legitimately be established through contract. Rousseau
states that 'the words "slavery" and "right" are contradictory, they
cancel each other out.'[100] There can be no such thing as a contract
between a master and slave that is to the advantage of each or that
involves reciprocity. Rousseau comments that a man who sells
himself into slavery does so in return for subsistence, but clearly
Rousseau does not see the grant of subsistence as giving the slave
anything in return for his services. Rather, subsistence is necessary
if any service is to be provided. The master owns the slave and
everything that is his, therefore, Rousseau writes, 'what right can
my slave have against me? If everything he has belongs to me, his
right is *my* right, and it would be nonsense to speak of my having a
right *against* myself.'[101] So any talk of slave contracts and mutual
exchange and duties is illogical, absurd, nonsense, completely
without meaning. Rousseau thinks that anyone who entered a
contract to be another's slave would not be in his right mind. He
would have lost the ability to appreciate his own status as a free man
and what that entails. To believe that natural freedom and equality
was manifest in slave contracts, meant that none of the individuals
involved could have understood the relationship in which they stood
one to another, since they had all renounced the necessary condition
of their free mutual interaction.

Rousseau argued that the story told by his fellow contract theorists
was about a fraudulent contract that merely endorsed the coercive

power of the rich over the poor. However, Rousseau did not extend his attack on his predecessors to their arguments about women and the marriage contract. The marriage contract was placed outside of the reach of the analogy with the illegitimate and absurd slave contract. Rousseau's conjectural history of the state of nature and his story of the social contract is very different from the stories of the other contract theorists, and thus helps disguise the fact that he, like all the rest, enthusiastically endorses the sexual contract. In other respects, Rousseau's rejection of the slave contract means that his interpretation of 'contract' has little in common with the theory that includes slavery, albeit as an extension of the employment contract. His theory precludes the reduction of contract between men to enforced submission, and, for Rousseau, not all contracts are legitimate, no free individual can make a contract that denies his own freedom.

The other contract theorists, to a great or lesser degree, all picture the individual, above all else, as a proprietor. This is true even of Kant, who states that 'a Contract by which the one party renounced his *whole* freedom for the advantage of the other, ceasing thereby to be a person and consequently having no duty even to observe a Contract, is self-contradictory, and is therefore of itself null and void.'[102] Apart from Rousseau, the classic contract theorists see the freedom of the individual as revolving round an act, the act of contract. The individual takes possession of himself and his freedom is then exercised through his ability to dispose of himself as he sees fit. Natural, equal freedom is turned into civil mastery and subordination, including slavery, which is held to be the exemplification of freedom because it originates in a voluntary contract. In contrast, the individual in Rousseau's contract story is not an owner, but a man whose individuality depends upon the maintenance of free relationships with other men. If he attempts to separate his capacities (services or labour power) from himself by alienating them through a contract he brings about a qualitative change in his relationship to others; freedom is turned into mastery and subjection. Slavery is thus the paradigm of what freedom is not, instead of an exemplification of what it is. For Rousseau, it therefore follows that any relationship that resembles slavery is illegitimate, and no contract that creates a relationship of subordination is valid – except the sexual contract.

4

Genesis, Fathers and the Political Liberty of Sons

To tell the story of the sexual contract a good deal of reconstruction has to be done. The amazing powers of Sir Robert Filmer's father have to be given their due, Freud's stories of political origins have to be considered alongside the more famous social contract stories and the story of the primal scene has to be told. Before I turn to these tasks, fraternity, the term that is usually missing in discussions of the social contract and civil society, must be restored to its rightful place. Attention is almost always directed to liberty and equality, but the revolutionary values are liberty, equality and *fraternity*. The revolution in which the slogan '*liberté, égalité, fraternité*' was proclaimed began in 1789, but the alliance between the three elements was forged much earlier. Modern patriarchy is fraternal in form and the original contract is a fraternal pact.

Most commentaries on the classic social contract theorists refer generally to 'individuals' making the original contract, with the implicit assumption that the 'individual' is a universal category that (in principle) includes everyone. In *Patriarchalism in Political Thought*, Schochet points out that in the seventeenth century it was taken for granted that fathers entered into the social contract on behalf of their families. When I first began to think about these questions I mistakenly assumed that the original contract was patriarchal because it was made by fathers. This cannot be the case; the reason that the contract is necessary is because fathers have been stripped of their political power. The participants in the original contract must be capable of creating and exercising political right, which they can no longer do as fathers. Locke's friend, James Tyrrell, wrote of the original contract that women were 'concluded by their Husbands, and [are] commonly unfit for civil business'. [1] But the male participants do not take part in the contract as husbands. Rather, the men who defeat the father, claim their natural liberty and, victorious, make the original contract, are acting as brothers; that is to say, as fraternal kin or the sons of a father, and by contracting together they constitute themselves as a civil fraternity. Fraternity, it has been said, 'is a word to conjure with at all times and by all fires'. [2] A very nice conjuring trick has been performed so that one kinship term, fraternity, is held to be merely a metaphor for the universal bonds of humankind, for community, solidarity or fellowship, while another kinship term, patriarchy, is held to stand for the rule of fathers which passed away along ago. The modern civil order can then be presented as universal ('fraternal') not patriarchal. Almost no one – except some feminists – is willing to admit that fraternity means what it says: the brotherhood of *men*.

The claim has been made that there is an 'inner contradiction' in the trilogy of liberty, equality, fraternity, since 'without a father there can be no [sons] or brothers.' [3] Patriarchal civil society may be fatherless but that does not make fraternity an inappropriate term. Remarkably little attention has been paid to fraternity compared to liberty and equality, but recent discussions of fraternity have paid implicit tribute to the fact that modern society is not structured by kinship. Fraternity is seen as a free union, and its proponents insist that 'fraternity' implies the existence of communal bonds that are civil or public, not confined to assignable persons, and that are freely chosen. [4] Such an interpretation of fraternity has become so widely accepted that, although feminists have long appreciated that community or socialist solidarity has usually meant that women are merely auxiliaries to the comrades, they have also spoken the language of fraternity. Simone de Beauvoir opens the last chapter of *The Second Sex* with the statement, 'no, woman is not our brother', and the final words of the book are, 'it is necessary, . . . that by and through their natural differentiation men and women unequivocally affirm their brotherhood.' [5] Again, when liberals, from the nineteenth century onward, attempted to redress the abstract character of the classical (liberal) contract theorists' conception of the individual by developing a more adequately social and communal view, they turned to the idea of fraternity. Gerald Gaus states in his recent study that, in the eyes of modern liberals, fraternity is 'the most powerful of communal bonds', and that the ideal of fraternity provides the 'preeminent conception of communal bonds in modern liberal theory'. Dewey, for instance, wrote of a 'fraternally associated public', and Rawls regards his difference principle as a 'natural meaning of fraternity'.[6]

Large claims have been made for fraternity; 'fraternity with liberty is humanity's greatest dream.'[7] Fraternity is 'a concept that has been the *cri de coeur* of modernity and, more recently, appropriated by America's radical academe'.[8] The communal bonds of fraternity have been seen as both completely general and diffuse or more local and particular. In the nineteenth century, James Fitzjames Stephen argued that fraternity was 'the creed of a religion', the religion of humanity, and that fraternity was 'the mere feeling of eager indefinite sympathy with mankind'.[9] More recently, fraternity has been characterized as 'at bottom, a certain type of social cooperation . . . a relation between a group of equals for the utmost mutual help and aid'.[10] Or, as Bernard Crick expresses it, addressing his fellow socialists, fraternity 'goes with simplicity, lack of ostentation, friendliness, helpfulness, kindliness, openness, lack of restraint between individuals in everyday life, and a willingness to work together in common tasks'.[11] More generally, John Dunn has declared that democracy is 'simply the political form of fraternity'.[12] But such statements do not explain why fraternity as kinship is now irrelevant, nor why the literal meaning of fraternity is not considered in most discussions. Nor is any indication given of why fraternity, rather than another term, should be used as a synonym for community, or why it belongs with liberty and equality in the famous revolutionary slogan.

The relevance of fraternity as a masculine bond is illustrated (though not acknowledged) by Wilson Carey McWilliams. McWilliams argues that to understand fraternity it is necessary to investigate societies in which kinship was the most important relationship. Traditionally, he states, maternal and paternal authority were distinguished: the mother 'seems universally associated with warmth, affection, and sensory gratification . . . with birth and nurture, . . . [and] mysteries'; paternal authority represented the 'abstract as opposed to the immediate', and it derived from 'what is outside or transcends' the community.[13] The childhood association of authority with a particular father has to be broken if the next generation of men is to assume social authority. McWilliams writes that 'the authority of the "male principle" must be raised above both father and son. In this sense, they cease to be father and son and become . . .

subject to the same higher authority, and hence brothers.'[14] Fraternity and politics are intimately connected. Political life, exemplified in the ancient *polis*, presupposes 'an idea of justice', or a law common to all, which transcends blood ties and applies alike to men of different kinship groups. McWilliams states that the 'separation of the "male principle" from blood descent becomes elevated to an explicit status in the construction of the state.'[15] In short, modern politics, including that of civil society, is the 'male principle'. However, an intense fraternal relationship is no longer possible. The Enlightenment (and the social contract theorists) undermined fraternity, which is now almost entirely lost in the modern state. Fraternity contributed to its own downfall; 'the values to which it is dedicated tend ultimately to suggest the idea of universal fraternity',[16] but universal brotherhood is an empty abstraction that leaves men lost and without identity and support. Nevertheless, McWilliams hopes that fraternity can be re-established in its old sense; it is 'one of the few moral ideals common to the diverse radical movements of [our] day'.[17]

McWilliams' account of the pre-modern world runs together two different forms of social life and so obscures some historically distinctive features of modern fraternity. Traditional society, in a fundamental sense, is kinship. The *polis*, however, stood apart precisely because the 'male principle', or the political order, was separated from 'blood descent'. Thus all men, when seen as equal subjects of the law that governed them, could be brothers. Public or civil fraternity has always been distinct from kinship. Civil fraternity refers not to a blood relation, to the sons of one father, but to men bound by a recognized common bond, such as that between the male citizens of the *polis*. Even so, civil fraternity has not always been universal; that is its distinctively modern feature. Unlike modern civil society, citizenship in the *polis* was defined ascriptively and was particular to a given city-state; for example, only Athenian-born males could be citizens of Athens. In the modern world, citizenship, for the first time, is (ostensibly) universal, and thus civil fraternity extends to all men *as men*, not as inhabitants of particular cities. This is why Fitzjames Stephen can write of fraternity as the religion of mankind, and Freud can tell a story of the civil order developing when men's sympathies included 'all men alike'.[18]

In the *polis* citizenship was upheld by the *phratries*, the brotherhoods, which were crucial for the sense of communal identity for which McWilliams yearns.[19] The ancient connection between the fraternities and the civil fraternity of citizenship that transcended them, draws attention to a major confusion in most discussions of fraternity. 'Fraternity' is used to refer to both *fraternity*, or the universal bond of community, and *fraternities*, or the small associations (communities) in which fellowship is close and brother can know and assist his brother, almost as if they were family members. The first usage points to the fact that in modern civil society fraternity goes beyond local attachments to encompass all men. But, as some conservatives and socialists and other communitarians have argued, and as McWilliams reiterates, the emergence of fraternity is part of the same process that has led to the decline of community in the sense of fraternities. When the loss of fraternity is mourned and suggestions for its revival put forward, most writers have fraternities in mind, not fraternity. The universal bonds of contract and citizenship are well established, and what is at issue is not so much civil fraternity (although many writers wish it to become more communal and participatory) as the bonds of the fraternities that give meaning and worth to a formally equal civil status.

The general use of 'fraternity' to refer to communal bonds is not perhaps surprising when the plural form lacks universal connotations. 'Fraternities' immediately tends to conjure up pictures of explicitly masculine and often secret associations. Fraternal orders typically have elaborate rituals to initiate their members into the fraternal secrets and into a rigid, hierarchical structure.[20] Fraternities include organizations far removed from the kinds of communities envisaged by socialist advocates of fraternity, such as Bernard Crick, who refers to 'the Fascist perversion of fraternity, the aggressive brother's band'. Crick also mentions 'the primal image of the brother's band organizing in shopfloor cells or in neighbourhood militias', which is an image shared by Right and Left.[21] Like other fraternities, this image embodies men's dreams of associations in which women have no place, except (sometimes) marginally, as auxiliaries. In *Three Guineas*, Virginia Woolf paints a picture of the public world as a mosaic of men's clubs, each with its appropriate costumes and ceremonial activities. Examples of 'community' in discussions of fraternity are, more often than not, examples of participation in the workplace and trades unions, in political parties and sects, in leisure activities, in which men participate in men's organizations. Crick has recently tried to rescue socialist fraternity from men; he suggests that 'sisterhood' is 'in some ways truly a less ambiguous image for what I am trying to convey by "fraternity"'. He argues that it is better to 'try to desex, even to feminize, old "fraternity", rather than to pause to rewrite most languages'.[22] A good deal more is required than a pause to deal with language. The language expresses and forms part of the patriarchal structure of our society, and the story of the creation of modern fraternal patriarchy is told in the tales of the social contract theorists.

There is no doubt that the classic social contract theorists won a total victory over Sir Robert Filmer and the other patriarchalists on the matter of the political right of fathers and the natural freedom of sons. The conflict centred on the question whether political power and subjection were natural or conventional, that is, created by individuals themselves. The contract theorists held that individuals, i.e., men, are born free and equal to each other and thus no natural relations of subordination and superiority can exist. To be legitimate, such relations must be created through mutual agreement or contract; 'since no man has any natural authority over his fellows, and since force alone bestows no right, all legitimate authority among men must be based on covenants.'[23] But, until Sir Robert Filmer formulated his classic patriarchal doctrine, the problem of nature, convention and political right was not always clear cut. Traditional patriarchal argument used the family as the metaphor for political order and understood all relationships of superior and subordinate to be like that of father and son. Schochet points out that, although the traditional argument could explain why fathers of families (and not their subordinates) were members of political societies, the difficulty remained that there was no way to explain why the fathers (rulers) were themselves political subjects.[24] One answer to this problem was provided by Dudley Digges in 1643. In what Schochet calls a 'curious union of consent with patriarchalism', Digges claimed that the 'King hath paternall powers from the consent of the people', and that 'it was our owne act which united all particular paternal powers in Him', (i.e., the King).[25]

   Digges' solution left something to be desired for all parties. Filmer shut off all possibility of riding both horses by uniting the divine right of kings with patriarchalism. He derived political right from God's paternal and monarchical grant to Adam. For Filmer, contract doctrine was subversive of all social and political order, and the 'main foundation of popular sedition'.[26] If consent were required for government, no one must be excluded, but how could it ever be said that everyone had agreed?; 'it is necessary to ask of every infant so soon as it is born its consent to government, if you will ever have the consent of the whole people.'[27] For Filmer, the *reductio ad absurdum* of contract argument was the corollary that 'women, especially virgins, [would] by birth have as much natural freedom as any other, and therefore ought not to lose their liberty without their own consent.'[28] If contract doctrine were correct, it would be impossible, Filmer states, 'ever lawfully to introduce any kind of government whatsoever'.[29] But, fortunately, there was no question of social contracts because individuals were not born free and equal, naturally knowing no government. Sons were born (were naturally) subject to their fathers; infants could not and did not consent to their father's authority. A son was subject at birth to the political power of his father, and through his father subject also to the paternal right of the monarch. Talk of social contracts was nonsense, and politically dangerous nonsense.

The contract theorists responded with two counter-arguments, both denying that title to political rule derived from the natural fact of generation. Hobbes and Pufendorf took contract to its radical conclusion, and insisted that an infant made, or could be said to make, a contract of submission to parental authority. The fact that an infant 'submitted' to a mother's power rather than be exposed was, for Hobbes, a sign of consent, and Pufendorf writes that the dominion of the parent rests on 'the presumed consent of the children themselves, and so on a tacit pact'. If an infant could have reasoned and appreciated how well his parents would care for him, there is no doubt that he would have gladly consented to their authority.[30] Hobbes and Pufendorf agree with the patriarchalist assumption that paternal power is political power but they argue that the power is based on convention. However, the patriarchalists' case rested on anthropologically convincing grounds. Hobbes and Pufendorf may have maintained the logical consistency of their theories on this point, but it was hardly plausible to characterize the relation between parent and tiny infant as consensual or contractual. Nor was the indentification of paternal and political right persuasive. In the modern world, fathers are not political rulers and the family and political (civil) society are seen as two very different forms of association.

The counter-argument that proved the downfall of classic patri-archalism involved responses that were the opposite of those of Hobbes and Pufendorf. First, all talk of contracts by infants was rejected. Instead of denying that children were naturally subject to their parents, Locke and Rousseau, for example, agreed that the natural duty of parents to care for their children gave them rightful authority, but, they argued against Filmer, parental power was temporary. Once out of their nonage, at the age of maturity, sons become as free as their fathers and, like them, must agree to be governed. Locke writes that:

> We are born Free, as we are born Rational; . . . Age that brings one, brings with it the other too. And thus we see how *natural Freedom and Subjection to Parents* may consist together, and are both founded on the same Principle. A *Child* is *Free* by his Father's Title, by his Father's Understanding, which is to govern him, till he hath it of his own. The *Freedom of a Man at years of discretion*, and the *Subjection* of a Child *to* his *Parents*, whilst yet short of that Age, are so consistent, and so distinguishable, that the most blinded contenders for Monarchy, *by Right of Fatherhood*, cannot miss this *difference*, the most obstinate cannot but allow their consistency.[31]

To establish the consistency of natural freedom and temporary subjection to parents was still not sufficient to reply to the classic patriarchalists. The crucial theoretical move for the construction of modern patriarchy was not concerned with the origin and duration of children's subjection but with the character of parental power.

Filmer's identification of paternal and political right gave rise to an insoluble problem. The 'inherent dilemma' in classic patriarchalism was that 'if kings are fathers, fathers cannot be patriarchs. If fathers are patriarchs at home, kings cannot be patriarchs on their thrones. Patriarchal kings and patriarchal fathers are a contradiction in terms.'[32] Filmer could not follow Digges' example and claim that the monarch gained his paternal (political) power through consent or convention. Thus, Filmer offered no way out of the dilemma that if fathers were the same as kings, wielding the same absolute power, then there could be no 'king', merely a multitude of father–kings. Hobbes avoided a similar problem by arguing that Leviathan's sword took precedence over the right of a master of a family; there could be only one political sovereign and his right could not be limited. However, Leviathan, the absolute, completely conventional, artificial twin of Filmer's natural father, was historically inappropriate for modern civil society and the principle of freedom of contract. The theoretical way forward was through the transformation of patriarchy, not its negation.

The second, and historically decisive, counter to classic patriarchalism was Locke's separation of paternal power from political power. A father's natural right over his sons was not political; political power is conventional and is created through contract. Locke states that 'these two *Powers, Political* and *Paternal, are so perfectly distinct* and separate; are built upon so different Foundations, and given to so different Ends, that every Subject that is a Father, has as much a *Paternal Power* over his Children as the Prince has over his.' A father therefore lacks 'any part or degree of that kind of Dominion, which a Prince or Magistrate has over his Subject'.[33] Similarly, Rousseau declares that the paths of a father and a political ruler 'are so different, their duty and rights so unlike, that one cannot confound them without forming false ideas about the fundamental laws of society and without falling into errors that are fatal to the human race'. Rousseau adds that he hopes his 'few lines' will be enough 'to overturn the odious system that Sir [Robert] Filmer attempted to establish in a work entitled *Patriarcha*'.[34]

The classic contract theorists also took issue with Filmer on another question. In the previous chapter, I mentioned that Hobbes argued that mothers, not fathers, had dominion over children in the state of nature, and that Locke spends a good deal of time arguing about the Fifth Commandment to support his stand that authority over children is parental not paternal. Recent feminist discussions of these theorists have drawn attention to their championing of the mother's familial authority, but this aspect of the conflict between the patriarchalists and contract theorists can be all too misleading about modern patriarchy. In practice, a mother's claim to, and her rights regarding, her children has been and, as so-called surrogate motherhood has shown very recently, remains a very important question. Theoretically, however, to focus on parents and children suggests that patriarchy is familial and that father-right is the problem. Moreover, in controversies over the meaning of 'patriarchy' and the interpretation of the classic texts, feminist discussions have failed to take into account the social meaning of fatherhood and paternal authority in classic and modern patriarchy. Filmer's father is seen in a common-sense way as one of two parents, and the full extent and significance of his powers is thus obscured. In the absence of an appreciation of the amazing capacities of Filmer's patriarchal father, the standard interpretation of the victory of the social contract theorists over the patriarchalists, and of the sons over the father, goes unchallenged. Without a closer look at the father, the fact that the sons eagerly embrace part of the father's inheritance goes unnoticed. Rousseau's claim that he wants to overthrow Filmer's odious system is exaggeration. Like the other contract theorists, he is keen to overthrow Filmer's identification of father-right with political right, but he is also more than willing to accept the father's legacy of sex-right and to transform it and make it his own.

Filmer argued that all law was of necessity the product of the will of one man. All titles to rule devolved from the original Divine grant of kingly right to Adam, the first father. Once it was recognized that '*the natural and private dominion of Adam* [is] the fountain of all government and propriety',[35] Filmer thought that the ground was swept from under the feet of the proponents of the doctrine of the natural freedom of mankind. He writes that 'the title comes from the fatherhood';[36] Adam's sons, and hence all succeeding generations of sons, were born into political subjection by virtue of Adam's 'right of fatherhood', his 'fatherly power', or the 'power of the father-hood'.[37] At the birth of his first son Adam became the first monarch, and his political right passed to all subsequent fathers and kings. For Filmer, fathers and kings were one and the same; paternal power was monarchical power, all kings ruled by virtue of their fatherhood and all fathers were monarchs in their families: 'the Father of a family governs by no other law than by his own will.'[38] Filmer argued that no government could be a tyranny because the king's will was law. Similarly, the will of the father was the absolute, arbitrary will of the *patria potestas*. Locke states that Filmer's father 'hath an Absolute, Arbitrary, Unlimited, and Unlimitable Power, over the Lives, Liberties, and Estates of his Children – so that he may take or alienate their Estates, sell, castrate, or use their Persons as he pleases';[39] and Laslett comments that Filmer 'did not adopt the capital punishment of children by their fathers, but he quoted examples of it from Bodin with approval'.[40] Filmer does say, however, that 'where there are only Father and sons, no sons can question the Father for the death of their brother.'[41]

Filmer's view of the origin of political right seems, therefore, to be straightforward. Political right derives from fatherhood. But patri-archy is more complex than Filmer's statements or its literal meaning suggests. Even in Filmer's classic formulation, patriarchy is about much more than the political right of fathers over sons. Fatherly power is only one dimension of patriarchy, as Filmer himself reveals. Filmer's apparently straightforward statements obscure the foundation of patriarchal right. Sons do not spring up like mushrooms, as Filmer was quick to remind Hobbes. If Adam was to be a father, Eve had to become a mother. In other words, *sex-right or conjugal right must necessarily precede the right of fatherhood.* The genesis of political power lies in Adam's sex-right or conjugal right, not in his fatherhood. Adam's political title is granted *before* he becomes a father.

Filmer makes clear that Adam's political right is originally established in his right as a husband over Eve: 'God gave to Adam . . . the dominion over the woman', and, citing *Genesis* 3:16, 'God ordained Adam to rule over his wife, and her desires were to be subject to his.'[42] (*Genesis* states that Eve's 'desire shall be to thy husband, and he shall rule over thee'.) Adam's desire is to become a father, but in no ordinary sense of 'father'. He desires to obtain the remarkable powers of a patriarchal father. Filmer briefly mentions Adam's original Divine grant of political right over Eve at various points, but it has a shadowy presence in his writings. In recent (patriarchal) commentaries on his texts, sex-right has completely disappeared. And, to be sure, when reading Filmer from the perspective of only half the contract story, conjugal right is not easy to discern under the cloak of Adam's fatherhood.

The biblical patriarchal image (here in Locke's words) is of 'nursing Fathers tender and carefull of the publick weale'.[43] The patriarchal story is about the procreative power of a father who is complete in himself, who embodies the creative power of both female and male. His procreative power both gives and animates physical life and creates and maintains political right. Filmer is able to refer to Adam's power over Eve so casually because classic patriarchalism declares women to be procreatively and politically irrelevant. The reason that Adam has dominion over 'the woman' is, according to Filmer (here following the patriarchal idea of fatherhood, which is very ancient), that 'the man . . . is the nobler and principal agent in generation.'[44] Women are merely empty vessels for the exercise of men's sexual and procreative power. The original political right that God gives to Adam is the right, so to speak, to fill the empty vessel. Adam, and all men, must do this if they are to become fathers, that is to say, if they are to exercise the *masculine* procreative or generative power. Men's generative power has a dual aspect. The genesis of new physical life belongs in their hands, not in the empty vessel. Masculine procreative power creates new life; men are the 'principal agents in generation'. Patriarchal argument thus refuses any acknowledgement of the capacity and creativity that is unique to women. Men appropriate to themselves women's natural creativity, their capacity physically to give birth – but they also do more than that. Men's generative power extends into another realm; they transmute what they have appropriated into another form of generation, the ability to create new political life, or to give birth to political right.

In view of the character of the extraordinary powers that classic patriarchalism arrogates to men, it is appropriate that the powers are contained in the name of 'father' and encompassed under the writ of fatherhood. The presence of conjugal right is very faint in Filmer's writings because (although at one level he must acknowledge it) Adam's original political right is subsumed under the power of fatherhood. For instance, after starting that Eve and her desires are subject to Adam, Filmer continues in the next sentence, 'here we have the original grant of government, and the fountain of all power placed in the Father of all mankind.' Adam is also Eve's father. In the story in the book of *Genesis*, Eve is created only after Adam and the animals have been placed on earth. God creates and names the animals and Adam but, we are told in *Genesis* 2:20, 'for Adam there was not found an help meet for him.' Eve is then created, but she is not created *ab initio* but *from* Adam, who is, in a sense, her parent, and Adam, not God, gives Eve her name. Filmer is therefore able to treat all political right as the right of a father because Eve is not only under the dominion of Adam, but he is (with God's help) the 'principal agent' in her generation. The father in classic patriarchal theory is not just one of two parents – he is *the* parent, and the being able to generate political right.

The classic patriarchalism of the seventeenth century was the last time that masculine political creativity appeared as a paternal power or that political right was seen as father-right. Classic contract theory is another story of the masculine genesis of political life, but it is a specifically modern tale, told over the dead political body of the father. In civil society the two dimensions of political right are no longer united in the figure of the father, and sex-right is separated from political right. Filmer's father, embodying both female and male capacities, stands at the end of a very long history of traditional patriarchal argument in which the creation of political society has been seen as a masculine act of birth, and in which women and their capacities have been seen, at best, as irrelevant, and, at worst, as dangerous to political order. Feminist scholars have recently begun to bring this tradition, particularly as exemplified in ancient Greece, out into the daylight. Nancy Hartsock has recently portrayed the *polis* as a community constituted by a masculine *eros*,[45] and various writers, including Mary O'Brien, have drawn attention to the ancient understanding of the political as a realm arising from an act of generation by men that transcended and opposed physical, i.e., womanly, generation.

Jean Elshtain comments of Plato, that his 'ideal, perhaps, would have been a kind of parthenogenesis whereby male elites could give birth to themselves both metaphorically and actually',[46] and several feminist scholars have drawn attention to Plato's (Diotima's) statement that some men, unlike those who turn to women, 'conceive in the soul . . . the most beautiful [conception], . . . that which is concerned with the ordering of cities and homes, which we call temperance and justice'.[47] In the Christian religion, Mary Daly claims, the creative force of the old goddesses was overcome and replaced by 'androgynous sweet Jesus'. And Jesus, that 'misbegotten and transsexed parthenogenetic daughter who incorporated both masculine and feminine roles, being lord, savior, and sacrificial victim, was the logical surrogate for the female principle'.[48] Nearer to modern times, Machiavelli's image of the political Founder is paternal, but the paternity is of a peculiar kind. Hanna Pitkin says of Machiavelli's accounts of the founding of Rome that, 'despite the imagery of birth in blood . . . no mother appears; it seems the issue is a purely masculine generation, singular paternity.'[49] More generally, Pitkin argues that, for Machiavelli, the free individual should 'be born from a father and nurtured by him alone. Cities and other human institutions have such a purely masculine birth'. The founding of a city 'should be the very opposite of a "natural" event: a masculine artifice, founded *against* the stream of natural growth and decay'.[50] Although the claim that men have the capacity to give political birth stretches across the centuries, the argument neither continues unchanged until the present (as some feminist discussions suggest), nor disappears by the eighteenth century after the defeat of classic patriarchalism by the social contract theorists. The stories of an original contract and the revolutionary assumption of natural individual freedom and equality mark a fundamental change in the long tradition of patriarchal argument.

When the father no longer embodies political right, patriarchy becomes fraternal, sex-right can no longer be subsumed under the power of fatherhood in the fashion of Filmer and masculine right over women is declared non-political. However, a contradiction soon became apparent in pictures of the state of nature in which women are denied the same natural capacities as men and excluded from the status of 'individual'. Very soon, for example, Mary Astell was asking 'if *all Men are born Free*, how is it that all Women are born Slaves?'[51] Many others, too, seized on the apparently emancipatory potential of contract doctrine, although the early feminist critics are never mentioned in discussions of contract theory in present-day textbooks. Sir Robert Filmer's alarmed reaction to contract theory had some basis. During the political ferment of the seventeenth century most forms of subjection came under scrutiny and attack, and the thin ends of various revolutionary wedges were clearly visible. Conjugal relations and the marriage contract were as central to political debate as the relation between king and subject and the social contract. The terms, or what were held to be the terms, of the two contracts were used to argue about the proper form of marriage and political rule. Royalists saw the right of husbands as unlimited and established for life, just like the right of the monarch. Their republican opponents argued that government was limited, like the powers given to husbands under the marriage contract, and that, in extreme cases, the conjugal or political tie could be broken.[52] But, with hindsight, Filmer's fears on one point, at least, were groundless. Masculine right was secured even as paternal right was defeated.

Several developments helped suppress the fact that the battle between classic patriarchalism and contract doctrine involved only one aspect of the father's political power. Women were deprived of an economic basis for independence by the separation of the workplace from the household and the consolidation of the patriarchal structure of the capitalism. The legal and civil standing of married women reached its nadir in the mid-nineteenth century. In the preceding century, Sir William Blackstone had succinctly stated the consequences, under the common law doctrine of coverture, when a woman entered into the marriage contract:

By marriage, the husband and wife are one person in law: that is, the very being, or legal existence of the woman is suspended during the marriage, or at least is incorporated and consolidated into that of the husband; under whose wing, protection, and *cover*, she performs everything; and is therefore called . . . a *feme-covert* . . . her husband, [is called] her *baron*, or lord.[53]

The economic and legal developments were accompanied by Locke's brilliant theoretical manoeuvre using the language of paternal right, which was central to the triumphal career of the patriarchal assertion that women's subjection to men was natural, and so outside of and irrelevant to the continuing controversies and struggles over political power in the state and economy.

The full theoretical and practical significance of Locke's separation of what he calls paternal power from political power is rarely appreciated. The standard (patriarchal) reading of his contract story focuses on the creation and separation of civil or political society – the new public world constituted by the universal bonds of contract between formally free and equal individuals – from the private familial world constituted by natural ties and a natural order of subordination. Paternal power is treated as the paradigm of natural subjection. Natural subjection has no place in conventional civil society, and so the paternal sphere drops out of theoretical and political sight; no attention is paid to Locke's use of 'paternal' in this context. I have already referred to the current use of 'paternalism' in arguments about prohibitions that the state may legitimately place on the consensual activities of citizens. The language of paternalism is a good illustration of the enduring strength of Locke's identification of subjection with fatherly power. I do not want to argue with Locke's claim that paternal power is not political, but it does not follow that paternal power is the paradigm of natural subjection, or that all forms of natural subjection are non-political. The 'paternal' sphere, created simultaneously with civil society, contains another example of natural subjection; the father is also a husband and, according to Locke, his wife is his natural subordinate.

There is good reason to confine the term 'political' to relationships among adults. That infants come into the world helpless, entirely dependent on their mother, or, today, when there are many substitutes for her breast, dependent on their parents or other adults, is a natural fact of human existence. Classic patriarchalism took the natural fact of childish dependence on (subordination to) the father to be the fundamental political fact about the world from which all else followed. However, in the civil world, the dependence of children has no political consequences, except to show how different paternal power is from political power. The protection that the parent must afford to the child if it is to flourish and mature comes to a natural end. The child develops and, once out of its nonage, is independent. The former child then stands as an equal to its parents and interacts in civil society alongside them as a citizen.

Political relationships among adults follow a different path from those between parents and children. There is no natural pattern of growth and completion, and there is no necessity that political relationships take the form of subordination and superiority ('protection'), but the form is so prevalent that it is not easy to envisage free political association. Political relations can be brought to an end, but, more typically, they are continually renewed (in the contemporary world, voting is seen as the legitimate means through which individuals are held to agree, and to renew their agreement, to be governed). Moreover, the parent–child relation is always recognized (although, of course, there can be considerable, bitter disagreements about the point at which nonage is concluded), but political relations are much harder to discern despite the fact – or perhaps because of the fact – that they are conventional. Liberals and socialists have battled for at least a century and a half over the question whether the relations that constitute the capitalist economy are political. In this case, the question has at least been put on the theoretical and practical agenda. Another set of relationships and the sphere that they constitute are, even now, rarely admitted to be political. Patriarchal right is still widely held to have a foundation in nature. When paternal power is seen as paradigmatic of natural subjection, critical questions about the designation of sexual and conjugal relations as natural as all too easily disregarded.

Locke's conjectural history of the state of nature provides an insight into the mechanisms at work in the theoretical construction of modern patriarchy. At first sight, Locke's story looks like another variant of the traditional patriarchal stories of the origins of society in the family, except that Locke, *contra* the classic patriarchalists, denies that the rule of the father in the family derives from his procreative power and he denies that his rule is political. Paternal right is not political right; only civil society is a properly political society. 'In the first Ages of the World', Locke's conjectural history runs, the fathers of families became monarchs. An 'insensible change' took place when the first sons reached maturity. The family needed government if the members of the family were to live together in harmony, and the sons agreed that no one was fitter to secure 'their Peace, Liberties, and Fortunes' than the father who had cared so tenderly for them in their earlier years. Locke stresses that the father became a monarch through the consent of his sons, not by virtue of his fatherhood; ' 'twas easie, and almost natural for Children by a tacit and scarce avoidable consent to make way for the *Father's Authority and Government.*'[54] Locke's story may seem to offer as curious a union of consent and patriarchalism as Dudley Digges' statements, but it becomes more curious still. Locke says nothing about the place of the mother in the father's transmogrification into a monarch, yet she must be a member of the family or there could be no sons. Indeed, Locke tells us that the original society was not formed of father and son, but of husband and wife: 'the *first Society* was between Man and Wife.' The first society, too, had a consensual genesis in a 'voluntary Compact between Man and Woman'.[55]

But what was the content of that compact? Locke agrees with Filmer that there is a natural foundation for a wife's subjection. Thus, Locke's first husband, like Adam, must have exercised conjugal right over his wife before he became a father. The 'original' political right or government was, therefore, not paternal but conjugal. Locke had no need to mention the wife when her husband became the family's monarch. Her subjection to his rule had *already* been secured through an earlier agreement. (Again, the question remains of why a contract is necessary when women's subjection, unlike that of grown sons, is natural). Eventually, Locke argues, social conditions become such that the rule of father–monarchs was no longer appropriate.[56] The sons, in an act of symbolic, if not actual, parricide, withdraw their consent to the father's power and claim their natural liberty. They then make the original contract and create civil society, or political society, which is separated into two spheres. During the genesis of civil society, the sphere of natural subjection is separated out as the non-political sphere. The non-political status of familial and private life is confirmed by Locke's label 'paternal power' for its constituent relationship. Sex-right or conjugal right, the original political right, then becomes completely hidden. The concealment was so beautifully executed that contemporary political theorists and activists can 'forget' that the private sphere also contains – and has its genesis in – a contractual relationship between two adults. They have found nothing surprising in the fact that, in modern patriarchy, women, unlike sons, never emerge from their 'nonage' and the 'protection' of men; we never interact in civil society on the same basis as men.

Women cannot be incorporated into civil society on the same basis as men because women naturally lack the capacities required to become civil individuals. But what exactly do women lack? The classic social contract theorists whom I discussed in the previous chapter are extremely vague on this crucial point. The meaning of Pufendorf's reference to the 'superiority' of the male sex, or Locke's pronouncement that a wife's subjection has a 'foundation in nature' is far from self-evident. The elaboration that they provide merely consists in references to the man's greater strength of body and mind, or his greater strength and ability. The contradiction between the assumptions of contract theory and appeals to natural strength was immediately obvious. Claims to rule could no longer be based on such natural attributes if the doctrine of individual freedom and equality was accepted. Mary Astell was quick to comment sarcastically that, if strength of mind and body went together, then ' 'tis only for some odd Accidents which Philosophers have not yet thought worth while to enquire into, that the sturdiest Porter is not the wisest Man!'[57] By 1825, when demands had already been heard for four decades or more for political rights to be extended to women, the utilitarian socialist William Thompson stated, equally sarcastically:

> If strength be the superior title to happiness, let the knowledge and skill of man be employed in adding to the pleasurable sensations of horses, elephants, and all stronger animals. If strength be the title to happiness, let all such qualifications for voters as the capacity to read and write, or any *indirect* means to insure intellectual aptitude be abolished; and let the simple test for the exercise of political rights, both by men and women, be the capacity of carrying 300 lbs. weight.[58]

Improvement in the social position of women, which has led to improvements in their health and physical condition, and techno- logical changes, have meant that the argument from strength, though it can still be heard today, has become more and more implausible. However, it should not be forgotten that, in practice, men continue to uphold their patriarchal right over women through 'strength', that is, through force and violence.

The claim that women's subordination was justified because of the greater natural ability of men was also immediately criticized by feminists. In 1696, for example, Elizabeth Johnson, in a preface to a volume of Elizabeth Rowe's poems, declared that when men, with strength and custom on their side, still

> would monopolise sense too, when neither that, nor learning, nor so much as wit must be allowed us, but all overruled by the tyranny of the prouder sex; . . . we then must ask their pardons if we are not yet so completely passive as to bear all without so much as a murmur . . . [We] appeal to all the world, whether these are not notorious violations on the liberties of freeborn Englishwomen. [59]

Since the seventeenth century, feminists have argued that it is lack of education that makes women appear less able. The apparently greater ability of men is a result of the defective education of women, the consequence of social (men's) contrivance, not nature. If both sexes received a similar education and had the same opportunities to exercise their talents, there would be no politically significant differences in the abilities of women and men. The problem with this argument is that what is at issue is assumed to be whether women have the same capacities as men and, hence, can do anything that men can do. Historically, the issue has had to be fought out, and the battle is not yet over, but struggle over this terrain presupposes that there is no political significance in the fact that women have an ability that men lack.

The theoretical war between the classic patriarchalists and the classic contract theorists reveals the political importance of women's ability to give birth, or, more accurately, in the case of the social contract story, the political importance of what the ability symbolizes or stands for. The arguments of Filmer and Locke show that the original political right is a man's right to have sexual access to a woman's body so that he could become a father. Filmer's father denies any procreative ability to women, appropriates their capacity and transforms it into the masculine ability to give political birth. The male individuals who act out the story of the original contract have no desire to become fathers in the classic patriarchal sense. The father as *patria potestas* lies defeated in the past. The sons' political aim is to inherit the father's capacity to create political right. In modern patriarchy the capacity that 'individuals' lack is politically significant because it represents all that the civil order is not, all that is encapsulated in women and women's bodies. The body of the 'individual' is very different from women's bodies. His body is tightly enclosed within boundaries, but women's bodies are permeable, their contours change shape and they are subject to cyclical processes. All these differences are summed up in the natural bodily process of birth. Physical birth symbolizes everything that makes women incapable of entering the original contract and transforming themselves into the civil individuals who uphold its terms. Women lack neither strength nor ability in a general sense, but, according to the classic contract theorists, they are naturally deficient in a specifically *political* capacity, the capacity to create and maintain political right.

Women must be subject to men because they are naturally subversive of men's political order. A fairly elaborate discussion of why this is the case is provided in Rousseau's contract story and conjectural history of the state of nature, and in Freud's contribution to the genre. Rousseau's argument, like Locke's, rests on the assumption that social life is natural to humans; 'the oldest of all societies, and the only natural one, is that of the family.'[60] A true state of nature would be an asocial state inhabited by languageless animals of various kinds, one species of which has the potential to develop into human beings. The males and females of the human species would encounter each other at random and engage sexually with each other as their desires dictated; no lasting unions would be formed. Once a child could forage for itself and left its mother, the two would be unlikely to recognize each other again. In the true state of nature, without language or sustained relationships, differences in natural attributes would not lead to the domination of some by others, or to the subjection of females. Natural isolated beings would find it impossible 'to understand what subjection and domination are'. If one seized what another had gathered, 'how will he ever succeed in getting himself obeyed . . . what would be the chains of dependence among men who possess nothing?' Nor could male humans dominate females; the sexes would lack the social and moral conceptions and desires that make sexual domination possible. Once physical desire had been satisfied (and Rousseau argues that desire would be less frequent and pressing than in the social state) that would be sufficient; male and female beings would go their separate and peaceful ways until sexual desire is felt again.[61]

Rousseau notes that it is very difficult to give a convincing account of how the transformation from natural animal life to social human life could have come about. But he argues that social life begins in the patriarchal family. The interrelated development of reason, language and social relationships is simultaneously the development of sexual difference, a difference that necessarily entails that women must be dependent on and subordinate to men. In 'a first revolution', families or small societies are formed, and then 'the first difference was established in the ways of life of the two Sexes, which until then had had but one. Women became more sedentary and grew accustomed to looking after the Hut and Children, while the man went in quest of the common subsistence.'[62] The rest of Rousseau's story of the transformation of human nature and the creation of a participatory civil order in the *Discourse on Inequality* is about the consciousness and activities of men. Elsewhere in Rousseau's writings, he makes very clear that women must 'tend the hut and the children' and bow to men's judgements if political order is not to be undermined.

'The physical', Rousseau argues in *Emile*, 'leads us unawares to the moral,'[63] We learn from a consideration of the physical difference between the sexes that their morality is also very different. Women, unlike men, cannot control their 'unlimited desires' by themselves, so they cannot develop the morality required in civil society. Men have passions, too, but they can use their reason to master their sexuality, and so can undertake the creation and maintenance of political society. Women have only modesty, and if they did not have this constraint, 'the result would soon be the ruin of both [sexes], and mankind would perish by the means established for preserving it . . . Men would finally be [women's] victims and would see themselves dragged to death without ever being able to defend themselves.'[64] But modesty is a precarious control of sexual desire. The story of Julie in *La Nouvelle Héloise* shows just how fragile it is, when, despite all Julie's efforts to live an exemplary life as a wife and a mother, she is unable to overcome her illicit passion and takes the only course she can to preserve the haven of family life at Clarens: she goes to her 'accidental' death.

Women lack the capacity to sublimate their passion and are a perpetual source of disorder, so they must 'be subjected either to a man or to the judgments of men and they are never permitted to put themselves above these judgments'.[65] Emile's tutor educates him to become master of himself, and so able to take his place as a participant in Rousseau's social contract. He can help create a participatory civil order in which male citizens are bound only by laws which they legislate for themselves. But Emile's education is complete and he becomes properly his own master only when, in the one explicit command ever given by his tutor, he is told to put duty before desire and to leave Sophie, his betrothed, and travel abroad. A man must prepare for marriage like a soldier preparing for battle. The tutor (Rousseau) tells Emile, who wants to marry without delay, that 'a man does not exercise for battle in the face of the enemy but prepares himself for it before the war. He presents himself at the battle already fully prepared.'[66] Emile obeys his tutor and spends nearly two years travelling and learning about politics, including the doctrine of *The Social Contract*, before his marriage. Women's bodies are so opposed to and subversive of political life, that Rousseau has Emile learn about citizenship before he is allowed to know the delights of being a husband. Emile is then fitted to marry, he is a soldier who can win the battle of the sexes and become Sophie's 'master for the whole of life'.[67] Sophie must yield to the 'primacy that nature gives to the husband'; in 'the nature of things, in the family it is the father who should command'.[68] Sophie's education, so thorough but so unlike Emile's, is designed to foster modesty, cleanliness and to make her pleasing to men, but it can never be sufficient to overcome her womanly propensity to disorderliness. As a husband and head of a family, Emile can take his place as a citizen, but Sophie, and all other women, must be rigorously excluded from political life if order is to prevail.

Rousseau argues that there must be 'a natural base on which to form conventional ties' – the natural base of marriage and the family. Rousseau writes that it is 'by means of the small fatherland which is the family that the heart attaches itself to the large one; . . . the good son, the good husband, and the good father . . . make the good citizen!'[69] To be a good husband and citizen a man must have a good, that is to say, obedient, wife, who upholds order in the sphere that is the natural foundation of civil life. The family is a woman's 'empire', and she 'reigns' by 'getting herself commanded to do what she wants to do'. However, if she does not want to do what is necessary to maintain her husband's conjugal mastery, then civil society is endangered. Her 'reign' consists in her ability 'to recognize the voice of the head of the house'; if she fails, the ensuing disorder leads to 'misery, scandal, and dishonor'.[70] All people, Rousseau cries, 'perish from the disorder of women'.[71] In a letter commenting on reactions to his *Politics and the Arts*, Rousseau says: 'I am not of your opinion when you say that if we are corrupted it is not the fault of women, it is our own; my whole book is undertaken to show how it is their fault.'[72] To avoid disorder the sexes must be segregated in all aspects of life, even, as at Clarens in *La Nouvelle Héloise*, in domestic life. Men must have their own social and political clubs so that they can educate themselves politically and reinforce their citizenship, out of the reach of women and their weakening, subversive influence.

Much nearer to our own day, Freud's conjectural history of the origin of social life presents a strikingly similar account of the differing political moralities of the sexes. He marks the passage from animal nature to human society as the point when 'the need for genital satisfaction no longer made its appearance like a guest who drops in suddenly.' In the absence of an oestrus cycle, 'the male acquired a motive for keeping the female . . . near him; while the female, who did not want to be separated from her helpless young, was obliged in their interests, to remain with the stronger male.'[73] So families were founded and 'civilization' began. Women's attachments remain particularized; women, Freud states, 'represent the interests of the family and of sexual life'. Men, on the other hand, are able to develop a sense of fraternity or community; they can universalize their sentiments away from the little world of the family. Men develop impulses 'with an *inhibited aim*' and so direct their attentions away from particular loved ones 'to all men alike', and toward 'a universal love of mankind'. Sexual difference is of fundamental significance for political order. Freud argues that 'the work of civilization has become increasingly the business of men, it confronts them with ever more difficult tasks and compels them to carry out instinctual sublimations of which women are little capable.' Women thus find that they are 'forced into the background by the claims of civilization' and they adopt a 'hostile attitude towards it'.[74] Moreover, the opposition between the sexes that is part of the origin and development of 'civilization' is recapitulated as human infants become little 'boys' and 'girls' and are differentiated into 'masculine' and 'feminine' beings. Women cannot overcome their hostility to men's participation in civil life or become capable of joining them in their civil tasks. Women remain a permanent threat to social and political order, because of their weaker, or even absent, super-ego, which is the 'internal representative' in each individual of the moral and political law, and which initiates 'all the processes that are designed to make the individual find a place in the cultural community'.[75] The different journeys that little boys and girls make through the Oedipus complex means, Freud argues, that women's super-ego is not as 'independent of its emotional origins' as men's, so that women 'show less sense of justice than men'.[76]

Standard discussions of the story of the original contract take none of this into account. No indication is given that the story is about masculinity and femininity and about the political significance of physical (natural) sexual difference – or that the structure of civil society reflects the division between the sexes. Rousseau and Freud reveal what it is in women's natures, what, in modern patriarchal terms, it means to be feminine, that entails that men must exercise the law of male sex-right. Women are creatures of unlimited desire, incapable of sublimating their passions in the manner of men who are to create themselves as civil individuals. The classic contract theorists (with the partial exception of Hobbes whose contractarianism is consistent enough to eliminate political significance from sexual difference in the natural condition) suggest that by nature men, not women, must take the initiative and control sexual activity. Rousseau makes it very clear in chapter 5 of *Emile* that women who are fit to be wives must indicate their desires in the most oblique fashion possible. They must say 'no' when they mean 'yes', a social practice that makes the separation of coerced from consensual sexual relations almost impossible. If men are to be masters of families they must have sexual access to women's bodies, but the access cannot be a matter of mutual agreement because women's and men's bodies do not have the same political meaning.

Women, their bodies and bodily passions, represent the 'nature' that must be controlled and transcended if social order is to be created and sustained. In the state of nature, social order in the family can be maintained only if the husband is master. Unlimited feminine desire must always be contained by patriarchal right. Women's relations to the social world must always be mediated through men's reason; women's bodies must always be subject to men's reason and judgements if order is not to be threatened. (Mozart's *The Magic Flute* provides a brilliant, dramatic presentation of this claim.) The meaning of the state of nature and civil society can be understood only in conjunction with each other. The 'foundation in nature' for masculine right is that women cannot develop the political morality required of participants in civil society. 'Femininity' and 'masculinity' in the state of nature are constructed theoretically to reflect women's deficiency so that the Rawlsian 'desired solution' can be obtained in civil society. Women are excluded from the status of free and equal individual because they lack the capacities to undergo that remarkable change that, Rousseau tells us, occurs in men when civil society and 'justice as a rule of conduct' are created.[77] Only men are able to develop the sense of justice required to maintain the civil order and uphold the civil, universal law as citizens. As Juliet Mitchell glosses Freud on this question, a woman 'cannot receive the "touch" of the law, her submission to it must be in establishing herself as its opposite'.[78]

The decision to move from the state of nature to civil society, and to establish the state and its universal laws, is based on a reasoned, rational assessment of the advantages of such a move to all men. Each 'individual' can see that he, along with all other individuals, will benefit if the endemic insecurities of a condition where each man, as master of a family, judges for himself on the basis of particular interests and desires, is replaced by a society in which all individuals are equally bound by universal laws. The making of the original contract thus presupposes that passion and partiality can be constrained by reason. Rousseau is emphatic that women cannot reason in the requisite fashion (and, in any case, they should be prevented from trying). Abstract principles and speculative truths are the preserve of men. Women should study the minds of the men to whom they are subject so that they know how to communicate with their masters. Rousseau was scornful of educated women; 'a brilliant wife is a plague to her husband, her children, her friends, her valets, everyone. . . . Outside her home she is always ridiculous . . . these women of great talent never impress anyone but fools.'[79] (Kant was even more scathing. He dismissed the woman scholar as follows; 'she uses her *books* in the same way as her *watch*, for example, which she carries so that people will see that she has one, though it is usually not running or set by the sun.')[80]

According to Rousseau and Freud, women are incapable of trans-
cending their sexual passions and particular attachments and
directing their reason to the demands of universal order and public
advantage. Women, therefore, cannot take part in the original
contract. They lack all that is required to create and then protect the
protection (as Hobbes puts it) afforded by the state and law to civil
individuals. Only 'individuals' can make contracts and uphold the
terms of the original contract. Women are 'the opposite' to the civil
law; they represent all that men must master to bring civil society
into being.

The story of the original contract tells a modern story of masculine
political birth. The story is an example of the appropriation by men
of the awesome gift that nature has denied them and its transmutation
into masculine political creativity. Men give birth to an 'artificial'
body, the body politic of civil society; they create Hobbes' 'Artificial
Man, we call a Commonwealth', or Rousseau's 'artificial and
collective body', or the 'one Body' of Locke's 'Body Politick'.
However, the creation of the civil body politic is an act of reason
rather than an analogue to a bodily act of procreation. The original
contract, as we are all taught, is not an actual event but a political
fiction; our society should be understood *as if* it originated in a
contract. The natural paternal body of Filmer's patriarchy is metaphorically put to death by the contract theorists, but the artificial
body that replaces it is a construct of the mind, not the creation of a
political community by real people. The birth of a human child can
produce a new male or female, whereas the creation of civil society
produces a social body fashioned after the image of only one of the
two bodies of humankind, or, more exactly, after the image of the
civil individual who is constituted through the original contract.

I have argued that the original contract is a fraternal pact; as
Pitkin remarks, 'what is supposed to follow partriarchal rule . . . is
the fraternal band of citizens in the *vivere civile* . . . by their pooled
masculinity jointly able to sustain civilization.'[81] The individuals
who enter the contract are brothers (sons of a father) who transform
themselves into a civil fraternity by contracting together. They are
bound together (so the familiar social contract story tells us) through
their common interest in upholding the civil laws that secure their
freedom. But they also have another fraternal bond constituted by
the forgotten dimension of the original contract. They also have a
common interest *as men* in upholding the terms of the sexual

contract, in ensuring that the law of male sex-right remains operative. Freud's versions of the contract story bring out more clearly than the stories of the classic writers that two dimensions of the father's political right are involved: his paternal right and his conjugal right. Even so, it is easy to be misled by Freud's account since the sexual contract is presented as a history of the origins of kinship, just as he presents the social contract as the history of the origins of civilization. Nevertheless, unlike the classic contract theorists, Freud explicitly states that the father's dominion over women, not merely his dominion over his sons, is the cause of their rebellion and the reason for his murder. In Freud's story, the parricide is actual, not metaphorical, and the sons commit their dreadful deed to gain the political liberty that will also bring sexual access to women.

Freud's writings are not usually considered in discussions of social contract theory, but Philip Rieff, for instance, interprets Freud's story of the parricide as a version of contract theory to be considered alongside the classic accounts.[82] Similarly, Norman O. Brown links Freud to the classic contract theorists, and, he states of the familiar stories, 'the battle of books reenacts Freud's primal crime.'[83] Moreover, there is warrant for this interpretation from Freud himself; in the version of the story in *Moses and Monotheism*, he calls the pact made by the brothers after the murder of the father 'a sort of social contract'.[84] Freud's equivalent of the state of nature is the primal horde – an idea he derived from Darwin – ruled over by the primal father who has the powers of a *patria potestas* and who keeps all the women of the horde for his own sexual use. One day, the sons rebel and kill the father (and, according to Freud, they then eat him, but I shall leave that complication aside in the present argument).

In Freud's theory, the parricide is not followed immediately by the original contract or the constitution of 'civilization'. Freud places Bachofen's epoch of mother-right between the murder and the original contract. However, mother-right is merely an interlude in 'primeval history' before the 'great progress' that occurs with the restitution of patriarchy in the new fraternal form of the brother clan.[85] The overthrow of mother-right (and Freud merely mentions its passing without telling a story about it) comes about because the sons' hatred of the father coexisted with admiration of his power; 'they hated the father who stood so powerfully in the way of their sexual demands and their desire for power, but they also loved and admired him.'[86] Eventually, their guilt at their awful deed leads them to take steps to ensure that it could never happen again. They realize that none of them could ever be a primal father, a *patria potestas* or father–monarch with absolute power. None of them is sufficiently strong to overcome the rest and they come to see that 'fights [among themselves] were as dangerous as they were futile.'[87] The point has been reached to make the original contract.

In *Psychoanalysis and Feminism* Juliet Mitchell argues that 'the law of the father' is established after the parricide, and that this law structures modern patriarchy. On the contrary, the law of the father, the untrammelled will of one man, holds sway before the father's murder. 'It is evident', Locke states, 'that Absolute Monarchy . . . is indeed *inconsistent with Civil Society*, and so can be no Form of Civil Government at all.'[88] The brothers' civil law has a completely different basis from the rule of the primal father. They establish their own law, which is based on the power of their bonds as a fraternity. Freud says that 'together they dared and accomplished what would have remained impossible for them singly.'[89] In killing the father, 'the sons had made the discovery that a combination can be stronger than a single individual.'[90] If brotherhood is to be maintained, fraternal relations must be regulated. 'In order to keep this new state of affairs in being', the brothers must have laws that bind them all equally and, conversely, give 'equal rights to all members of the brother horde'.[91] The social contract *replaces* the law of the father with impartial, public laws to which all stand as equal civil individuals. Paternal rule gives way to civil society. So runs half of Freud's tale.

Freud's accounts of the *social* contract follow the familiar pattern, but he leaves no doubt that the brothers' contract is about very much more than reclamation of their liberty and their right to civil government. They hate the father because 'he stood so powerfully in the way of their sexual demands.' Although the classic tales are not explicit about everything that is at stake, all the stories of original contracts have a singular feature in common. Freud's stories, like those of Sir Robert Filmer and the contract theorists, begin with a father who is, already, a father. The arguments about 'original' political right all begin after physical genesis, after the birth of the son that makes a man (a husband) a father. But a father cannot become a father unless a woman has become a mother, and she cannot become a mother without an act of coitus. Where is the story of the true origin of political right? In the stories of political origins, sex-right is incorporated into father-right, and this nicely obscures the fact that the necessary beginning is missing. All the stories lack a political book of genesis. The stories lack what, borrowing from another part of Freud's work, I shall call the story of the *primal scene*.

The tales as usually told leave the origin of political right shrouded in obscurity. This is not for decency's sake, for parricide, whether theoretical or actual, is hardly a decent story. In part, the obscurity comes from the transmutation of physical birth into masculine political birth. More importantly, a section of the story of political origins must be *repressed* if the claim is to be made that modern society is built on the defeat of patriarchy, or if the law of male sex-right is to be ignored and the claim made that sexual relations are consensual and non-political. Freud rejects the suggestion that the parricide was not an historical event but merely a powerful impulse, never acted upon, that led the sons to imagine the death of their father. He insists that we cannot escape 'the necessity of tracing back the beginning of our cultural possession, of which we rightly are so proud, to a horrible crime which wounds all our feelings'.[92] He ends *Totem and Taboo* with the words, 'in the beginning was the deed.' But which deed? Before a father can be murdered by his sons a woman has to become a mother: was that deed connected to a 'horrible crime'? There are no stories of the primal scene in modern political theory on which I can draw as I have drawn on the stories of the original contract. In chapter 3, however, in order to explain how it could come about in Hobbes' state of nature that a female individual, who is equal in strength and wit to a male individual, could forcibly be subjugated, I had to develop a version of the story of the primal scene.

Sex-right must necessarily precede paternal right; but does the origin of political right lie in a rape, another 'horrible crime'? The crime of the parricide is at least followed by a major revolution. The brothers put to excellent use the political power they have wrested from the father; they make an original contract as well as committing a crime. What of the other original deed and its consequences? Freud denies that the primal scene involves a rape, a crime. Significantly, the primal scene is not discussed in Freud's speculative accounts of the origins of civilization, but is introduced in one of his therapeutic case histories, the case of the Wolf Man. The term 'primal scene' is used in the analysis of the Wolf Man's recollection of his observation and interpretation, as a child, of parental sexual intercourse. To the child, his father appeared to be attacking his mother. Freud notes that, to a child, 'a coitus in the normal position . . . cannot fail to produce the impression of being a sadistic act.'[93] Freud argues that the child's interpretation is a misinterpretation; what the child sees as aggression by the father is actually normal, consensual sexual activity. It is important to note that an actual example of conjugal sexual relations is not necessarily at issue here. Freud also says that what the infant Wolf Man saw was not sexual intercourse between his parents, but an event that was part of an infantile fantasy that drew on the phylogenetic inheritance of humans; the original primal scene, according to Freud, was present to the child.[94]

There are two good reasons for reading this incident in the case history in a different way from Freud himself. Suppose, first, that the infant Wolf Man observed his parents; Freud's interpretation depends on the assumption that 'consent' has genuine meaning in sexual relations, so that consensual intercourse can be clearly distinguished from enforced submission. However, in most legal jurisdictions, the marriage contract still gives a husband right of sexual access to his wife's body whether or not, in any instance of marital relations, she has consented. The young Wolf Man may have accurately interpreted what he saw; we can never know. Moreover, in sexual relations more generally, the belief is still widely held that women say 'no' when they mean 'yes', and the empirical evidence about rape and the way in which rape cases are dealt with in the courts shows, sadly, that there is widespread lack of ability to understand what consensual intercourse means; all too often, enforced or unwilling submission is treated as consent.[95] As a startling example of this point, consider a case of rape and murder in 1986 on an American college campus. The crime, according to a press report, 'was witnessed in part by two college security guards who evidently misunderstood what they were seeing. The guards said they did nothing because they thought the couple were engaging in consensual sexual relations'.[96]

Second, if the Wolf Man was reporting an infantile fantasy, Freud's own account of political origins makes his interpretation of the primal scene most implausible. The will of the primal father, the *patria potestas*, is absolute and unbounded; in the beginning his is the deed. His will is law, and no will counts but his own; thus, it is completely contradictory to suggest that the will of the woman is relevant in the primal scene. Yet her will must be relevant if sexual intercourse is consensual. It makes nonsense of the idea of the all-powerful primal father to imply that, before he becomes a father, his will is constrained in any way by the will of another being or the desire of a woman for coitus. Even if the story of the primal scene is written to incorporate a woman of unlimited, unbridled sexual appetite, so that she 'tempts' the man, the act could not occur at her behest if the man (the father) is to have dominion. His will must prevail. The original deed is *his* deed, and the passionate woman must be subject to his will if his order is to prevail.

There is as much, or as little, reason to call the original rape a crime as there is to call the parricide a crime. As Freud tells us, neither deed, when committed, is properly a 'crime', because the original contract brings morality and, hence, crime into being. Another psychoanalytic theorist was quite certain of the status of the deed in the primal scene. Gregory Zilboorg, in a discussion of what he calls the 'primordial deed', states that he long felt that Freud's words 'were even more fittingly applied to the act of primordial rape than to the murder of the father'.[97] Zilboorg wrote during the Second World War under the impetus of the 'sexual slavery' of women under the Nazis and a crisis in psychoanalytic thought. The crisis arose from Freud's assumption that 'man's primary superiority' was central to the explanation of the construction of masculinity and femininity.[98] In the best tradition of stories of origins, Zilboorg offers his argument as a history of humankind. He argues, against Freud, that the earliest stage of human life was a 'gynaecocentric period', or a matriarchy; mother-right preceded the primal horde.[99] Mother-right was overthrown when, 'one day [a man] became sufficiently conscious and sure of his strength to overpower the woman, to rape her'. Taking issue with all the stories in which men's discovery of paternity is the driving force that institutes the patriarchal family and civilization, Zilboorg speculates that the primordial deed had nothing to do with paternity; 'the act was not that of love and of anticipated fatherhood, nor of tender solicitude;. . . . It was an assault. . . . It was a phallic, sadistic act.'[100]

Zilboorg argues that the original deed was prompted purely by 'the need to possess and master'. The subjugation of women provided the example required to enable men to extend their possession and mastery beyond their immediate needs. Economic mastery quickly followed sexual mastery. Zilboorg claims that 'the idea of the family was originally born not out of love but out of the drive for economic exploitation.' Once women had been enslaved and families formed, men had the concept of slavery and the means to extend their mastery: 'he found himself free to limit and to conquer other human beings; and he was fully secure in that his "wife" – that is to say, his female slave – would roast his meat and attend to any other of his needs.'[101]

The origin of political right must either be repressed or reinterpreted if the creation of civil society is to be represented as a victory over patriarchy, and the sexual contract is to remain hidden. In Freud's stories, the fact that the sexual contract forms part of the original pact is much clearer than in the classic tales. Nevertheless, the patriarchal reading is so well established that only half Freud's story is usually acknowledged. Admittedly, there is another factor that inhibits recognition of the sexual contract. In Freud's argument, the sexual contract appears in the guise of a conjectural history of the origins of kinship. Freud tells the story of the origin of *both* spheres of modern civil society. 'Civilization', i.e., the public world or civil society, and 'kinship', i.e., the private or familial world, are brought into being through the same fraternal contract.

In *Moses and Monotheism*, Freud states that the brothers erect three laws after the parricide. One prohibition, against parricide (or killing the totem, the father-substitute), needs no further comment; the dreadful deed will not occur again. A second law gives equal rights to the brothers. I have already referred a number of times to the crucial place of this law in the social contract, but equal rights are just as important in the sexual contract. The sexual contract is signalled by the third law, which prohibits incest or, positively, institutes exogamy or an orderly system of marriage. Freud uses the term 'incest' in this context to refer to sexual relations within a particular social group; say, the original primal horde or patriarchal family. The prohibition against incest means that men must look for wives from outside the group to which they belong by virtue of 'blood descent'. Freud's use of 'incest' is thus different from the narrow (euphemistic) use, typical today, to refer to carnal relations (rape) between father and daughter, or between siblings, in the same family. (In Britain, for example, the Prohibited Degrees of Marriage, which caused such controversy about deceased wives' sisters in the nineteenth and early twentieth centuries, and which

depended on a much wider sense of 'incest', have long since ceased
to have social meaning.)

Freud makes some rather cryptic comments about the laws
established through the original pact. He states of the law granting
equal rights to the brothers that it 'ignores the father's wishes. Its
sense lies in the need of preserving permanently the new order which
was established after the death of the father'. This law marks the
overthrow of the father's absolute political right. He would have
wished his form of rule to continue, so his wishes were ignored.
Freud states of the laws against incest and parricide that these 'two
prohibitions work in the direction of what the murdered father
would have wished; they, so to speak, perpetuate his will.'[102] The
father would, of course, endorse a law prohibiting parricide – but he
would not object to exogamy because it consolidates sex-right while
placing it on a different footing. The primal father wanted none of
his sons to take his place and have exclusive, unlimited access to all
the women. When the primal horde gives way to kinship and
marriage, the father's legacy of sex-right is shared equally among all
the brothers.

Freud writes of the brothers' 'renunciation of the passionately
desired mothers and sisters of the horde', and claims that they 'all
equally renounced the women whom they desired.' This is a very
misleading way of putting the matter. The brothers do not renounce
the women, or, at best, the renunciation is only temporary, during
the period of matriarchy that comes after the parricide; the brothers
are then homosexual. The historic movement to 'civilization' (civil
society) takes place with the establishment of orderly, universal
heterosexual relations. Each of the brothers has seen the futility of
desiring to have all the women to himself. Freud remarks that the
brothers' rivalries over the women they had seized from the father
threatened to destroy their new fraternal organization. So, he says,
'there was nothing left for the brothers, if they wanted to live
together, but to erect the incest prohibition. . . . Thus they saved
the organization which had made them strong.'[103] None of the
brothers can ever be a primal father, but it does not follow that they
renounce patriarchal sex-right. Instead, the right is extended to all
the brothers through the law of exogamy (kinship). That is, the
brothers *make a sexual contract*. They establish a law which confirms
masculine sex-right and ensures that there is an orderly access by
each man to a woman. Patriarchal sex-right ceases to be the right of

one man, the father, and becomes a 'universal' right. The law of male sex-right extends to all men, to all members of the fraternity.

In the stories of the classic contract theorists the sexual contract is very hard to discern because it is *displaced onto the marriage contract*. Most of the classic theorists argue that marriage and family life are part of the natural condition. Men enjoy the natural 'superiority of their sex' and, when women become wives, they are assumed always to agree to enter into a marriage contract which places them in sub-jection to their husbands. 'In the beginning', in the state of nature, the 'first' husband exercised a conjugal right over his wife, and all husbands enjoy this original political right by virtue of their masculine natures. An orderly system of marriage – or the law of exogamy – exists in the state of nature; each man has access to a woman. The antinomy state of nature/civil society in the classic texts thus *presupposes* the sexual contract. When the momentous move is made from the natural condition into civil society, marriage and the patriarchal family are carried over into the new civil order. There is no need for the classic contract stories to include an account of the sexual contract. The original contract that creates civil society (which encompasses both the public and the private spheres) implicitly incorporates the sexual contract. In these stories, marriage and the patriarchal family appear as the natural, necessary foundation of civil life. The natural foundation already exists (the sexual contract is presupposed) so that there is no need to tell a story about its origins. However, like Freud, Hobbes argues that marriage law is created through the original pact; Hobbes' state of nature contains no 'matrimonial laws'. The standard readings of Hobbes and Freud see no political significance in the genesis of marriage law or the law of exogamy. From a patriarchal perspective, political right is either father-right or civil (public) right. Conjugal relations are presented as natural and private, and so the law of male sex-right and the sexual contract completely disappear.

My interpretation of Freud's very brief remarks is endorsed in Lévi-Strauss' extremely lengthy conjectural history of the origins of 'culture'. The momentous step from nature to culture, he maintains, comes about through the institution of the prohibition against incest, or the law of exogamy. This law has a unique status; it is a social rule which, like the laws of nature, is universal. The prohibition of incest marks the great dividing-line between nature and culture, or civilization. The law is the means through which nature is transcended. Once exogamy is the rule, men must find wives from outside their own social group (family). Lévi-Strauss states of the law of exogamy, that 'on the only possible basis it institutes freedom of access for every individual to the women of the group . . . all men are in equal competition for all women.'[104] No man can claim his mother or his sister, but he can claim the sister of another man, and this is the case for all men. Every man can have sexual access to a woman, and so he can avoid bachelorhood, one of the two great 'social calamities' (the other is to be an orphan; Lévi-Strauss does not mention the fate of spinsters); all men can obtain a woman (wife), one of the 'valuables *par excellence* . . . without which life is impossible, or, at best, is reduced to the worst forms of abjection'.[105] I noted in the previous chapter that Lévi-Strauss sees marriage as the archetype of exchange, and it is now clear why. Marriage, or the orderly exchange of women, which gives equal sexual access to all men, is the original exchange that constitutes culture or civilization. Once culture is created, women cease to be mere 'natural stimulants' and become signs of social value.[106] Lévi-Strauss also stresses that (like language) the law of exogamy binds men together; when men become brothers-in-law, communal (fraternal) bonds are constituted and strengthened.

Lévi-Strauss writes of marriage that 'the woman figures only as one of the objects in the exchange, not as one of partners between whom the exchange takes place.'[107] Feminists who have used Lévi-Strauss' idea of 'the exchange of women' to tell stories of the origins of patriarchy have overlooked a very odd feature of this exchange. Certainly, in the story of the creation of the prohibition against incest (the original pact) women are the object of the contract, the object of the exchange of words or other signifiers of agreement among men. Women cannot be participants; their nature rules out that possibility. Once an orderly system of marriage is established, however, women are not merely objects that are exchanged; women are not merely signs of value or property that is exchanged like any other material property. Women are parties to the marriage contract. In the traditional marriage service, one man (a father) 'gives away' a woman (daughter) to another man, but this 'exchange' is not marriage, but a preliminary to marriage. Marriage is constituted by a contract *between* a man and a woman.

Moreover, the 'exchange' that is embodied in marriage is not at all like the exchange of material property; marriage is a long-term social relationship between the sexes in which, in return for protection from a husband, a wife gives obedience. The classic stories of the original contract raise the question of how women, naturally lacking the capacities of 'individuals' who make contracts, always enter into the marriage contract, and why it is held that women must enter into this contract. The question is more pressing in Lévi-Strauss' conjectural history in which women are reduced to the status of property and, like slaves, are merely exchanged among their masters; how can a being with such a status enter into a contract? If women are purely objects of exchange and signs, then they cannot take part in contract – but their inability to participate creates a major problem for contract doctrine. The reason that women enter into the marriage contract in the classic stories, and must do so (a reason on which I shall elaborate in detail in chapter 6), is that, if universal freedom is to be presented as the principle of civil society, all individuals, including women, must enter into contracts; no one can be left out. In civil society, individual freedom is exhibited through contract.

Freud and Lévi-Strauss write in the grand tradition of theoretical speculation about the origins of human society, civilization and culture. But, as I argued in chapter 2, there is no good reason to read their stories of origins in this light. Rather, they should be read as stories of the origin of civil society, a culturally and historically specific form of social order. Exogamous marriage may or may not be a universal feature of human social life, but its social meaning does not remain unchanged across history or across cultures. In particular, marriage and the kinship alliances established through the 'exchange of women' occupy a very different place in the traditional societies from which Lévi-Strauss draws his copious ethnographic data than in modern civil society. Traditional societies are structured by kinship relations, but the move from the state of nature – from the primal horde or from Lévi-Strauss' nature – to *civil* society is a move into a social order in which 'kinship' is sloughed off into its own separate private sphere and reconstituted as the modern family. The story of the original contract tells of the genesis of a society that is structured into two spheres – although we are usually told only half the story and so we only hear about the origin of the public 'universal' sphere.

To tell the missing half of the story, to uncover the sexual contract and the origins of the private sphere, is necessary for an understanding of modern patriarchy. Yet, it is very difficult to reconstruct the story of the sexual contract without losing sight of the fact that the two spheres of civil society are, at one and the same time, both separate and interwoven in a very complex manner. To state that the social contract and the sexual contract – the original contract – creates the two spheres, can be seriously misleading in so far as such a formulation suggests that patriarchal right governs only marriage or the private sphere. In the classic tales the sexual contract is displaced into the marriage contract, but this does not mean that the law of male sex-right is confined to marital relations. Marriage is extremely important, not least because the private sphere is constituted through marriage, but the natural power of men as 'individuals' extends to all aspects of civil life. Civil society (as a whole) is patriarchal. Women are subject to men in both the private and public spheres; indeed, men's patriarchal right is the major structural support binding the two spheres into a social whole. Men's right of access to women's bodies is exercised in the public market as well as in private marriage, and patriarchal right is exercised over women and their bodies in ways other than direct sexual access, as I shall show when I consider the connection between the marriage contract and the (public) employment contract.

Once the father is politically dead and his partriarchal power has been universalized, that is, distributed to all men, political right is no longer centred in one pair of hands or even recognized for what it is. When the brothers make the original pact they split apart the two dimensions of political right that were united in the figure of the patriarchal father. They create a new form of civil right to replace paternal right, and they turn their legacy of sex-right into modern patriarchy, which includes the marriage contract. Patriarchal right is extended in an orderly fashion to the fraternity (all men) and given legitimate social expression. Civil individuals form a fraternity because they are bound together by a bond *as men*. They share a common interest in upholding the original contract which legitimizes masculine right and allows them to gain material and psychological benefit from women's subjection.

The civil sphere gains its universal meaning in opposition to the private sphere of natural subjection and womanly capacities. The 'civil individual' is constituted within the sexual division of social life created through the original contract. The civil individual and the public realm appear universal only in relation to and in opposition to the private sphere, the natural foundation of civil life. Similarly, the meaning of civil liberty and equality, secured and distributed impartially to all 'individuals' through the civil law, can be understood only in opposition to natural subjection (of women) in the private sphere. Liberty and equality appear as universal ideals, rather than the natural attributes of the men (the brothers) who create the social order within which the ideals are given social expression, only because the civil sphere is conventionally considered on its own. Liberty, equality *and* fraternity form the revolutionary trilogy because liberty and equality are the attributes of the fraternity who exercise the law of male sex-right. What better notion to conjure with than 'fraternity', and what better conjuring trick than to insist that 'fraternity' is universal and nothing more than a metaphor for community.

The idea of a fraternal patriarchy might seem to be undermined because, the objection can be raised, brothers do not share a common bond, they are often in competition or hostile to each other, even committing fratricide. In the bibilical story, Adam is given dominion over Eve – and Cain murders Abel. McWilliams remarks that fraternal unity is always temporary, 'hostility between brothers . . . is the logical rule.'[108] This may be 'logical' when brothers in the family are looking for the approval of a father and hoping to inherit his power, but in civil society the 'male principle' operates on a new footing. The brothers who enter into the original contract transform themselves into civil individuals, whose fraternal relations are between equals. In both the public and private spheres of the civil order, competition is no longer personal rivalry between kin (brothers) that can lead to murder, but is instituted socially as the impersonal pursuit of interests in the competition of the market and the competition for women in marriage. Public (market) competition is regulated by the laws of the state, and competition for wives is regulated by marriage law and by social norms. Furthermore, in the masculine sexual competition, unlike the competition in the market, *all members of the fraternity can win a prize*. Most men become husbands, but that is by no means the only way that members of the fraternity can exercise their masculine right.

Still, the marriage contract is the best place to begin to illustrate how patriarchal political right is continuously renewed and reaffirmed through actual contracts in everyday life. Marriage is a relationship about which everyone knows something and most of us know a good deal, although what women know and what men know is often, for good reason, very different. The sexual contract is made only once, but it is replicated every day as each man makes his own 'original' marriage contract. Individually, each man receives a major part of his patriarchal inheritance through the marriage contract. There are echoes of the story of the primal scene and the slave contract lingering round the marriage contract. When a woman becomes a 'wife' her husband gains right of sexual access to her body (once called 'conjugal rights' in legal language) and to her labour as a housewife. In the next chapter I shall look at the mutually interdependent construction of the wife as a 'housewife' and the husband as a 'worker', and at the relationship between the marriage contract and the employment contract. Conjugal relations are part of a sexual division of labour and structure of subordination that extends from the private home into the public arena of the capitalist market.

5

Wives, Slaves and Wage Slaves

The story of the sexual contract is fundamental to an understanding of modern patriarchy, but the world in which the classic contract theorists told their stories was foreign in many ways to the social world we inhabit today. When Rousseau died in 1778, economic production was not yet completely separated from the household, the capitalist market was still being formed as an independent sphere of activity and families included servants, apprentices and slaves, as well as the master, his wife and children. At first sight, the modern patriarchal family of the classic contract theorists may look indistinguishable from the pre-modern form, or from the family in Filmer's patriarchalism, since the inhabitants are the same. The crucial change is the claim that the modern family has its origins in contract, not in the father's procreative power. The civil master of a family attains his right over his wife through contract, his right over his servant was contractual and, according to some classic contract theorists and defenders of American slavery, so was his right over his slave. The 'family', in the sense in which the term is used today, emerged only after a long process of historical development. The many figures that populated the family in the seventeenth and eighteenth centuries gradually disappeared until the couple of husband and wife took the centre of the stage, and the marriage contract became constitutive of domestic relations.

The old, domestic contracts between a master and his (civil) slave and a master and his servant were labour contracts. Slaves and servants labour at the behest of their masters. The marriage contract, too, is a kind of labour contract. To become a wife entails becoming a housewife; that is, a wife is someone who works for her husband in the marital home. But what kind of labourer is a (house)wife? How does the conjugal labour contract resemble or differ from other domestic labour contracts, or from the present-day employment contract? What form of subordination is involved in being a (house)wife? What is the significance of the fact that only women become (house)wives? Over the past three centuries, feminists have compared wives to slaves, servants and, the predominant comparison today, workers. But none of the comparisons, taken singly, serves fully to capture patriarchal subjection.

Feminist discussions do not usually consider the similarities and differences between slaves, servants and workers and whether the subjection of wives might throw light onto other forms of subordination. Nor is the fact that civil slaves, servants, workers and housewives are all constituted through contract given much weight. In the absence of knowledge of the story of the sexual contract, the classification of contracts as, for example, conjugal, or between a master and servant, can appear arbitrary indeed. Consider the following definition from *A Treatise on the Law of the Domestic Relations* published in the United States in 1874: 'a master is one who has legal authority over another; and the person over whom such authority may be rightfully exercised is his servant.' A civil slave, a wife or a worker are all 'servants' according to this definition. The volume includes an extensive discussion of the 'disabilities' of wives under coverture which seems to leave no doubt that a wife was the 'servant' of her husband. Yet she is not classified as such. Husbands and wives are discussed separately from masters and servants. The author remarks innocently that 'the relation of master and servant presupposes two parties who stand on an unequal footing in their mutual dealings; yet not naturally so, as in other domestic relations, . . . This relation is, in theory, hostile to the genius of free institutions.'[1]

'Free institutions' presuppose parties who stand to each other as equals. The domestic relations of master–slave and master–servant, relations between unequals, have given way to the relation between capitalist or employer and wage labourer or worker. Production moved from the family to capitalist enterprises, and male domestic labourers became workers. The wage labourer now stands as a civil equal with his employer in the public realm of the capitalist market. A (house)wife remains in the private domestic sphere, but the unequal relations of domestic life are 'naturally so' and thus do not detract from the universal equality of the public world. The marriage contract is the only remaining example of a domestic labour contract, and so the conjugal relation can easily be seen as a remnant of the pre-modern domestic order – as a feudal relic, or an aspect of the old world of status that has not yet been transformed by contract. Feminists sometimes portray the contemporary wife as like a serf and argue that the family is a 'quasi-feudal institution'.[2] On the other hand, socialists, rejecting the claim that the worker is a free labourer, have argued that 'unfree labour is not a feudal relic, but part of the essential relations of capitalism.' How, then, are capitalist relations to be characterized? One writer claims that, under capitalism, 'status relations are the mode of achieving contractual relations.'[3] If a wife resembles a serf, this is not because a feudal relation lingers on; nor does the employment contract rest on relations of status. Modern marriage and employment are contractual, but that does not mean that, substantively, all resemblance to older forms of (unfree) status have vanished. Contract is the specifically modern means of creating relationships of subordination, but, because civil subordination originates in contract, it is presented as freedom. Arguments about feudal relics and status overlook the comparisons and oppositions created by original contract. Contractual relations do not gain their meaning from the old world but in contrast to the relations of the private sphere.

Private domestic relations also originate in a contract – but the meaning of the marriage contract, a contract between a man and a woman, is very different from the meaning of contracts between men in the public sphere. The marriage contract reflects the patriarchal ordering of nature embodied in the original contract. A sexual division of labour is constituted through the marriage contract. In Hobbes' state of nature, when a male individual conquers (contracts with) a female individual he becomes her sexual master and she becomes his servant. Rousseau's conjectural history of the development of civil society tells how women must 'tend the hut', and in *La Nouvelle Héloise* Julie superintends the daily domestic business at Clarens. The story has been told again more recently – this time as science – by the sociobiologists. E. O. Wilson's story of the genesis of the contemporary sexual division of labour in the earliest stages of human history is held to reveal that the division is a necessary part of human existence. The story begins with the fact that, like other large primates, human beings reproduce themselves slowly:

Mothers carry fetuses for nine months and afterward are encumbered by infants and small children who require milk at frequent intervals through the day. It is to the advantage of each woman of the hunter–gatherer band to secure the allegiance of men who will contribute meat and hides while sharing the labor of child–rearing. It is to the reciprocal advantage of each man to obtain sexual rights to women and to monopolize their economic productivity. [4]

That is to say, science reveals that our social life is as if it were based on a sexual contract, which both establishes orderly access to women and a division of labour in which women are subordinate to men.

In Zilboorg's interpretation of the primal scene, women become sexual and economic slaves in the family. The co-operative socialist William Thompson provided a similar conjectural history of the origin of marriage. He argued that, 'in the beginning', men's greater strength, aided by cunning, enabled them to enslave women. Men would have turned women into mere labourers except that they depend on women to satisfy their sexual desires. If men had no sexual desire, or if the propagation of the species did not depend on men's intervention in a form which also provided sexual gratification, there would have been no need for the institution in which 'each man yokes a woman to his establishment, and calls it a *contract.*' Women are 'parcelled out amongst men, . . . one weak always coupled and subjected to one strong'. [5] John Stuart Mill offered a similar argument later in the nineteenth century; 'from the very earliest twilight of human society, every woman (owing to the value attached to her by men, combined with her inferiority in muscular strength) was found in a state of bondage to some man. . . . [Marriage] is the primitive state of slavery lasting on . . . [it] has not lost the taint of its brutal origin.' [6]

Until late into the nineteenth century the legal and civil position of a wife resembled that of a slave. Under the common law doctrine of coverture, a wife, like a slave, was civilly dead. A slave had no independent legal existence apart from his master, and husband and wife became 'one person', the person of the husband. Middle- and upper-class women of property were able to avoid the full stringency of the legal fiction of marital unity through the law of equity, using devices such as trusts and pre-nuptial contracts. [7] But such exceptions (compare: not all slave-masters use their power to the full) do nothing to detract from the strength of the institution of

coverture as a reminder of the terms of the conjugal relation established by (the story of) the original contract. Sir Henry Maine
remarks in *Ancient Law* that:

> I do not know how the operation and nature of the ancient Patria
> Potestas can be brought so vividly before the mind as by reflecting on
> the prerogatives attached to the husband by the pure English
> Common Law, and by recalling the rigorous consistency with which
> the view of a complete legal subjection on the part of the wife is
> carried by it.[8]

The Married Women's Property Act in Britain (1882) – which had
been preceded from the 1840s by such Acts in some American states
– was one of the great landmarks in the struggle to end coverture
and gain recognition for married women as civil individuals. But it
was only one landmark, and some decisive reforms in the legal
standing of wives are so recent that most of us still bear marks of
subjection, notably that we are known by our husbands' names.

The comparison of women and wives with slaves was frequently
made from the late seventeenth century onward. In the previous
chapter I cited Mary Astell's statement that, unlike men, who were
born free, women were born slaves, and in the eighteenth century
many novelists made similar statements. For example, in Daniel
Defoe's *Roxana* (published in 1724), the heroine proclaims that she
thinks a woman 'was born free, and . . . might enjoy that Liberty to
as much Purpose as the Men do'. She continues, 'the very Nature of
the Marriage-Contract was, in short, nothing but giving up Liberty,
Estate, Authority, and every-thing, to the Man, and the Woman
was indeed a meer Woman ever after, that is to say, a Slave.'[9] The
comparison of wives and slaves reverberated through the women's
movement in the nineteenth century. Women were very prominent
in the abolitionist movement and they quickly made the connection
between the condition of slaves and their own condition as wives.
John Stuart Mill wrote in *The Subjection of Women* that 'there remain
no legal slaves, except the mistress of every house.'[10] A year later, in
1870, the American feminist Laura Curtis Bullard declared:

> Slavery is not yet abolished in the United States. . . . It was a
> glorious day for this republic when she shook herself free from the
> disgrace of negro slavery, . . . It will be a still more glorious day in

her annals when the republic shall declare the injustice of a slavery of sex, and shall set free her millions of bond women![11]

To be a slave or a wife was, so to speak, to be in a perpetual nonage that wives have not yet entirely cast off. Adult male slaves were called 'boys' and adult married women were – and still are – called 'girls'. As befitted civilly dead beings, the slave was brought to life by being given a name by his master (servants were also given another name by their masters if their own was 'unsuitable'; 'Mary' was very popular). When a woman becomes a wife, her status was/is singled out by the title 'Mrs'. A wife was included under her husband's name and, still today, can be called 'Mrs John Smith'. Elizabeth Cady Stanton, the great American suffragist, refused to give up her name of Cady when she married Henry Stanton, and in 1847 she wrote that she seriously objected to 'being called Henry. Ask our colored brethren if there is nothing to a name. Why are the slaves nameless unless they take that of their master?'[12] Under coverture, a wife was required to live where her husband demanded, her earnings belonged to her husband and her children were the property of her husband, just as the children of the female slave belonged to her master. But perhaps the most graphic illustration of the continuity between slavery and marriage was that in England – as Thomas Hardy's *The Mayor of Casterbridge* reminds us – wives could be sold at public auctions.

Samuel Menefee lists 387 recorded cases of wife-selling, beginning with an isolated reference from 1073, and then occurring regularly from 1553 through to the twentieth century. He argues that the sale of slaves and the sale of wives existed independently; the abolition of the slave-trade had no effect on the trade in wives. Wives, however, were a good deal cheaper to buy than slaves – and even cheaper than corpses.[13] The wife usually stood to be auctioned with a halter round her neck (the popular belief seems to have been that the sale was valid only if the halter were in place); sometimes the halter was fixed round a waist or an arm, and occasionally decorated with ribbon, 'perhaps to lessen the humiliation of the symbol'.[14] Halters, as Menefee notes, were part of livestock sales, but one might speculate that the symbolism goes further. Livestock are driven by men with whips, so the halter may at one remove have symbolized the slave-master's whip. Menefee's conclusion about wife-selling is that wife sales alleviated friction in social life, providing one solution to intersecting problems of marriage, divorce and support. Based on well-known market mechanisms, with numerous symbolic parallels, wife-selling represented a conservative and traditional social solution to the dilemmas faced by individuals, relieving stress on the social fabric with a minimal strain on the communal *status quo*.[15]

The sale of wives enabled a husband to avoid supporting his wife and children, and the purchaser 'could insure himself against an action for *crim. con.*', i.e., criminal conversation.[16] If a wife committed adultery, her sale could enable her lover to avoid action under the law of criminal conversation. The law was based on the assumption that a wife was (like) property; a husband could sue another man for damages for restitution – for injury to his property – if his wife committed adultery. A successful case was brought in Dublin as recently as 1979.[17] No doubt, wife-selling provided an informal solution to marital breakdown in the absence of divorce. But why did the solution take this form? Menefee says nothing about the significance of the institution of wife-selling for the structure of marital relations and the subjection of wives, let alone the implications for the operation of the law of male sex-right.

American slave-owners sold their slaves, not their wives. However, the figure of the slave-owner's wife was a peculiarly dramatic symbol of patriarchal right for other (white) wives of the period. As a husband, the slave-master had right of sexual access to his wife – but he also, as a master, had sexual access to his female slaves. Mary Chestnut, wife of a plantation owner, wrote in her diary in 1861, that 'Mrs. Stowe [author of *Uncle Tom's Cabin*] did not hit the sorest spot. She makes Legree a bachelor.'[18] The slave-master/husband was 'sole father of a "family, black and white"', and protector of his family.[19] The term 'family' is beautifully ambiguous here. In 1800, Thomas Jefferson compiled a 'Census of My Family' which included his slaves.[20] But Jefferson's 'family' (in one sense of the term) resulted from his marriage and from his long union with his slave Sally Hemings, who was his wife's half-sister. In his brilliant study, *Roll, Jordan, Roll*, Eugene Genovese notes that masters were particularly concerned about their male slaves beating their wives, even as those masters themselves might with impunity seize and beat the black wives; the slave-master 'thought nothing of stripping a woman naked and whipping her till she bled'.[21]

In Britain, in the same period, it was widely believed that a husband had the right physically to chastize his wife provided that he used a stick no bigger than a man's thumb. Nineteenth-century feminists, like feminists today, were greatly concerned about injuries to wives inflicted by their husbands. Frances Power Cobbe published an influential article in 1878, 'Wife Torture in England', and, in a speech in the House of Commons, supporting women's suffrage during the debates on the Second Reform Bill, John Stuart Mill said that 'I should like to have a Return laid before this House of the number of women who are annually beaten to death, kicked to death, or trampled to death by their male protectors.'[22] A husband owned the property in his wife's person and a man was fully a proprietor and master only if he could do what he willed with his own.

His right to do as he willed was given *de jure* sanction by the legal category of 'conjugal rights'. Even today, the comparison between marriage and slavery remains relevant in one respect in those states of the United States and Australia, as well as in Britain, where the law still sanctions marital rape. Lord Hale's *The History of the Pleas of the Crown* laid down in the eighteenth century that 'the husband cannot be guilty of a rape committed by himself upon his lawful wife, for by their mutual matrimonial consent and contract the wife hath given up herself in this kind unto her husband, which she cannot retract.'[23] Until 1884 in Britain, a wife could be jailed for refusing conjugal rights, and, until 1891, husbands were allowed forcibly to imprison their wives in the matrimonial home to obtain their rights. The marriage contract, on this matter, is a contract of specific performance. Rousseau's advice to Sophie when she became Emile's wife was that she could secure her woman's empire and 'reign by means of love' if she rationed Emile's access to her body and so made herself precious. She must be modest, not capricious, so that Emile could 'honor his wife's chastity without having to complain of her coldness'.[24] But it is hard to see the relevance of this advice; only Emile could decide whether access would be 'rationed'. The husband's conjugal right is the clearest example of the way in which the modern origin of political right as sex-right is translated through the marriage contract into the right of every member of the fraternity in daily life.

The denial of bodily integrity to wives was a major reason why William Thompson called marriage the 'white–slave code'. He implicitly suggests that, without the sexual contract, men would not have entered the social contract and created the state; men's conjugal mastery looks as if it 'compensate[s] them for their own cowardly submission almost everywhere to the chains of political power'.[25] John Stuart Mill went so far as to argue that wives were worse off than female slaves:

> No slave is a slave to the same lengths, and in so full a sense of the word, as a wife is . . . however brutal a tyrant she may unfortunately be chained to – though she may know that he hates her, . . . he can claim from her and enforce the lowest degradation of a human being, that of being made the instrument of an animal function contrary to her inclinations.[26]

At about the same time, in the United States, Elizabeth Cady Stanton declared that 'society as organized today under the man power, is one grand rape of womanhood'.[27]

In most legal jurisdictions, despite some recent reforms, husbands still own the sexual property in their wives' persons. The comparison of wives with slaves, unfortunately, is not yet completely redundant. Still, the comparison cannot now be pressed any further, although in the early stages of the current revival of the women's movement the argument was again made that a wife was a slave. One reason advanced to support this characterization was that a wife who works full time in the conjugal home is not entitled to pay. Wives are housewives and housewives, like slaves, receive only subsistence (protection) in return for their labours; Sheila Cronan asked, 'does this not constitute slavery?'[28] Her juxtaposition of a description of the Alabama slave-code of 1852 and a description of the duties of a wife in about 1972 does not, as she argued, show that a wife is a slave. Wives are not civilly dead as they once were, but are now, for most purposes, juridically free and equal; we have won citizenship. A juridically free and equal citizen cannot be an actual slave (which is not to say that conditions of wage labour may not, at times, look like that of slavery); at most, a citizen could contract to be a civil slave. Perhaps a wife is like a civil slave. The marriage contract can still, in principle, last for a lifetime, and the civil slave contract also runs for life.

The difficulty with this analogy is that the civil slave contract is an extended employment contract and a civil slave is a special kind of wage labourer. A wife, as feminists have continually emphasized, is not paid a wage for her labour; she is not employed. Furthermore, employment is part of the public civil world, and a wife labours in the private home. Perhaps, then, despite the fact that a wife receives no pay, she is more like a servant, who also is a domestic labourer. A wife is now usually the only other adult member of the family, or if there are others they, too, rely on her labours.

In the past, a wife's position in the master's family was never exactly comparable to that of other subordinates. The wife of an American slave-master, for example, had her own jurisdiction over the slaves (but a married woman had no power of manumission), even though she was also subject to her husband. The most apt characterization of the position of the wife was that she was the first slave of the master; or, more generally, as many of the early feminists insisted, a wife was merely the first servant of the master of the family. Mary Astell's pointed comment was that a woman 'has no Reason to be fond of being a Wife, or to reckon it a Piece of Preferment when she is taken to be a Man's Upper-Servant'.[29] Lady Chudleigh summed up the matter neatly in 1703:

Wife and servant are the same,
But only differ in the name.[30]

A few years later, Daniel Defoe stated that he did not 'take the State of Matrimony to be designed as that of Apprentices who are bound to the Family, and that the Wife is to be us'd only as the upper Servant in the House'.[31] And in 1792, in *A Vindication of the Rights of Woman*, Mary Wollstonecraft criticized the patriarchal claim that woman was 'created merely to gratify the appetite of man, or to be the upper servant, who provides his meals and takes care of his linen'.[32] At the end of the nineteenth century, Thorstein Veblen called a wife 'the chief menial of the household'.[33]

There is, though, one fundamentally important difference between wives and other labourers. Only *women* become (house)wives and provide 'domestic service', even though all masters demand 'service' from their subordinates. As Genovese makes clear, many slave-owners wished not just to be masters but good masters, and the prevailing ideal of the good master was that he protected his slaves and fulfilled certain responsibilities towards them. The ideal for slaves was that they showed gratitude and rendered faithful service –

an impossible requirement, of course, to demand of a piece of
property.[34] And 'faithful service' is precisely what all masters desire,
including husbands. My late father-in-law's indenture paper as an
apprentice printer, which he signed as a boy of fourteen in 1918,
includes clauses binding him to 'truly and faithfully serve' his master,
'his secrets keep, and his lawful commands willingly obey'. The
specific content of the 'faithful service' demanded by a husband,
however, is determined not only by the marriage contract but by the
'foundation in nature' that gives rise to the sexual contract and the
sexual division of labour. The provision of 'domestic service' is part
of the patriarchal meaning of femininity, of what it is to be a woman.

In 1862, a commentator on the problem of 'surplus women' in
Britain stated that female servants were not part of the problem:

> They are in no sense redundant, . . . they discharge a most
> important and indispensable function in social life; they do not follow
> an obligatory independent, and therefore for their sex an unnatural,
> career – on the contrary, they are attached to others and are
> connected with other existences, which they embellish, facilitate, and
> serve. In a word, they fulfill both essentials of woman's being; *they are
> supported by, and they minister to*, men.[35]

Leonore Davidoff has shown how familial ties often entailed
domestic service for women; 'female kin could be and were used as
domestic servants without pay.' Female family members and domestic service were identified so closely that, although residential
servants might contract with a master for a year at a time, the wages
paid were seen as an extension of bed and board, or protection, and
'legally the payment of wages had to be explicitly stated in the
contract, otherwise it could be assumed that the service was being
given voluntarily.' By the mid-nineteenth century, domestic service
had become predominantly women's work. Significantly, a wife
could not enter domestic service unless she had obtained her
husband's permission. He had right over her services. If the
employer failed to obtain the husband's permission, he 'could be
sued for "loss of services", in exactly the same way as an employer
could be sued for enticing away a servant. In lay terms, a woman
could not serve two masters'.[36]

Until very recently, the law of consortium confirmed that a wife
stood to her husband as a servant to a master. If his wife was

negligently injured by a third party, a husband could sue for loss of consortium which 'in addition to housework and child care, . . includes her love, affection, companionship, society, and sexual services'.[37] The loss through wrongful injury of the wife's ability to work in the home was seen in the same light as an injury to a servant which also, necessarily, injures a master. The law was not abolished in Britain or the state of New South Wales in Australia until the 1980s. In the United States only a small minority of states have abolished the law; most (rather oddly, although, as I shall show in the next chapter, in keeping with the standpoint of contract) have extended the right to sue to wives. In New South Wales in 1981, a successful case was brought under the law of consortium and a husband was awarded damages of $40,000.[38]

Only during the last fifty years in Britain has a wife become the sole servant in the family. The emergence of the little world of the married couple and their children, now taken for granted as constituting a proper 'family', was completed only relatively recently. The persistence of the older understanding of the 'family' is illustrated in the Report on the 1851 Census in Britain, in which the Registrar General stated that 'the English family, in its essential type, is composed of a husband, wife, children, and servants.' He adds that it is formed 'less perfectly but more commonly, of husband, wife, and children'.[39] In American cities in the middle of the last century, between 15 and 30 per cent of all households had resident domestic servants. The great majority of these servants were women (at that time, usually white women) and most women in paid employment were domestic servants.[40] In Australia in 1901, almost half the women in paid employment were in some kind of domestic service (not all in private homes), and throughout the nineteenth century the demand for servants was greater than the supply, which was perhaps not surprising when a woman well-trained as a servant was eminently suitable as a wife.[41] Servants were also objects of desire for some upper-class men in the complex, intricately demarcated world of class and sex in nineteenth-century Britain. (Perhaps the most dramatic recorded example was the long liaison between the servant, Hannah Cullwick and the gentleman, Arthur Munby.)[42] Until the 1930s, very many families in Britain, including those of modest means in the skilled working class, could keep servants or a maid of all work. Domestic service was a major area of employment. In 1881 one person in every twenty-two was a domestic servant, the majority of residential servants were female, and one-third of all women aged between fifteen and twenty were in service.[43]

A (house)wife now performs the tasks once distributed between servants of different rank or undertaken by the maid of all work. Her 'core' jobs are cleaning, shopping, cooking, washing-up, laundering and ironing.[44] She also looks after her children, frequently cares for aged parents or other relatives, and is sometimes incorporated to a greater or lesser degree as an unpaid assistant in her husband's work. This aspect of being a wife is visible in many small shops or in the activities of the wives of clergymen and politicians, but the same service is provided, less visibly, to husbands in all kinds of occupations. A wife, for example, contributes research assistance (to male academics), acts as hostess (to a business man's clients), answers the phone and keeps the books (for a small business man).[45] However, as Christine Delphy has argued, to list the tasks of a housewife tells us only so much. The list cannot explain why exactly the same services can be bought in the market, or why a particular task is performed without pay by a wife, yet she would get paid for providing the service if she worked, for example, in a restaurant or for a firm of contract cleaners.[46] The problem is not that wives perform valuable tasks for which they are not paid (which has led some feminists to argue for state payment or wages for housework). Rather, what being a woman (wife) *means* is to provide certain services for and at the command of a man (husband). In short, the marriage contract and a wife's subordination as a (kind of) labourer, cannot be understood in the absence of the sexual contract and the patriarchal construction of 'men' and 'women' and the 'private' and 'public' spheres.

One of the features of the unfree labour of the slave, or the labour of a residential servant, is that they must serve their masters at all times. A wife, too, is always available to provide for her husband. Thus, (house)wives work extremely long hours. Evidence from the United States and Soviet Union indicates that there was no significant decrease in the hours that housewives worked each week between the 1920s and 1960s, although a decline may have occurred in the United States between 1965 and 1975. But the decline was from a very high level; American time-budgets in the 1960s and 1970s show that housewives worked around 55 hours each week, and where there was a child under a year old the working week stretched to nearly 70 hours.[47] Wives in Britain in 1971 worked on average 77 hours a week.[48] Husbands contribute very little; one recent, very detailed empirical study of the division of conjugal labour in the United States concluded that 'very little could be found that affected how much husbands did.'[49] The presence of a husband may also increase the workload in the home; 'the husband may be a net drain on the family's resources of housework time – that is, husbands may require more housework than they contribute.' Heidi Hartmann estimates that a husband generates about eight hours extra housework each week.[50]

A wife obtains her means of support ('protection') from her husband, and also the means to perform her tasks. She is dependent on the benevolence of her husband and can only endeavour to obtain a 'good master'. Davidoff's comment about the Victorian and Edwardian husband is not irrelevant today; if he gave his wife 'extra' money, or 'helped' in the house 'it was much in the same tradition as the "kindly" squire and his lady who gave charitable extras to their retainers and villagers.'[51] The services a wife is expected to supply and the amount of support she obtains is entirely dependent on the will of her husband; 'it is impossible for married women to improve their own standard of living by improving their services. The only solution for them is to provide the same services for a richer man.'[52] However, a wife cannot guarantee that her husband will be generous, whether he is a proletarian or capitalist. Yet economists, for example, have assumed that husbands are always benevolent. The law of coverture haunts neo-classical economic analyses of the family. Economists take for granted that there can be a single welfare function for the whole family; that is to say, the welfare function of the husband – the 'one person' who represents his wife (and children) – can stand for all the rest. Even socialist writers, such as George Orwell in his famous *The Road to Wigan Pier*, were oblivious to the greater poverty and deprivation among working-class wives than among their husbands.[53] Wives typically denied themselves the basic necessities so that their husband and children could be fed, and there is no reason to suppose at present, in a period of very high, long-term unemployment and of cuts in welfare benefits, that wives will act any differently. Even at the best of times, there can be conflict between the requirements of the husband's recreations and the (house)wife's demand for support from the breadwinner.

The housewife is frequently presented as being in a very different position from a worker, a servant or a slave; a housewife is her own boss. Housewives see freedom from control as their great advantage; they stress that they can decide what to do and how and when to do it, and many housewives have strong, internalized standards of what constitutes a good job of work.[54] Wives, like the strikingly high proportion of male workers who tell investigators that they are satisfied with what, to an outsider, appear to be extremely unsatisfactory jobs, make the best of their lot; life can be insupportable otherwise. Certainly, during the daytime, during 'working hours', the housewife is alone at her place of work, unless her husband also works from his home, or the home is 'above the shop'. But the husband, the boss, is there at other times. Discussions of housework often overlook the expectations and requirements of the husband. The demands of *his* work largely determine how the housewife organizes her time. Meals are served, for instance, according to his hours of work, and he has views about how he wants his home and children to look – and he has means of enforcing his expectations by destruction of meals and physical violence in the last resort.

That wives should be housewives now appears so natural that, in the very popular British television series *Minder*, the wife of one of the two main characters is never seen on the screen and is referred to as ''er indoors'. Some effort is now required to appreciate the historical and cultural specificity of this arrangement. In Britain in the seventeenth century, wives were subordinate to their husbands but they were not economic dependents. Another breach in the law of coverture allowed married women to trade as *feme sole*, and women engaged in a wide variety of occupations. By the middle of the nineteenth century, to have a wife as a full-time housewife had become the goal for husbands of all respectable classes. But, as I have already noted, many or most wives, for a long time, were upper servants, not 'housewives' as the term is now understood. Moreover, only relatively few wives today are full-time housewives, but the continuing strength of the social ideal of the 'housewife' is a tribute to the power of the sexual contract.

Many working-class wives have always been in paid employment from economic necessity. In 1851, a quarter of the married women in Britain were in paid employment.[55] The social standing of these women under coverture was contradictory to say the least. The status of 'wife' affirmed that a woman lacked the capacities of an 'individual'; she became the property of her husband and stood to him as a slave/servant to a master. A wife was civilly dead. At the same time, since many wives entered the employment contract, their standing as 'individuals', capable of entering contracts was also affirmed. Just as slave-masters could not but help recognize the humanity of their human property – what use was it to brandish a whip at a mere possession? – women's capacity as 'individuals' could never be denied completely. Entry into the employment contract seems to show beyond any doubt that women possess the requisite capacities to be individuals and parties to contracts. To make a contract in the public world of the capitalist market, to become a wage labourer, presupposes that an individual owns the property in his person; he can then contract out his labour power, part of that property, in the employment contract. Women, too, it seems, can become workers.

Many feminists have argued that a wife's subordination to her husband is like that of worker to capitalist. Not only do women become workers, but the marriage contract is like the employment contract and constitutes the (house)wife as a worker in the conjugal home. To see the marriage contract as if it were an employment contract is, however, to forget the sexual contract once again. A (house)wife is not like a worker, and women cannot become 'workers' in the same sense as men. The marriage contract is not like an employment contract; rather the employment contract presupposes the marriage contract. Or, to make this point another way, the construction of the 'worker' presupposes that he is a man who has a woman, a (house)wife, to take care of his daily needs. The private and public spheres of civil society are separate, reflecting the natural order of sexual difference, and inseparable, incapable of being understood in isolation from each other. The sturdy figure of the 'worker', the artisan, in clean overalls, with a bag of tools and lunch-box, is always accompanied by the ghostly figure of his wife.

One reason why the comparison between wives and workers has been so attractive to feminists is that, like socialists, they have focused on the coercive conditions of entry into contracts. Employers control the means of production and so are able to set the terms of the employment contract to their advantage; workers own only the property in their labour power, and have no genuine choice about whether or not to enter the employment contract. Using the techniques of contemporary analytical philosophy, G. A. Cohen recently argued that proletarians, though formally free not to remain workers

– they can, for example, become small shopkeepers, and a particular worker, or even most workers, are free to escape from the proletariat in this way – nevertheless are forced to sell their labour power; workers are 'collectively unfree, an imprisoned class'.[56] Similarly, women collectively are coerced into marriage although any woman is free to remain single. William Thompson compared women's freedom to decline to marry with that of the freedom of peasants to refuse to buy food from the East India monopoly which had already cornered all the supplies; 'so by male-created laws, depriving women of knowledge and skill, excluding them from the benefit of all judgment and mind-creating offices and trusts, cutting them off almost entirely from the participation, by succession or otherwise, of property, and from its uses and exchanges – are women kindly told, "they are free to marry or not".'[57] In 1909, Cicely Hamilton argued in *Marriage as a Trade* that marriage was virtually the only way in which women could earn their livelihood; marriage is 'essentially . . . a commercial or trade undertaking'.[58] Women's trade differed from the trades of men because women had no choice of employment; there was only one trade for them, which they were compelled to enter.

Today, when many workers, objectively, can obtain the resources to rise into the petite bourgeoisie, so many more women than in the last century, or in 1909, can obtain the educational qualifications and skills that enable them to find jobs and support themselves. Nevertheless, everyday observation reveals that few women are to be found in highly paid positions in the professions or business. The capitalist market is patriarchal, structured by the sexual division of labour. The sexual segregation of the labour force, and the preservation of workplaces as arenas for fraternal solidarity, have remained remarkably stable during the twentieth century.[59] Most women can find paid employment only in a narrow range of low-status, low-paid occupations, where they work alongside other women and are managed by men, and, despite equal-pay legislation, they earn less than men. Marriage thus remains economically advantageous for most women. Moreover, the social pressures for women to become wives are as compelling as the economic. Single women lack a defined and accepted social place; becoming a man's wife is still the major means through which most women can find a recognized social identity. More fundamentally, if women exercised their freedom to remain single on a large scale, men could not become husbands – and the sexual contract would be shaken.

Coercion to enter the marriage or employment contract casts doubt on the validity of the contract; but to concentrate on economic coercion does little to question the practice of contract. If entry into the marriage and employment contracts were voluntary, would feminists and socialists cease their criticism? One difficulty with the comparison of a wife with a worker is that too little attention is paid to the specific manner in which workers are subject to capitalists. The Marxist analysis of capitalist exploitation is applied to conjugal relations. At the meeting of the National Women's Suffrage Association in 1878 in the United States, it was unanimously agreed that 'man, standing to woman in the position of capitalist, has robbed her through the ages of the results of her toil.'[60] A more recent account states that, if we 'focus on the parallel with the role of the bourgeoisie in relation to the proletariat', it is clear that the husband 'benefits directly from the exploitation and oppression of the wife within marriage'.[61] The comparison between workers and wives has been central to the contemporary controversy over the relationship between capitalism and patriarchy. Heidi Hartmann, for example, claims that there is a 'partnership', in which 'the material base upon which patriarchy rests lies most fundamentally in men's control over women's labor power', just as the capitalist controls the worker's labour power.[62] And Christine Delphy argues that 'marriage is the institution by which unpaid work is extorted from a particular category of the populations, women–wives.' The marriage contract is a work contract, 'the contract by which [the wife's] labour power is appropriated by her husband'.[63]

The *locus classicus* for the argument that wives are like workers is, of course, Engels' conjectural history of *The Origin of the Family, Private Property and the State*. Engels argues that 'the first class oppression' was that of male oppression of the female sex, and he states that 'within the family [the husband] is the bourgeois and the wife represents the proletariat'. However, he also claims that in the monogamous family the wife became 'the head servant', and that 'the modern individual family is founded on the open or concealed domestic slavery of the wife.' Engels' famous statement about the oppression of wives thus uses all three feminist terms of comparison; the upper servant, the slave and the worker. Despite his references to the slave and the servant, Engels treats all subordination as class subordination; all 'workers' lack freedom in the same way whether they are located in public workplaces or the private workplace of the home, whether they receive protection or the token of free exchange, the wage. Sex is irrelevant to subordination, and the position of wives is best understood as exactly like that of proletarians. Thus, Engels argued that the solution to the subordination of wives in the home was 'to bring the whole female sex back into public industry'.[64] If wives became public workers like their husbands, the married couple would stand together as equals against capitalism, and the husband would have lost the means through which he could control his wife's labour power in the home.

Engels' solution assumes that the original contract was purely a social contract and that the terms of the social contract are universal; conjugal relations in the family are like those in the market. That is to say, he assumes that men have no stake *as men* in their power over women; a husband's interest in his wife's subordination is exactly like that of any capitalist who has another man labour for him. Engels also assumes that sexual difference is irrelevant in the capitalist market. Once women enter into paid employment then, as workers, they become their husbands' equals. The category of 'worker' is universal and applicable to all who enter the capitalist market and sell their labour power.

Contemporary feminists soon ran into difficulties with these assumptions. When the current revival of the organized feminist movement focused attention on housework, many socialists and feminists assumed initially that what became called 'domestic labour' could be brought within the orthodox Marxist critique of capitalism.[65] This approach led to a series of dead-ends; little insight could be gained into the subordination of a wife by seeing her merely as another (unpaid) worker in the interest of capital. The theoretical impasse in the domestic labour debate provoked new interest in the concept of patriarchy. Once it was apparent that the subjection of wives could not be subsumed directly under class subordination, the way was opened for new theoretical categories to be used to understand conjugal power. However, as the 'dual systems' account of the relationship between capitalism and patriarchy illustrates, patriarchy is all too frequently merely joined to existing analyses of class. The model of bourgeois and proletarian is still seen as appropriate for marriage, even though the husband's appropriation of his wife's labour is also seen as patriarchal power. That the wife's subjection

derives from the fact that *she is a woman* has received acknowledgment, but the full political implications of patriarchal right
remain obscured.

The dual systems argument assumes that patriarchy is a feudal
relic, part of the old world of status, and that feminist criticism of
this relic must be added to the existing socialist critique of
capitalism. But 'class' and the 'worker' can wear the trousers (to
borrow a formulation that philosophers are fond of using) in the
'partnership' between capitalism and patriarchy only because half
the original contract is ignored. No hint is given that capitalism and
class have been constructed as modern patriarchal categories. The
social contract is about the origins of the civil sphere and capitalist
relations. Without the *sexual* contract there is no indication that the
'worker' is a masculine figure or that the 'working class' is the class
of men. The civil, public sphere does not come into being on its own,
and the 'worker', his 'work' and his 'working' class cannot be
understood independently of the private sphere and his conjugal
right as a husband. The attributes and activities of the 'worker' are
constructed together with, and as the other side of, those of his
feminine counterpart, the 'housewife'. A (house)wife, a woman,
naturally lacks the capacities required of a participant in civil life,
and thus she cannot participate as a worker on the same basis as her
husband. Women have now won civil and juridical standing almost
equal to men's, but they are not incorporated into workplaces on the
same basis as male workers. The story of the original contract shows
how sexual difference gives rise to a patriarchal division of labour,
not only in the conjugal home between the (house)wife and her
husband, but in the workplaces of civil society.

A (house)wife is not a worker who happens to be located outside
the workplace and who is subject to her husband; she is not a
'worker' at all. The work of a housewife – housework – is the work of
a sexually subject being who lacks jurisdiction over the property in
her person, which includes labour power. But sale of labour power,
in contrast to sale of labour or the person, is what makes a man a
free worker; the ability to contract out a piece of property in
exchange for a wage is, it is held, what distinguishes the worker, the
wage labourer, from unfree labourers and slaves. A (house)wife does
not contract out her labour power to her husband. She is not paid a
wage – there is no token of free exchange – because her husband has
command over the use of her labour by virtue of the fact that he is a

man. The marriage contract is a labour contract in a very different sense from the employment contract. The marriage contract is about *women's* labour; the employment contract is about *men's* work.

The connection between the sexual division of labour and the sub-ordination of wives was emphasized in various radical circles in the early nineteenth century, especially by the Owenite co-operative socialists, including William Thompson. They attacked 'single family arrangements' and, in their model communities established between the 1820s and 1840s, they attempted (not altogether suc-cessfully) to combat marital subjection through communal forms of housework.[66] If Marx and Engels had not dismissed their predecessors so summarily and scathingly as utopians, they would have found it far harder to forget the sexual contract, and to treat the private sphere as the politically irrelevant, natural basis from which the worker emerges to contract out his labour power and engage in political struggle in the workplace. Socialist criticism of the employ-ment contract might then have continued to be informed by feminist criticisms of the marriage contract and an appreciation of the mutual dependence of conjugal right and civil equality.

Men resisted their transformation into workers. It was not until late in the nineteenth century that civil society developed into an 'employment society', in which 'work' was the key to citizenship and full (male) employment became the central political demand of the working-class movement.[67] But while men clung to their older ways of life, they also fought to keep the new status of worker as a masculine privilege. They did not join in their wives' resistance to being turned into housewives. Brecht once wrote of the worker that:

> He wants no servants under him,
> And no boss over his head.[68]

If this were true of (some? many?) workers in their places of work, it was true of virtually none of them at home. Few husbands were willing to relinquish their patriarchal right to a servant.

The labour of a (house)wife is aptly termed domestic servitude, or, more politely, domestic service. Housework is not 'work'. Work takes place in the men's world of capitalism and workplaces. The meaning of 'work' depends on the (repressed) connection between the private and civil spheres. A 'worker' is a husband, a man who supports/protects his wife, an economic dependent (subordinate). That is to say, a worker is a 'breadwinner'. The difference between 'work' and what a wife does is established in popular language and in official statistics; the labours of housewives are not included in official measurements of national productivity. The construction of the male worker as 'breadwinner' and his wife as his 'dependent' can be charted in the classifications of the Census in Britain and Australia. In the Census of 1851 in Britain, women employed in unpaid domestic work were 'placed . . . in one of the productive classes along with paid work of a similar kind'. This classification changed after 1871, and by 1911 unpaid housewives had been separated from the economically active population. In Australia, an initial conflict over the categories of classification was resolved in 1890 when the scheme devised in New South Wales was adopted. The Australians divided up the population more decisively than the British, and the 1891 Census was based on the two categories of 'breadwinner' and 'dependent'. Unless explicitly stated otherwise, women's occupation was classed as domestic, and domestic workers were put in the dependent category.[69]

A worker supports/protects his (house)wife by earning a wage. Receipt of a wage in return for contracting out labour power distinguishes the (free) worker from the slave; the worker is a *wage labourer*. There is no free exchange between master and slave; the slave receives only the subsistence (protection) that enables him to continue to labour. The conventional view of the wage is that the crucial token of exchange has no taint of protection and servitude clinging to it. But the 'wage', like the 'worker', is a category that depends on the connection between the civil world of contract and the private realm of protection. A large element of protection remains embodied in the wage. The worker contracts out his labour power, so that he appears to receive a wage as an individual in exchange for the employer's use of his services. Only since equal-pay legislation has been introduced over the past decade or so, is the wage becoming an individual wage. When husbands became 'breadwinners' and their wives became economic 'dependents', the wage became a *family wage*. Wages are paid to the male worker as a husband/breadwinner to maintain himself *and* his dependents, not merely in exchange for the sale of his own labour power. A 'living wage' for a man is a wage that can support himself and his wife and family at a decent level.

The family wage was enshrined in law in Australia in 1907 in the famous Harvester Judgement in the Commonwealth Arbitration Court. Justice Higgins ruled in favour of a legally guaranteed minimum wage – and defined a living wage as sufficient to keep an unskilled worker, his wife and three children in reasonable comfort. Today, it is still 'standard trade union practice to draw up pay claims for low-paid workers which refer to the need to maintain the level of living of a standard married man with two children'.[70] The worker as protector of his dependents was also seen by political economists as the true creator of the next generation of wage labourers. The father and his family wage, not the mother, provided the necessary subsistence to maintain children. The political economists were thus able to see the mother's labours as 'the raw material on which economic forces acted, the elements of nature with which human [i.e., civil] societies were built'. The father/breadwinner gained 'the status of value-creator'.[71] Or, to make the point a different way, men as wage labourers share in the masculine capacity to create and nurture new political life.

However, the family wage has always been as much an ideal as a reality. Many, perhaps most, working-class families have been unable to survive on the husband's wage alone, and, as feminists pointed out many years ago, not all male workers have families, while many women have had to support dependents, including aged parents. But precisely because the wage has been seen as a family wage, women's earnings have been regarded as a 'supplement' to a husband's wage. Women are assumed to be wives, and wives are assumed to be economically dependent on their husbands, obtaining their subsistence in return for domestic service. Therefore, wages have been sexually differentiated. Women workers are paid less than men – and so an economic incentive for women to become wives is maintained. The conviction that a 'wage' is what is due to a male breadwinner, was nicely illustrated as recently as 1985 in the United States, in the claim that 'women have generally been paid less [than men] because they would work for lower wages, since they had no urgent need for more money. Either they were married, or single and living at home, or doubling up with friends.'[72]

Women workers have often been invisible in the chronicles of the working class. The figure of the miner, and the solidarity and fraternity that he embodies, has often represented 'the worker', yet in 1931 the British Census recorded twice as many domestic servants as miners.[73] Nor have male workers been eager to have women work alongside them, especially if the women were married. Paid employment for wives threatens both the husbands' right of command over the use of their services and the fraternal order of the workplace itself. In 1843 in Britain, the Poor Law Commissioners noted that the husband 'suffered' if his wife was in paid employment; 'there is not the same order in the cottage, nor the same attention paid to his comforts.'[74] Whether or not the family wage enabled some sections of the working class to obtain better living standards than would otherwise have been the case (as trades unions claimed), the history of the labour movement leaves no doubt that the insistence on a family wage was an important strategy through which men were able to exclude women from many areas of paid work and bolster the husband's position as master in the home.

Sometimes wives have simply been excluded from employment; for example, women were compelled to resign from the Australian public service upon marriage from 1902 until 1966, and the ban was not lifted in the State of Victoria until as recently as 1973. More generally, women's employment has been restricted by 'protection' due to those who lack ownership of the property in their persons. One of the best known examples is the judgement in the case *Muller v. Oregon* in the United States in 1908, in a period of great conflict over freedom of contract. In 1905 (in *Lochner v. New York*), the Supreme Court ruled that a law limiting the work of male bakers to eight hours per day was unconstitutional. In *Muller v. Oregon* the Court ruled that it was permissible to restrict the working hours of women workers. The Court's reasoning harks back to the story of the sexual contract; the argument appeals to man's strength, woman's physical structure and child-bearing function and her dependance on man. The Court maintained that although 'limitations upon personal and contractual rights may be removed by legislation, there is that in [woman's] disposition and habits of life which will operate against a full assertion of [civil] rights'. Woman is 'properly placed in a class by herself, and legislation designed for her protection may be sustained, even when like legislation is not necessary for men and could not be sustained'.[75]

For women, the terms of the sexual contract ensure that all men, and not just craftsmen, form an aristocracy of labour. Married women have entered the paid labour force on a large scale over the past thirty years, but husbands can still be found who believe that their wives must obtain their permission to work; many husbands would prefer their wives to be full-time housewives and try 'to limit and diminish their wife's job'.[76] Some wives do both their unpaid and paid work at home, often because their husbands prefer them to do outwork. When both spouses leave the home 'to go to work', the action has a very different meaning for the husband than for his wife. Spending eight hours each day in the workplace and bringing home a wage packet is central to masculine identity, to what it means to be a man; in particular, hard, dirty manual labour has been seen as *man's* work. Certain kinds of detailed, clean work have been designated 'women's work', but it does not follow that such work is seen by either men or women as enhancing femininity. Popular receptiveness to the contemporary anti-feminist movement indicates that many people still see paid employment as detracting from womanhood.

Many married women work part time, often because no other jobs are available (in the United States in 1980 almost a quarter of all jobs in the private sector were part-time),[77] but also because they can then devote the major part of their energies to domestic service, and so avoid conflict with their husbands. A wife who is in paid employment never ceases to be a housewife; instead she becomes a *working wife*, and increases the length of her working day. Evidence from the United States shows that married women workers spend less time on housework than full-time housewives, but their working week is longer, averaging 76 hours. Their husbands, in contrast, do not increase their contribution to domestic tasks, and are able to use the time when they are not at work for leisure activities. Wives continue their domestic service on their 'days off'.[78] In one British study, 'all the men (except one) drew a strong distinction between part-time and full-time work, a distinction not shared by their wives. What was crucial for the men was that *they* should remain the primary breadwinner.'[79]

The worker is conventionally discussed, by defenders of socialism and capitalism alike, as if the fact of his masculinity and that he is a husband is quite irrelevant to his working-class consciousness. 'Fraternity' is assumed to mean community, not the brotherhood of men. Recent feminist research, especially in Britain, has begun to reveal how the terms of the original fraternal contract are upheld in the everyday life of the workplace and the working-class movement. In *Brothers*, a fascinating study of British printers, Cynthia Cockburn has shown in detail how the workplace and trades unions are organized as fraternal territory, where 'it was unthinkable' that a girl could be part of an apprenticeship system so clearly 'designed to produce a free *man*', where 'skilled' work is the work done by men, and where manhood is tested and confirmed every day.[80] One of the most graphic illustrations of the practical strength of the sexual contract in daily life is that both men and women see women workers as less than full members of the workplace.

Women factory workers, doing jobs comparable to those of un-skilled male workers, 'still feel they are housewives, even when they are at work'.[81] Other women, doing traditional 'women's work', and working exclusively with other women, also 'saw their job as secondary to their main work *inside* the home'. The women recognized that to enter paid employment was to cross a boundary; they saw their female workplace 'as part of another world – the male one – and therefore essentially dominated by men. Their excursions into it were merely as migrant labour – almost as trespassers'.[82] Even more strikingly, married women workers who took over their shoe factory and ran it as a democratic co-operative from 1972–6, saw each other 'fundamentally, . . . as wives and mothers'. Despite their identification with the co-operative, their difficult economic and political fight to keep it going and the increased knowledge and confidence that came from running a democratic workplace, they were not 'workers'. The women's perception of themselves is not, as many popular accounts suggest, a consequence of 'socialization'; rather, their consciousness accurately reflects their structural position as women and wives. Their wages were economically necessary, but their husbands still saw wives' incomes as supplementary; the women spent their earnings on 'extras' for their home and their children, so that 'their basic position as economic dependants' remained unchanged. The women also continued to perform domestic service as housewives. Although their responsibilities as workers had increased dramatically, the only change at home was that two husbands began to help with the washing-up. One husband succinctly expressed the law of male sex-right when he commented, 'I don't keep a dog and bark myself.'[83]

The law of male sex-right operates in the workplace in its other sense, too. Cockburn found that, as in other male clubs, the 'social currency of the composing room is women and women-objectifying talk, . . . the wall is graced with four-colour litho "tits and bums".

Even the computer is used to produce life-size print-outs of naked women'.[84] What is now labelled 'sexual harassment' helps maintain men's patriarchal right in the public world. Women workers are frequently subject to persistent, unwelcome sexual advances, or their promotion or continuing employment is made conditional upon sexual access. Much more is at issue than 'discrimination' in employment. Sexual domination is part of the structure of subordination in the workplace. In another factory, 'sexual banter and pranks became something more than a laugh – it became the language of discipline.'[85]

Such language is very different from the language of contract or exploitation usually used to discuss capitalist employment. The familiar language is used for relations between men; another language, the language of patriarchal discipline, is required for relations between men and women. Even as workers, women are subordinated to men in a different way than men are subordinated to other men. Women have not been incorporated into the patriarchal structure of capitalist employment as 'workers'; they have been incorporated as *women*; and how can it be otherwise when women are not, and cannot be, men? The sexual contract is an integral part of civil society and the employment contract; sexual domination structures the workplace as well as the conjugal home. To be sure, men are also subordinates as workers – but to see the worker as no more than a wage slave fails to capture a vital dimension of his position in civil society; he is that curiosity, an *unfree master*.

When contemporary feminists compare wives with workers they assume that the worker is, at the same time, both a subordinate and a master. The worker who is subordinate to the employer is also a master at home. Many feminists also argue explicitly that, as a husband, the worker emulates the capitalist and appropriates the labour power of his wife. The argument forgets that the marriage contract is not an employment contract in which labour power or services are contracted out for use by another. 'Labour power' is an inappropriate category to use in arguments about conjugal relations, but that is not the only problem when the comparison of workers and wives is put in these terms.

To understand contract, including the employment contract, the category of labour power (services) is vital – but also, as Marx was well aware, extremely misleading. The claim that *labour power* is contracted out, not labour, bodies or persons, enables proponents of contract to argue that the employment contract, like other contracts about property in the person, constitutes a free relation. When feminists argue that a husband appropriates the labour power of his wife in exactly the same way that a capitalist appropriates the labour power of a worker, they are implicitly joining hands with contract. To compare a wife to a worker because the latter is a subordinate, requires that the idea of labour power is rejected; that is to say, critical attention must be directed to the employment contract along with the marriage contract. To criticize the employment contract is not, as Philmore asserts, to fall into a *reductio ad absurdum* but to add another political fiction, the fiction of labour power, to the political fiction of the original contract.

If a husband did indeed contract for use of his wife's labour power, she would, according to contract doctrine, be a free worker. By accepting the category of labour power at face value, feminists leave themselves unable to criticize other contracts about property in the person, such as the prostitution contract and the contract with the so-called surrogate mother, which are contracts that, necessarily, involve women, and which are defended precisely on the grounds that services (labour power), and nothing more, is contracted out in free, fair exchange. The prostitution and surrogacy contracts (which I shall discuss in detail in chapter 7) are contracts made in the public world of the capitalist market – although they do not spring readily to mind in this context – and their defenders assimilate the two contracts to the paradigm of the free employment contract. For feminists to enter onto the terrain of contract through uncritical use of 'labour power', is to offer contract theorists the opportunity to appear as opponents of patriarchy. Contractarians can argue that a husband is a master only in an uncivil form of marriage. Marriage should become genuinely contractual, like the employment contract, the exemplar of contract. If marriage is a genuinely dissoluble contract, entered by two civil individuals who can, free from constraints, bargain with each other about the disposition of the property in their persons, conjugal relations will finally lose the taint of their coercive, patriarchal past. I shall look at the feminist version of this argument in the next chapter.

The patriarchal construction of 'civil society' is so powerful that most discussion of marriage and employment assume that the employment contract will illuminate the subordination of wives.

That is to say, the public sphere is always assumed to throw light onto the private sphere, rather than vice versa. On the contrary, an understanding of modern patriarchy requires that the employment contract is illuminated by the structure of domestic relations.

A good deal can be learnt about the employment contract by considering its relationship to the domestic labour contracts entered into by a master with his slave, servant and wife. In the 1980s, marriage has still not lost all trace of its 'brutal origins' – and nor has the employment contract. The figures of the worker and the housewife are relatively late arrivals in the story of civil society. The old law of Master and Servant in England, the origins of which went back beyond the Statute of Artificers in the days of Good Queen Bess, was not repealed in its entirety until 1875, when the Employer and Workman Act recognized the formally equal standing of the two parties to the contract. The (domestic) labour contract then became a (civil) employment contract. Before ·the transformation was completed, legal authorities had great difficulties in deciding exactly how a servant differed from a slave. Britain was not a slave society, but there were considerable numbers of slaves in British families in the seventeenth and eighteenth centuries. In 1772, Lord Mansfield stated that slaves were sold in Britain 'with as little reserve as they would have been in any of our West India possessions'.[86] At the time, according to the not necessarily reliable figure cited in standard texts, there were some 15,000 blacks in Britain, the majority of whom might have been slaves.

Slaves were first imported in substantial numbers into Britain towards the end of the sixteenth century and, until well into the next century, they were commonly termed servants. In 1677 the Solicitor General ruled that 'negroes ought to be esteemed goods and commodities within the Acts of Trade and Navigation', and their status as property was confirmed in judgements in common law.[87] British lawyers gave many contradictory opinions and judgements about the status of slaves ranging from the view (1706) that 'by the common law no man can have property in another . . . there is no such thing as a slave by the laws of England'; to the opinion (1729) that 'a slave coming from the West Indies to Great Britain or Ireland, with or without his master, doth not become free, and that his master's property in him is not thereby determined or varied.'[88] Popular belief held that slavery was outlawed in the Somerset case in 1772 – feminists in the nineteenth century, for example, cited the case when attacking coverture – but only the forced export of slaves from Britain was prohibited; ownership of the persons of blacks as property was not disturbed. Lord Mansfield, judge in the Somerset case, was clearly not alone when he declared that he hoped the question of human property would never 'be finally discussed. For I wou'd have all Masters think they were Free and all negroes think they were not because then they wo'd both behave better'.[89]

Sir William Blackstone's famous exposition of common law provides a remarkable example of trimming on the question of free and coerced labour (probably to bring his views into line with those of his mentor and patron Lord Mansfield).[90] In the first edition of the *Commentaries*, in book I, chapter 1, Blackstone wrote that the 'spirit of liberty is so deeply implanted in our constitution, . . . that a slave or negro, the moment he lands in England, falls under the protection of the laws, and with regard to all natural rights becomes *eo instanti* a freeman'. In the second edition, Blackstone added the clause, 'though the master's right to his service may probably still continue'. By the fourth edition (from which I have been citing Blackstone) his text reads that the slave falls under the protection of the law, 'and so far becomes a freeman; though the master's right to his service may *possibly* still continue'. Certainly, his original statement sat very oddly with another argument in the first edition, in book I, chapter 14 (unaltered in subsequent editions), that:

> A slave or negro, the instant he lands in England, becomes a freeman; that is, the law will protect him in the enjoyment of his person, and his property. Yet, with regard to any right which the master may have lawfully acquired to the perpetual service of John or Thomas, this will remain exactly in the same state as before; for this is no more than the same state of subjection for life, which every apprentice submits to for the space of seven years, or sometimes for a longer term.[91]

Or, Blackstone might also have added, the slave's status was little different from the subjection for life and the perpetual service required of a wife. Domestic contracts are hard to differentiate from one another.

A worker and the employment contract were separated from a servant and a domestic labour contract only in the late nineteenth century, and contractarians now argue that a (civil) slave contract is merely an extended employment contract. How then does the free worker differ from servants and slaves? One participant in the controversy over paternalism has stated that 'many perfectly reasonable employment contracts involve an agreement by the employee virtually to abandon his liberty to do as he pleases for a daily period, and even to do (within obvious limits) whatever his boss tells him.'[92] Such statements beg the question why, if the employment contract creates a free worker, he must 'abandon his liberty', or, perhaps more accurately, the need to ask this question never arises when, for three centuries, contract doctrine has proclaimed that subjection to a master – a boss, a husband – is freedom. Moreover, the problem of freedom is misrepresented here. The question central to contract theory does not involve the general liberty to do as you please, but the freedom to subordinate yourself in any manner that you please. If all involved 'did as they pleased', economic production – and social life – would be very difficult if not impossible. The issue is not abstract, unconstrained liberty, but the social relations of work, production, marriage and sexual life. Are relations between women and men to be politically free, and is there to be collective participation in the task of deciding what is to be produced and how it is to be produced; or is political right to be exercised by men, husbands, bosses, civil masters?

Free labour, or employment, is said to be separated from unfree labour because, first, the worker stands on an equal footing with the employer as a juridically free and equal citizen; second, because the employment contract (unless it is a contract of civil slavery) is temporally limited; third, because unfree labourers receive protection, but the worker receives a wage, the token of a free exchange; and fourth, because a worker does not contract out himself or even his labour, but his labour power or services, part of the property in his person. The worker and the unfree labourer appear to be at opposite poles. The criteria held irrevocably to separate the free wage labourer from an unfree labourer, as I pointed out in chapter 3, are eminently permeable. To be sure, a juridically free and equal citizen cannot be property, but defenders of slavery in the Old South who claimed that the institution originated in a contract, also argued that slaves were not the property of their owners. Consideration of the arguments of the classic contract theorists about the distinction between free and coerced labour also raise grave doubts whether the second criterion is very robust.

The contractarians have performed a service by defending the 'civilized' slave contract, so revealing the extreme fragility of the criterion of temporal limitation of the employment contract as a distinguishing mark of a free worker. Consider Hegel's statement:

> I can give [someone else] the use of my abilities for a restricted period, because, on the strength of this restriction, my abilities acquire an external relation to the totality and universality of my being. By alienating the whole of my time, as crystalized in my work, and everything I produced, I would be making into another's property the substance of my being, . . . my personality.[93]

Socialists typically respond to such statements by arguing, correctly, that it is virtually impossible to distinguish the piecemeal contracting out of labour power from the alienation of the whole lifetime of a man's labour. But the response does nothing to counter the contractarian argument that to deny the individual the right to alienate the property in his person for as long as he sees fit is an arbitrary restriction. The contractarian argument is unassailable all the time it is accepted that abilities can 'acquire' an external relation to an individual, and can be treated as if they were property. To treat abilities in this manner is also implicitly to accept that the 'exchange' between employer and worker is like any other exchange of material property. Labour power is exchanged for a wage, and receipt of a wage is the third criterion that is held to distinguish a free worker from an unfree labourer.

A worker receives a wage – but the wage is not easily distinguished from protection. I have already shown how the fact that the worker is also a husband/breadwinner means that protection is part of the wage. But protection is also involved in the wage in another sense. Workers are usually bound to employers by more than the cash nexus. Trades unions have won many more benefits for workers than improved wages, and in giant bureaucratic enterprises, run on a day-to-day basis by an hierarchy of managers who enforce impersonal rules, protection is provided in the form of a wide array of extra-wage benefits and perquisites. For example, an American mining company operating in Queensland, Australia, provides housing for employees, carefully graded according to status, and, in the best tradition of the village squire, gives workers' wives two turkeys for Christmas.[94] Contemporary capitalist managers enforce workers' obedience by regular evaluations of personal character and work-habits and, at higher levels, loyalty and commitment. That is, they demand 'faithful service', which is valued as highly as productivity.[95]

The reason why the wage embodies protection is that the employment contract (like the marriage contract) is not an exchange; both contracts create social relations that endure over time – social relations of subordination. Marx commented that the capitalist 'obtains the productive force which maintains and multiplies capital', and he obtains this force through a process which is *'qualitatively different from exchange, and only by misuse* could it have been called *any sort of exchange at all'*.[96] Ironically, the contractarian ideal cannot encompass capitalist employment. Employment is not a continual series of discrete contracts between employer and worker, but (as Coase made clear) one contract in which a worker binds himself to enter an enterprise and follow the directions of the employer for the duration of the contract. As Huw Benyon has bluntly stated, 'workers are paid to obey.'[97] The employment contract is open-ended, not a contract of specific performance, and the employer alone gains the ultimate right to decide what the content of the contract will be.

Alan Fox has argued that the Act of 1875 left the employment contract 'virtually unrecognizable as contract'; that is, contract in which the two parties freely bargain. If worker and employer negotiated the terms, duration and conditions of the employment contract until a mutually beneficial result were reached, all aspects of employment would have to be open to negotiation. No employer could accept such an arrangement. Fox argues that 'the damaging implication of pure contract doctrine for the employer would have been that it could not allow him to be the sole judge of whether his rules were arbitrary or exceeded the scope of his authority.'[98] If unrestricted bargaining took place, the employer's possession of the political right that makes him an 'employer' would have disappeared; hence, instead of 'pure contract' there is the employment contract, which is enforced by the employer. His task is much easier if the wage includes protection that binds the subordinate more closely to the contract. Extra-monetary benefits, or, in the case of the marriage contract, 'generous' housekeeping money or 'help' around the house, are obvious examples. There are, of course, other means to enforce both contracts; husbands use physical violence, there are an impressive array of coercive measures, sanctioned by the state, available to employers and the wider structure of patriarchal capitalism makes disobedience costly for both wives and workers.

Feminist and socialist critics of the marriage contract and employment contract severely weaken their criticism when they rely on the categories 'exchange' and 'labour power'. When argument is couched solely in terms of labour power, critics tend to concentrate on the absence of a fair exchange between capitalist and worker; that is, they concentrate on exploitation (both in the strict Marxist sense of extraction of surplus value and the more popular sense of unjust and unfair treatment). Subordination can then be seen as arising from exploitation (or as part of exploitation) rather than as the relation that makes exploitation possible. Marx provides an illustration of this point. In his polemic against Lassalle in the *Critique of the Gotha Progamme*, Marx argues that Lassalle takes wages at face value as payment for the worker's labour, instead of seeing that wages are payment for labour power. Marx stresses that the worker can only gain his livelihood if he works for nothing for a certain time for the capitalist (i.e., the latter expropriates surplus value). Capitalism depends on the extension of this free labour by such means as lengthening the working day; '*consequently*', Marx states, 'the system of wage labour is a system of slavery.'[99] But wage slavery is not a consequence of exploitation – exploitation is a consequence of the fact that the sale of labour power entails the worker's subordination. The employment contract creates the capitalist as master; he has the political right to determine how the labour of the worker will be used, and – consequently – can engage in exploitation.

If the free worker is to stand at one pole and the slave in his absolute servitude is to stand at the other – or, conversely, if the employment contract is to be extended into the civil slave contract – it is necessary to make a sharp distinction between the sale of the slave himself (he is a commodity or piece of property) and the sale of the worker's labour power (a commodity external to himself, the owner). The 'individual' owns his labour power and stands to his property, to his body and capacities, in exactly the same external relation in which, as a property owner, he stands to his material property. The individual can contract out any of his pieces of property, including those from which he is constituted, without detriment to his self. However, although labour power is property, a commodity, it is not quite the same as other material property. One difficulty is that,

> with most commodities the contract of sale, and acquisition of the use-value, are concluded more or less at the same time. In the case of wage-labour there is a problem for the capitalist in that after hiring the worker he must find ways of enforcing performance of work with desired quality and in maximum quantity.[100]

Socialists have not been alone in noticing that labour power is an extremely odd commodity. T. H. Green, for example, a liberal writing in 1881, argued that 'labour . . . is a commodity which attaches in a peculiar manner to the person of man. . . . [Labour] differed from all other commodities inasmuch as it was inseparable from the person of the labourer.' Green insisted that it followed from this peculiarity of labour that freedom of contract, the right of the individual to do what he wills with his own, is never unlimited. He argued that a slave contract cannot be a valid contract, albeit entered into voluntarily, since it prevents any further exercise of a man's freedom and free use of his capacities. Restrictions can legitimately be placed on the sale of this commodity so that all men can remain in a position 'to become a free contributor to social good' and enjoy their freedom on the same footing as others.[101] Green does not spell out exactly why it is that the curious attachment of labour power to the person means that freedom of contract must be curtailed. Unless the case is made in full, contractarians can always respond that the restriction is arbitrary paternalism. The question that is bypassed in all the argument about the duration of the employment contract, fair wages and exploitation is *how* this peculiar property can be separated from the worker and his labour. All the parties to the argument, in other words, tacitly accept that individuals own property in their persons.

The answer to the question of how property in the person can be contracted out is that no such procedure is possible. Labour power, capacities or services, cannot be separated from the person of the worker like pieces of property. The worker's capacities are developed over time and they form an integral part of his self and self-identity; capacities are internally not externally related to the person. Moreover, capacities or labour power cannot be used without the worker using his will, his understanding and experience, to put them into effect. The use of labour power requires the presence of its 'owner', and it remains as mere potential until he acts in the manner necessary to put it into use, or agrees or is compelled so to act; that is, the worker must labour. To contract for the use of labour power is a waste of resources unless it can be used in the way in which the new owner requires. The fiction 'labour power' cannot be used; what is required is that the worker labours as demanded. The employment contract must, therefore, create a relationship of command and obedience between employer and worker.

Capitalist employment, and the argument that the worker is the exemplar of a free labourer, who, paradoxically, can exemplify his freedom by entering into a civil slave contract, depends on the claim that the worker is not a commodity; labour power is the commodity that can be subject to contract. The idea of the individual as owner is thus central to an understanding of the employment contract. That the idea of ownership of property in the person *is a political fiction* is equally central to understanding the employment contract. The political fiction is all too often overlooked today by both socialists and feminists. The worker and his labour, not his labour power, are the subject of contract. The employment contract, necessarily, gives the employer political right to compel the worker to use his capacities in a given manner, or the right to the worker's obedience:

> Here is a real peculiarity of labor-power. The enjoyment of the use-value of any other commodity is non-problematic: . . . not so with labor-power. Its 'use value' is not delivered, it is not offered, it is not consumed. It must be extracted. This process of extraction engages the energies of armies of supervisors, time-motion men, guards, spies, and bosses of all descriptions. [102]

In short, the contract in which the worker allegedly sells his labour power is a contract in which, since he cannot be separated from his capacities, he sells command over the use of his body and himself. To obtain the right to the use of another is to be a (civil) master. To sell command over the use of oneself for a specified period is not the same as selling oneself for life as another's property – but it is to be an unfree labourer. The characteristics of this condition are captured in the term *wage slave*.

The term wage slave ceased to be fashionable among socialists a long time ago. In its own way, 'wage slave' is as indispensable as 'patriarchy'. Both terms concentrate the mind on subordination, and, at a time when contract doctrine is so popular, such reminders are necessary if feminist criticism of the marriage contract and socialist criticism of the employment contract are not to tip over into collusion with contractarianism. The attractions of contract for socialists who cling to the political fiction of labour power are not hard to discern. The fiction suggests that capitalism can be replaced by contract-socialism (as it might be called). There is no need, it may seem, for employers to have command over the use of workers' labour or to have an employment contract. What is required is that the conception of the individual owner be universalized. All individuals, as it were, become subcontractors or petty entrepreneurs, and 'employees' and 'wage labourers' disappear. Owners of labour power contract directly with each other about the terms and conditions of work, and so make mutually advantageous use of the property in their persons. Contract-socialism cannot, however, eliminate the need for a boss, as contractarian attempts to amend Coase's argument in the direction of 'pure contract' inadvertently reveal.

A firm, according to Alchian and Demsetz, is a 'privately owned market', and the employer is a 'central common party to a set of bilateral contracts [which] facilitates efficient organization of the joint inputs in team production'. The story they tell is less a political fiction than a political fairy tale. The 'central common party' is claimed to have no more and no less rights than other members of the team; any member is able to terminate his contract if he so desires. However, to avoid the problem of 'shirking' (or free riding) a 'monitor' is required. The monitor, in turn, will be constrained from shirking if he has a right to 'any residual product above prescribed amounts'. To perform his task, the monitor must be able to discipline members of the team and must have the right to revise the terms of individual contracts, and to 'terminate or alter every other input's contract'. He alone has the right to 'expand or reduce membership, alter the mix of membership, or sell the right to be the residual claimant-monitor of the team', but his own association with the team remains unaltered. Alchian and Demsetz suggest that, in the absence of 'several input owners', the classic firm becomes a 'socialist firm'.[103] In the contract-socialist firm, all the contracting parties are owners of the property in their persons. But 'individuals' are self-interested and thus shirking is an endemic problem. The only way that bilateral contracts can be enforced is for the contracting parties to turn themselves into bosses (monitors) and wage slaves. To begin with contract in the capitalist market is to end with the firm. Contracts about property in the person inevitably create subordination.

The wage slave is subject to the discipline of the employer – but the workplace is also structured by patriarchal discipline. Women workers are not wage slaves in the same sense as male workers, and nor is the subordination of the wage slave the same as that of a wife. Both employer and husband have right of command over the use of the bodies of workers and wives, but although each husband has his own specific demands, the content of the labour of a housewife is determined by the fact that she is a woman. The content of the labour of the worker is determined by the capitalist, but since capitalism is patriarchal, the labour of women workers is different from that of male workers. Because the subjection of wives derives from their womanhood and because the sexual division of labour extends into the workplace, it is tempting for feminists to conclude that the idea of the individual as owner is anti-patriarchal. If women could be acknowledged as sexually neuter 'individuals', owners of the property in their persons, the emancipatory promise of contract would seem to be realized. Or so many critics of the marriage contract now argue.

6

Feminism and the Marriage Contract

From at least 1825, when William Thompson published his attack on the 'white slave code' of marriage, feminists have persistently criticized marriage on the grounds that it is not a proper contract. In 1860, for example, Elizabeth Cady Stanton stated, in a speech to the American Anti-Slavery Society, that 'there is one kind of marriage that has not been tried, and that is a contract made by equal parties to lead an equal life, with equal restraints and privileges on either side.'[1] Marriage is called a contract but, feminists have argued, an institution in which one party, the husband, has exercised the power of a slave-owner over his wife and in the 1980s still retains some remnants of that power, is far removed from a contractual relationship. Some recent discussions of marriage assume that conjugal relations are purely contractual – 'husbands and wives contractually acquire for their exclusive use their partner's sexual properties'[2] – and feminists sometimes take criticism of the marriage contract to contractarian conclusions. One feminist legal scholar, for example, has argued that marriage should be modelled on economic contracts and that there should be a move from 'public marital policy to private contract law'.[3] However, not all feminist critics of the marriage contract conclude that marriage should become a purely contractual relationship.

Marriage, according to the entry under 'contract' in the *Oxford English Dictionary*, has been seen as a contractual relationship since at least the fourteenth century, and Blackstone states that 'our law considers marriage in no other light than as a civil contract.'[4] The attraction of contractual marriage for feminists is not hard to see. Feminist criticism takes a 'contract' to be an agreement between two equal parties who negotiate until they arrive at terms that are to their mutual advantage. If marriage were a proper contract, women would have to be brought into civil life on exactly the same footing as their husbands. Many feminists, especially in the United States, now advocate what are called 'intimate contracts' or 'marriage contracting' instead of the marriage contract.[5] Negotiation of a clear-cut agreement, that may even include advance provision for dissolution, has obvious advantages over the marriage contract. Critics of marriage contracting have pointed out that, since few women can earn as much as men, only a few middle-class and professional women are likely to be in a position to negotiate an intimate contract. But the problems with a purely contractual view of marriage run much deeper.

Feminist writers have stressed the deficiencies of a contract in which the parties cannot set the terms themselves. They have also pointed to the respects in which the marriage contract differs from economic contracts, but, by and large, their criticisms offer little insight into *why* this contract is so curious. Nor have they explained why legal authorities, despite Blackstone's firm statement, have also expressed similar doubts about the contractual character of marriage. For example, in Schouler's *A Treatise on the Law of the Domestic Relations* we find, 'we are then to consider marriage, not as a contract in the ordinary acceptation of the term; but as a contract *sui generis*, if indeed it be a contract at all; as an agreement to enter into a solemn relation which imposes its own terms.'[6] A few years later, in 1888, a judge in the United States stated:

> when the contracting parties have entered into the married state, they have not so much entered into a contract as into a new relation, . . .
> It was of contract that the relation should be established, but, being established, the power of the parties as to its extent or duration is at an end. Their rights under it are determined by the will of the sovereign as evidenced by law.[7]

More recently, in a reference to marriage towards the end of *The Rise and Fall of Freedom of Contract*, Atiyah remarks that 'we are not here dealing with matters conventionally classified as contract.'[8] But legal writers are very reticent about why the marriage contract is unlike other contracts.

Blackstone explained the singular situation of married women as follows; under coverture, for a man to contract with his wife, 'would be only to covenant with himself: and therefore it is also generally true, that all compacts made between husband and wife, when single, are voided by the intermarriage'.[9] Blackstone, like the classic contract theorists, assumes that women both are, and are not, able to enter contracts. If a man and a woman agreed to draw up the terms of their contract when they married, the contract would be void. A married woman lacks a civil existence so she could not have made a contract with her husband. No wonder there are still problems about the contractual character of marriage! To concentrate on the defects of the marriage contract as contract deflects attention from the problems surrounding women's participation in this agreement. In particular, enthusiastic embrace of contractarianism by some contemporary critics presupposes that contract is unproblematic for feminists. The solution to the problem of the marriage contract is presented as completion of the reforms that have eroded coverture; wives can take their place as 'individuals', and contract appears once again as the enemy of the old world of status or patriarchy. All the anomalies and contradictions surrounding women and contract, brought to light in the story of the sexual contract, remain repressed.

William Thompson's *Appeal of One Half the Human Race, Women, Against the Pretensions of the Other Half, Men, to Retain them in Political, and Thence in Civil and Domestic, Slavery*, laid the foundation for subsequent feminist criticism of marriage as a contractual relation. The vehemence of his polemic has rarely been equalled, but Thompson places little weight on a proper contract as a solution to the problems of conjugal relations. In this respect, his argument differs not only from much contemporary feminist argument but also from John Stuart Mill's much better known *The Subjection of Women*. According to Thompson, political rights for women and an end to the economic system of individual competition (capitalism) are the crucially important changes that are needed. Only political rights can bring an end to 'the *secrecy* of domestic wrongs',[10] and free relations between the sexes will be possible only within a social order based on 'labour by mutual co-operation', or co-operative socialism.

Thompson built model dwellings for his workers on his Cork estate and established mechanics institutes – he argued that women should be admitted to the institutes, to libraries and other educational establishments. He worked out a detailed scheme for co-operative, communal socialism but he died before his plan could be fulfilled. The co-operative or utopian socialists included communal housework in their blueprints for their new communities and, in the *Appeal*, Thompson emphasizes that provision for children, for instance, would be a communal responsibility. When women contributed to all the work of the community along with men, and could make equal call on communal resources in their own right, the basis of sexual domination would be undermined. When man had 'no more wealth than woman, and no more influence over the general property, and his superior strength [is] brought down to its just level of utility, he can procure no sexual gratification but from the voluntary affection of woman'.[11] Once women had secured their civil and political rights and were economically independent in the new world of voluntary co-operation, they would have no reason to be subject to men in return for their subsistence and men would have no means to become women's sexual masters.

The *Appeal* was occasioned by the argument of John Stuart's father, James Mill, that women did not need the vote because their interests were subsumed in the interests of their fathers or their husbands. Unlike his fellow utilitarians then and now, and the economists who incorporate members of the family into one welfare function, Thompson extended his individualism to women. He argued that the interests of each individual member of a family must be counted separately and equally. Individual interests of wives and daughters could not be subsumed under those of the master of the family, nor could his benevolence be assumed to be sufficient to ensure that their interests were protected. Thompson says that close examination must be made of the 'so mysteriously operating connexion in marriage', and of the 'moral miracle, of the philosophy of utility of the nineteenth century – of reducing two identities into one'.[12] The marriage contract was the means through which the 'moral miracle' was wrought, but it was anything but a contract. Thompson cries that it is an 'audacious falsehood' to refer to marriage as a contract.

> A contract! where are any of the attributes of contracts, of equal and just contracts, to be found in this transaction? A contract implies the voluntary assent of both the contracting parties. Can even both the parties, man and woman, by agreement alter the terms, as to *indissolubility* and *inequality*, of this pretended contract? No. Can any individual man divest himself, were he even so inclined, of his power of despotic control? He cannot. Have women been consulted as to the terms of this pretended contract?[13]

Women were forced to enter into this supposed contract. Social custom and law deprived women of the opportunity to earn their own living, so that marriage was their only hope of a decent life. The marriage 'contract' was just like the contract that the slave-owners in the West Indies imposed on their slaves; marriage was nothing more than the law of the strongest, enforced by men in contempt of the interests of weaker women.

Thompson makes the very important point that no husband can divest himself of the power he obtains through marriage. I have found in discussing this subject that confusion easily arises because we all know of marriages where the husband does not use, and would not dream of using, his remaining powers, and it thus seems that feminist criticism is (today, at least) very wide of the mark. But this is to confuse particular examples of married couples with the *institution* of marriage. Thompson carefully draws a distinction between the actions of any one husband and the power embodied in the structure of the relation between 'husband' and 'wife'. To become a 'husband' is to attain patriarchal right with respect to a 'wife'. His right is much diminished today from the extensive power he enjoyed in 1825, but even if a man does not avail himself of the law of male sex-right, his position as a husband reflects the institutionalization of that law within marriage. The power is still there even if, in any individual case, it is not used. Christine Delphy makes the same point: 'the particular individual man [may] not play a personal role in this general oppression, which occurs before his appearance on the scene: but, reciprocally, no personal initiative on his part can undo or mitigate what exists before and outside his entrance'.[14] Thompson adds the further important observation that, even if a husband renounces his power, his wife's freedom is always contingent on his willingness to continue the renunciation.

Some husbands may, as Thompson puts it, allow their wives equal pleasure to their own. However, the wife's enjoyment depends entirely on the benevolence of her husband and what he does, or does not, *permit* her to do. The husband can make the marital home into a prison and cut off 'his household slave from all sympathy but with himself, his children, and cats or other household animals'. A wife can be excluded from all intellectual and social intercourse and pleasures, and can be prevented from forming her own friendships; 'is there a wife who dares to form her own acquaintances amongst women or men, without the permission, direct or indirect, of the husband . . . or to retain them when formed?'[15] If a husband chooses to forego all his legal powers, his wife still has 'but the pleasures of the slave, however varied', because her actions are always contingent upon the permission of her husband.[16] Thompson claims that in these matters wives are worse off than the female slaves of the West Indies, and husbands have wider jurisdiction than slave-masters.

In one respect the marriage contract differs from slavery or from the extended employment contract of civil slavery. Slavery originated in and was maintained through physical coercion. In the civil slave contract, like the employment contract, service (labour power) is exchanged for subsistence or wages. Civil slavery cannot be maintained through time unless the worker (slave) is obedient to the commands of the employer; obedience is constitutive of contract. As Thompson emphasizes, in the marriage contract a wife explicitly agrees to obey her husband. The marriage contract is distinguished by reserving for wives 'this gratuitous degradation of swearing to be slaves'. Thompson wonders why it is that men do not find the 'simple pleasure of commanding to be sufficient, without the gratification of the additional power of taunting the victim with her pretended *voluntary* surrender of the control over her own actions?'.[17] The vow of obedience is now no longer always included in the marriage ceremony but nor has it entirely disappeared, and I shall come back to this feature of the marriage contract.

Just as wives' social pleasures depend on the benevolence of their husbands, so, Thompson argues, do their sexual pleasures. In his brief conjectural history of the origins of marriage, Thompson speculates that men's sexual desires led them to set up 'isolated breeding establishments, called married life', instead of using women merely as labourers.[18] With the establishment of marriage and the pretence of a contract, men's domination is hidden by the claim that marriage allows equal, consensual sexual enjoyment to both spouses. Husbands, it is held, depend upon the voluntary compliance of their wives for their pleasure. Thompson declares this to be an 'insulting falsehood'; a husband is physically strong enough, and is allowed by public opinion and the law, to compel his wife to submit to him, whether she is willing or not. She, however, has no right to enjoyment at all; she can beg, like a child or a slave, but even that is difficult for women who are not supposed to have sexual desires. Thompson concludes that 'sexual desires increase tenfold the facility of exercising, and of continuing for life, the despotism of men in marriage.'[19] Thompson's argument implies that, to bring the audacious falsehood of the marriage contract to an end, not only sweeping political and economic changes are required, but also a radical change in what it means to be a masculine or feminine sexual being; the original contract must be declared null and void.

Four decades later, John Stuart Mill drew much less far-reaching conclusions from his attack on the marriage contract as a contract. In some ways this is rather surprising, since there are some striking parallels between Mill's arguments in *The Subjection of Women* and Thompson's *Appeal*. But there are also some important differences. The suggestion has recently been made that Mill had 'unconsciously' taken over Thompson's argument 'almost word for word'.[20] Be that as it may, it is curious that Mill does not mention Thompson, whom he met in 1825, the year that the *Appeal* was published. Mill was sympathetic to co-operative socialism, and in the 1820s and 1830s he went to meetings at the South Place Chapel in London, a radical gathering-place, where Anna Wheeler sometimes lectured. Anna Wheeler's contribution to the *Appeal*, which has come down to us with William Thompson's name on the cover, is, perhaps, more clear cut than Harriet Taylor's role in *The Subjection of Women*, published in the name of John Stuart Mill.

Women had a very large hand in both the *Appeal* and *The Subjection of Women*. The controversy about the contribution of Harriet Taylor to Mill's works has continued for many years, and offers a fascinating glimpse into the patriarchal bastion of political philosophy, often fiercely defended by women; Diana Trilling, for instance, announced that Harriet Taylor had 'no touch of true femininity', no intellectual substance, and was 'a monument of nasty self-regard, as lacking in charm as in grandeur' – clearly quite unfitted to associate with a male theorist admitted to the pantheon of Great Western Philosophers. Gertrude Himmelfarb has blamed Taylor's undue influence for Mill's lapses from the path of moderation, most notably in his feminism. Philosophers must clearly choose their wives with care or women's natural political subversion will undermine the work of the mind.[21] As a friend of a writer ignored by political theorists and dismissed by Marxists as utopian, Anna Wheeler has suffered only from neglect. In the 'Introductory Letter to Mrs. Wheeler', with which Thompson opens the *Appeal*, he states that he had hoped that she would continue the work begun by Mary Wollstonecraft, 'but leisure and resolution to undertake the drudgery of the task were wanting.' Only a few pages were written by Anna Wheeler herself; 'the remainder are our joint property, I being your interpreter and the scribe of your sentiments.'[22]

John Stuart Mill was one of the rare men who not only supported the feminist movement but attempted to put his sympathies into practice. His criticism of the marriage contract was summed up in a statement that he drew up two months before he and Harriet Taylor were married in 1851. Mill completely rejected the legal powers that he would acquire as a husband – though his rejection had no legal standing – undertaking 'a solemn promise never in any case or under any circumstances to use them'. He states that he and Harriet Taylor entirely disapproved of existing marriage law, because it 'confers upon one of the parties to the contract, legal power and control over the person, property and freedom of action of the other party, independent of her own wishes and will'. Mill concluded his declaration by stating that Harriet Taylor 'retains in all respects whatever the same absolute freedom of action and freedom of disposal of herself and of all that does or may at any time belong to her, as if no such marriage had taken place; and I absolutely disclaim and repudiate all pretension to have acquired any such rights whatever by virtue of such marriage'.[23]

Mill agrees with Thompson on several issues. He argues, for example, that women have no alternative, they are compelled to marry. 'Wife' is the only position that their upbringing, lack of education and training, and social and legal pressures realistically leave open to them. Mill also distinguishes between the behaviour of individual husbands and the structure of the institution of marriage. He argues that defenders of existing marriage law rely on the example of husbands who refrain from using their legal powers, yet marriage is designed for every man, not merely a benevolent few, and it allows men who physically ill-treat their wives to do so with virtual impunity. Again, like Thompson, Mill argues that to become a wife is tantamount to becoming a slave, and in some ways is worse; a wife is the 'actual bond-servant of her husband: no less so, as far as legal obligation goes, than slaves commonly so called'.[24] Mill is much more reticent than Thompson about a wife's sexual subjection, although, as I have already noted, he drew attention to the right of a husband to compel his wife to grant his 'conjugal rights'.

Where Mill parts company with Thompson is that he denies that there is any connection between conjugal domination and a wife's position as housewife and economic dependant. Mill calls for reform of marriage law to bring the marriage contract in line with other contracts. Echoing Pufendorf, he notes that 'the most frequent case of voluntary association, next to marriage, is partnership in business', but marriage compares very unfavourably with business. No one thinks that one partner in a business must be the absolute ruler; who would enter a business partnership if that were the case? Yet, if power were placed in the hands of one man, the arrangement would be less dangerous than in marriage, since the subordinate partner can always terminate the contract; such a course is not open to a wife (and Mill, who was very cautious in public on the highly charged question of divorce, adds that even if a wife could withdraw from a marriage she should do so only as a last resort). In business, theory and experience both confirm that the appropriate arrangement is for the conditions of partnership to be negotiated in the articles of agreement. Similarly, Mill argues, in marriage, the 'natural arrangement' is a division of powers between husband and wife, 'each being absolute in the executive branch of their own department, and any change of system and principle requiring the consent of both'.

How is the division to be made? Mill suggests, on the one hand, that an arrangement will be made according to the capacities of the partners; they could 'pre-appoint it by the marriage contract, as pecuniary arrangements are now often pre-appointed'. On the other hand, as feminist critics have recently pointed out, Mill is ultimately inconsistent in his argument. He falls back on the appeals to custom and nature that he had rejected at an earlier stage of his argument in *The Subjection of Women*. Mill, like the classic social contract theorists, assumes that sexual difference necessarily leads to a sexual division of labour, a division that upholds men's patriarchal right. He remarks that, because a husband is usually older than his wife, he will have more authority in decision-making, 'at least until they both attain a time of life at which the difference in their years is of no importance'. However, he does not say why the husband would be willing to relinquish his power, or how the appropriate time of life is to be recognized. Again, Mill notes that the spouse (and he disingenuously writes, 'whichever it is') who provides greater support will have a greater voice, but his own argument ensures that the wife's voice will remain subordinate.[25]

Mill states that when the family is reliant on earnings for support, 'the common arrangement, by which the man earns the income and the wife superintends the domestic expenditure, seems to me in general the most suitable division of labour between the two persons.' Mill assumes that when women have equal opportunity in education and thus 'the *power* of earning', and marriage has been reformed so that husbands are no longer legally sanctioned slave-masters, a woman, by virtue of becoming a wife, will still choose to remain in the home, protected by her husband. He explicitly equates a woman's choosing to marry with a man's choice of a career. When a woman marries and has a household and family to attend to, she will renounce all other occupations 'which are not consistent with the requirements of this'.[26] Even if marriage became a freely negotiable contract, Mill expected that women would accept that they should render domestic service.

Harriet Taylor was much closer to William Thompson on this issue. In 1851 in *The Enfranchisement of Women*, she responded to the objection that opening all occupations to both sexes on merit would lead to too many competitors and the lowering of wages and salaries. Taylor argued that, at worst, such an enlargement of opportunity for women would mean that a married couple could not then earn more than the man could now earn on his own. The great change would be that the wife 'would be raised from the position of a servant to that of a partner'. As long as economic life was governed by competition the exclusion of half the competitors could not be justified. She added that she did not believe that 'the division of mankind into capitalists and hired labourers, and the regulation of the reward of labourers mainly by demand and supply, will be for ever, or even much longer, the rule of the world'.[27]

Most of the reforms to marriage law demanded by feminists in the nineteenth century have now been enacted. Nevertheless, contemporary feminists still emphasize that the marriage contract diverges in significant respects from other contracts. Some of their arguments resemble those of Thompson and Mill, others highlight yet further peculiarities of marriage as a contract.[28] For example, contemporary feminists point out that the marriage contract, unlike other valid contracts, requires that one party gives up the right to self-protection and bodily integrity. They have also pointed out that the marriage contract does not exist as a written document that is read and then signed by the contracting parties. Generally, a contract is valid only if the parties have read and understood its terms before they commit themselves. If very large amounts of property are involved in a marriage today, a contract will sometimes be drawn up that resembles much older documents, common when marriage was a matter for fathers of families and not the free choice of two individuals. The fact that most marriages lack any document of this kind, illustrates one of the most striking features of the marriage contract. There is no paper headed 'The Marriage Contract' to be signed. Instead, the unwritten contract of marriage, to which a man and a woman are bound when they become husband and wife, is codified in the law governing marriage and family life. [29]

There is another reason, too, why there is no written document. A man and a woman do not become husband and wife by putting their signatures on a contract. Marriage is constituted through two different acts. First, a prescribed ceremony is performed during the course of which the couple undertake a speech act. The man and woman each say the words 'I do'. These words are a 'performative utterance'; that is to say, by virtue of saying the words, the standing of the man and woman is transformed. In the act of saying 'I do', a man becomes a husband and a woman becomes a wife. Bachelors and spinsters are turned into married couples by uttering certain words – but the marriage can still be invalidated unless another act is performed. Second, the marriage must also be 'consummated' through sexual intercourse. Kant was emphatic about this:

> The Contract of Marriage is completed only by conjugal cohabitation. A Contract of two Persons of different sex, with the secret understanding either to abstain from conjugal cohabitation or with the consciousness on either side of incapacity for it, is a *simulated Contract*; it does not constitute a marriage. [30]

The story of the sexual contract explains why a signature, or even a speech act, is insufficient for a valid marriage. The act that is required, the act that seals the contract, is (significantly) called *the sex act*. Not until a husband has exercised his conjugal right is the marriage contract complete.

Contemporary feminists have also emphasized the fact that a married couple cannot determine the terms of the marriage contract to suit their own circumstances. There is not even a choice available between several different contracts, there is only *the* marriage contract. Married women first obtained some power to contract for themselves after Married Women's Property Acts were passed in the nineteenth century – in Britain a wife's personal liability for contracts was acknowledged by Parliament only in 1935 – but, as Lenore Weitzman has noted, despite major reforms since then, two legal restrictions have been maintained on contract between husband and wife. 'First, no contract could alter the essential elements of the marital relationship, and second, no contract could be made in contemplation of divorce.' A married couple cannot contract to change the 'essentials' of marriage, which are seen as 'the husband's duty to support his wife, and the wife's duty to serve her husband'.[31] The relation of protection and obedience cannot legally be altered, so that, for example, a married couple cannot contract for the wife to be paid by her husband for her work as a housewife. Couples do have some scope for making their own arrangements, but it is important to note that William Thompson's point about the permission of the husband remains relevant; individual variations are made within 'a relationship of *personal* dependency. The couple work out together what the husband wants [the wife] to do . . . within certain general parameters'.[32] The general parameters are set by the law governing marriage, and feminist legal scholars often follow other legal authorities in arguing that, therefore, marriage is less a contract than a matter of *status*.

But 'status' in which sense? Some discussions suggest that the old world of status has lingered on into the modern world. Thus, in *The Subjection of Women*, John Stuart Mill argues that 'the law of servitude in marriage is a monstrous contradiction to all the principles of the modern world', and that women's subordination is 'a single relic of an old world of thought and practice exploded in everything else'. The 'peculiar character of the modern world . . . [is] that human beings are no longer born to their place in life, . . . but are free to employ their faculties, and such favourable chances as offer, to achieve the lot which may appear to them most desirable'.[33] At present this principle applies only to men; to be born a woman still entails that a place in life is already waiting. Marriage, Mill argues, must thus be brought into the modern world; the relics of status must be eliminated and marriage must be moved from status to contract. In the old world of status, men and women had no choice about the social positions they occupied as husbands and wives. Mary Shanley has remarked of marriage in the seventeenth century, that 'the "contractual" element in marriage [was] simply the *consent* of each party to marry the other, . . . To contract a marriage was to consent to a status which in its essence was hierarchical and unalterable'.[34] Feminist critics of the marriage contract often make a similar point about contemporary marriage; for example, the marriage contract 'is not, in fact, a contract between the spouses, but rather they agree together to accept a certain (externally defined) status'.[35]

Emphasis on 'status' as an externally defined position overlaps with 'status', as used by legal writers, to refer to regulation of, and restriction on, freedom of contract by the state. Status, they argue, is then incorporated into contract. Feminist legal scholars, too, present marriage as either an exception to the movement from status to contract or as part of a reversal back to status. For example, Weitzman argues that marriage is not yet a contract, in which the parties freely negotiate the terms, but has moved 'from a status to a status-contract'. Men and women can choose whether or not to marry, just as they choose whether or not to enter other contracts, but, once they decide to marry, 'the contract analogy fails, because the terms and conditions of the relationship are dictated by the state. The result is that marital partners have lost the traditional privileges of status and, at the same time, have been deprived of the freedom that contract provides.'[36] Marjorie Shultz recognizes that there has been a shift from Maine's use of 'status' to 'legal conditions imposed on the individual by public law, not usually as a result of birth characteristics, but through choice or consent'. Nevertheless, she still refers to a movement from contract back to status. In marrying, 'spouses can contract into a status "package" with little control over its substantive terms.' She argues that the movement from contract should be reversed; marriage should be purely a matter of contract, since contract 'offers a rich and developed tradition whose principal strength is precisely the accommodation of diverse relationships'.[37] Exactly; the contract tradition can even accommodate the relation between master and slave.

To argue for the assimilation of marriage to the model of economic contract in the heyday of freedom of contract (if such a period ever existed) is to assume that the public and private worlds can be assimilated and to ignore the construction of the opposition between the world of contract and its 'natural foundation' within civil society. Contract appears as the solution to the problem of patriarchal right (status) because contract is seen as a universal category that can include women. Contract in the public world is an exchange between equals (between 'individuals') so it appears that, if contract is extended into the private sphere, inequalities of status between men and women in marriage must disappear. The husband exercises political right over his wife, and only men can be 'husbands'. Status in yet another sense must also be replaced by contract.

Contemporary feminist critics have pointed out that, unlike other contracts, the marriage contract cannot be entered into by any two (or more) sane adults, but is restricted to two parties, one of whom must be a man and the other a woman (and who must not be related in certain prescribed ways). Not only does a 'husband' obtain a certain power over his wife whether or not he wishes to have it, but the marriage contract is sexually ascriptive. A man is always a 'husband' and a woman is always a 'wife'. But what follows from this criticism? The argument that marriage should become a properly contractual relation implies that sexual difference is also an aspect of 'status'. Legal writers argue that there has been a movement back from contract to status because substantive social characteristics of parties to contracts are treated as relevant matters in decisions whether certain contracts should be permitted or regulated. Freedom of contract (proper contract) demands that no account is taken of substantive attributes – such as sex. If marriage is to be truly contractual, sexual difference must become irrelevant to the marriage contract; 'husband' and 'wife' must no longer be sexually determined. Indeed, from the standpoint of contract, 'men' and 'women' would disappear.

The completion of the movement from status to contract entails that status as sexual difference should disappear along with 'status' in its other senses. There can be no predetermined limits on contract, so none can be imposed by specifying the sex of the parties. In contract, the fact of being a man or a woman is irrelevant. In a proper marriage contract two 'individuals' would agree on whatever terms were advantageous to them both. The parties to such a contract would not be a 'man' and a 'woman' but two owners of property in their persons who have come to an agreement about their property to their mutual advantage. Until recently, there was no suggestion that status in the sense of sexual difference would also give way to contract. To sweep away the last remnants of status in marriage can have consequences not foreseen by Thompson or Mill who did not object to the fact that *women* became wives; they strongly objected to what being a *wife* entailed. Earlier feminist attacks on the indissoluble marriage contract and its non-negotiable terms were directed at the husband's conjugal right, not at the sexually ascriptive construction of 'wife' and 'husband'. The contemporary attack on sexual difference, apparently much more radical than older arguments, suffers from an insuperable problem; the 'individual' is a patriarchal category. Contract may be the enemy of status, but it is also the mainstay of patriarchy. Marriage as a purely contractual relation remains caught in the contradiction that the subjection of wives is both rejected and presupposed, a point illustrated in the argument over the marriage contract between Kant and Hegel.

The contractual conception of marriage presupposes the idea of the individual as owner. The marriage contract establishes legitimate access to sexual property in the person. Kant was the contract theorist who came closest to presenting a view of marriage as nothing other than a contract of sexual use. Marriage, for Kant, is 'the Union of two Persons of different sex for life-long reciprocal possession of their sexual faculties'.[38] Locke remarked that marital society established through the marriage contract, 'consist[s] chiefly' in the spouses' 'Communion and Right in one anothers Bodies'.[39] But, as the story of the original sexual contract reveals, the right is not to one another's bodies; the right is that of masculine sex-right. Kant endorsed the sexual contract, but, paradoxically, he also rejected the idea of the individual as owner of the self (property in the person) and he had to go to some rather startling lengths to maintain a self-consciously contractual view of marriage.

   Kant's view of marriage offers a particularly clear example of the simultaneous denial and affirmation that women are 'individuals', or in Kant's terminology, 'persons'. On the one hand, his philosophy rests on the assumption that, by virtue of being human, everyone has reason, and so possesses the capacity to act according to universal moral laws and to participate in civil life. On the other hand, human capacity is sexually differentiated. Women lack political or civil reason. Kant's rather banal observations on the characters of the sexes owe everything to Rousseau. He tells us that women are creatures of feeling, not reason, so that it is useless to attempt to enlarge women's morality to encompass universal rules. Women only act if the action is pleasing to them. They are incapable of understanding principles so, for women, the good must be made pleasing. Women know 'nothing of *ought*, nothing of *must*, nothing of *due*'.[40] The tenaciousness with which male philosophers cling to the sexual contract is illustrated by the recent comment that, 'whatever Kant's conclusion about woman's role, his analysis of her condition is still worthy of his great name.'[41]

Men are governed by reason and are their own masters. Self-mastery is demonstrated in the way a man gains his livelihood, by 'not allowing others to make use of him; for he must in the true sense of the word *serve* no-one but the commonwealth'. If social circumstances require a man to be another's servant or enter into the employment contract and labour at the behest of another, he lacks the criterion for possession of a 'civil personality' and so is excluded from citizenship. Kant attempts to distinguish men who serve others, such as a barber or labourer, from a wig maker or tradesman who is an independent master. A tradesman, for instance, 'exchanges his property with someone else', while the labourer 'allows someone else to make use of him'. Kant, rather despairingly, adds that it is hard to define the criteria for self-mastery.[42] Or, at least, it is hard in the case of *men*, because all men have the potential for self-mastery; mere accidents of fortune and circumstance make some men servants, used by another, and disqualify them as civil personalities or individuals. The case of women appears to pose no difficulties.

Kant states that 'women in general . . . have no civil personality, and their existence is, so to speak, purely inherent.'[43] They must, therefore, be kept well away from the state, and must also be subject to their husbands – their masters – in marriage. Kant claims that birth cannot create legal inequality because birth is not an act on the part of one who is born. He argues that the equality of legal subjects cannot be forfeited through contract; 'no legal transaction on his part or on that of anyone else can make him cease to be his own master.'[44] Kant fails to mention that the marriage contract is an exception to this argument. Even if women were men's civil equals, they would forfeit their standing upon entering into the marriage contract. But all women lack a civil personality and so the marriage contract merely confirms the natural sexual inequality of birth. At the same time, Kant's contractual view of marriage presupposes that his own explicit statement about women's 'inherent' lack of civil standing is invalid. If civil equality between the sexes does not exist, if women are not property owners and their own masters, Kant cannot sustain his curious category of 'personal right' and his account of the marriage contract.

Personal right, Kant writes, 'is the Right to the *possession* of an external object as a Thing and the *use* of it as a Person'.[45] The marriage contract takes a different form from other contracts. In the marriage contract an individual acquires a right to a person – or, more exactly, as Kant states, 'the Man acquires a Wife'[46] – who thus becomes a *res*, a thing, a commodity or piece of property. But because both parties become things, and each is the possession of the other, they both, according to Kant, thereby regain their standing as 'rational personalities'. They make use of each other not as property but as persons. Kant's discussion of the idea of personal right and his argument about how and why a married couple must be things and persons is tortuous – and contradictory.

He states that there is always a danger that sexuality will bring humans down to the level of the beasts. The question, according to Kant, is 'how far [a man] can properly make use of [this desire from nature] without injury to his manhood. . . . Can [the sexes] sell themselves or let themselves out on hire, or by some other contract allow use to be made of their sexual faculties?'[47] Kant answers that such use is not permissible. The reason he gives is that property in the person cannot be separated from the individual owner. To acquire 'part of the human organism' – to take possession only of the sexual property of another individual – is to acquire the individual as property, a *res*, since the human organism is a unity.[48] Indeed, Kant argues that it is impossible to use only *part* of a person 'without having at the same time a right of disposal over the whole person, for each part of a person is integrally bound up with the whole'. Kant concludes that 'the sole condition on which we are free to make use of our sexual desire depends upon the right to dispose over the person as a whole – over the welfare and happiness and generally over all the circumstances of that person.'[49]

Kant's rejection of the idea of property in parts of the person is very odd. If marriage is, as he defines it, nothing more than a contract of mutual sexual use – mutual use of sexual property (faculties) in the person – then there is not the slightest need for him to argue in terms of use of persons, and least of all to argue that persons are used as things. To have right over a person as a thing, as a piece of property, is to have the power of a slave-master – but Kant's husband does not have such a power. Kant argues that, if *both* parties to the contract acquire the same right, they each give themselves up and win themselves back. They are simultaneously owner and owned. They become persons again, unified into one will. The reason for all these very unconvincing theoretical manoeuvres becomes clear once the story of the sexual contract has been told.

Kant does his best to have his philosophical cake and eat it. If he is to maintain his claim that all human beings have the rational capacity to act according to universal moral principles, then the two parties to the marriage contract must be of equal standing. Moreover, if their standing is to be maintained, they must engage in an equal exchange of property; or an equal exchange of themselves as property. Therefore, Kant implies, women, like men, are individuals or persons. If this is the case, there is no need for Kant to insist that the married couple are property for each other. If the person is a unity, if sexual faculties are inseparable from the self, then why do not the husband and wife remain as persons for each other? The reason is not hard to discern. Kant excludes women from the category of persons or individuals. Women can only be property. Personal right exists only in the private sphere of marriage and domestic relations. In the public realm, individuals interact as civil equals, and even a man whose circumstances place him in the position of a servant does not also become property. The social contract, which creates civil freedom and equality, depends on the sexual contract, which creates patriarchal (personal) right; civil equality depends on personal right. What it is to be master of oneself in civil life becomes clear in contrast to men's mastery of women in marriage. Kant's pervasive influence on contemporary political theory is not surprising in view of his adept sleight of hand through which the sexual contract is concealed by marriage as a contract of mutual sexual use.

A moral miracle (as William Thompson would call it) turns women's natural subjection into marital equality. Nature has given us sexual desire so that we will procreate, but this is not the only end for which to marry; 'enjoyment in the reciprocal use of the sexual endowments is an end of marriage', and it is legitimate to marry with this end in view.[50] But if men and women wish to use their sexual property they *must* marry. 'Matrimony is the only condition in which use can be made of one's sexuality. If one devotes one's person to another, one devotes not only sex but the whole person: the two cannot be separated.'[51] Kant not only declares that mutual sexual use outside of marriage dehumanizes a man and a woman (they remain as mere property for each other), but that the use is 'in principle, although not always in effect, on the level of cannibalism'. To consume a body with teeth and mouth instead of a sexual organ merely provides a different form of enjoyment. Only the marriage contract can turn use of sexual property, in which 'one is really made a *res fungibilis* to the other', into the use of a person.[52] But it is the *husband* who has use of a person, not the wife. Kant's marriage contract establishes the husband's patriarchal right; *he* possesses his wife's body, which is to say her person, as a thing, but she has no corresponding right. 'Personal right' is the right of a husband as a civil master.

And there is no doubt that he is a master. The unity of wills is represented by the will of the husband. Kant claims that a 'relation of equality as regards the mutual possession of their Persons, as well as of their Goods exists between husband and wife'. He rejects the suspicion – a suspicion voiced very loudly from a variety of quarters by the 1790s, when the *Philosophy of Law* appeared – that there is something contradictory about postulating both equality and legal recognition of the husband as master. He states that the husband's power over his wife

> cannot be regarded as contrary to the natural Equality of a human pair, if such legal Supremacy is based only upon the natural superiority of the faculties of the Husband compared with the Wife, in the effectuation of the common interest of the household; and if the Right to command is based merely upon this fact.[53]

Although Kant states that, if either spouse ran away, 'the other is entitled, at any time, and incontestably, to bring such a one back to the former relation, as if that Person were a Thing', it is clear that the right is only likely to be exercised by the master of the family. The master, Kant says, also has the same right to bring back servants who abscond, 'even before the reasons that may have led them to run away, . . . have been judicially investigated'.[54] In amplifying his notion of personal right, Kant uses the revealing example of the difference between pointing to someone and saying 'this is my father', which means only that I have a father and here he is, and pointing to someone and saying 'this is my wife.' To point to a wife is to refer to 'a special juridical relation of a possessor to an object viewed as thing, although in this case it is a person'.[55] Kant notes that personal right is distinct from possessing a man who has lost his civil personality as a slave – but to possess a wife is to possess someone who, naturally, has no civil personality, although she is not called a slave.

Hegel attacked Kant's marriage contract, declaring that it was 'shameful' to see marriage 'degraded to the level of a contract for reciprocal use'.[56] Hegel also rejected the doctrine of the social contract. He denied that the state should be understood as if it was, or could be, generated from an original contract. Commentators on Hegel's theory invariably conclude that Hegel opposes contract theory. In the absence of the whole story of the original contract such a conclusion appears entirely reasonable, and it can be forgotten that, despite his criticism of Kant's marriage contract, Hegel argues that marriage originates in a contract. The extensive area of common ground that he shares with contract doctrine, notably the patriarchal construction of civil society, masculinity and femininity, can then also be overlooked.

Hegel rejects the keystone of contract theory, the idea of the individual as owner. He also rejects the contractarian ideal of social life as nothing but contract, all the way down. On these issues, he is the most profound critic of contract. However, Hegel's arguments are fatally compromised by his acceptance of the sexual contract. In order to incorporate women into civil society while excluding them, Hegel re-enacts the contradictions of Kant's theory. Hegel attacks Kant's claim, that individuals become property in marriage, but his own marriage contract, like Kant's, assumes that women are not, and cannot be, and yet are, individuals. Hegel dismisses the marriage contract of mutual use or exchange of property, but still advocates a contract that constitutes a wife as subject to her husband.

Hegel regards it as shameful to substitute the one-sided, contractual individual as owner, or person–thing, for the complexity of human personality and ethical life. The individual as owner and contract-maker is what Hegel calls an 'immediate self-subsistent person', and although this is one element, or 'moment', in the individual personality and in social life, it is not and cannot be the whole.[57] To see marriage as a contract entered into by owners of the sexual property in their persons, or to see spouses as property, is completely to misunderstand marriage and its place in modern civil life. Purely as contract, marriage is open to the contingency, the whim and caprice, of sexual inclination. The marriage ceremony becomes merely the means to avoid unauthorized use of bodies (or sexual cannibalism). On the contrary, for Hegel, marriage is a distinct form of ethical life – part of the universal family/civil society/state – constituted by a principle of association far removed from contract.

The marriage contract, according to Hegel, could not be more different from other contracts; the marriage contract 'is precisely a contract to transcend the standpoint of contract'.[58] From the standpoint of contract, two individuals who contract together recognize each other as property owners and mutually will that they should use each other's property. The owner is related externally to his property and so, as it were, stands outside the contract and is unchanged by it. Similarly, the self of Kant's person–thing is unaffected by this curious status. The unity of will of the two parties is sheer coincidence. In contrast, Hegel's marriage contract changes the consciousness and standing of the man and woman who marry and a public, duly authorized ceremony is thus essential to marriage. A husband and wife cease to be 'self-subsistent' individuals. They become members of a little association which is so closely unified that they are 'one person'. Hegel writes that, in marrying, the spouses 'consent to make themselves one person, to renounce their natural and individual personality to this unity of one with the other. From this point of view, their union is a self-restriction, but in fact it is their liberation, because in it they attain their substantive self-consciousness'.[59] The husband and wife are bound together through a rational, ethical bond which unites them internally in their association and not externally as property owners. The end of marriage is not mutual sexual use; sexual passion is merely one 'moment' of marriage, a moment that disappears as it is satisfied. The marriage contract creates a substantive relation constituted by 'love, trust, and common sharing of their entire existence as individuals'.[60]

A husband and wife are bound together neither by contract, nor sexual inclination, nor even by love, as 'love' is usually understood. They are incorporated by 'ethico-legal love' which transcends the fickleness of ordinary, romantic love.[61] Hegel states that love is 'the most tremendous contradiction'.[62] The contradiction comes about because the lovers' first impulse is to obliterate their individuality in total unification with the loved one. However, in opposition to this desire, they also discover that their sense of themselves as autonomous beings is strengthened through the relationship with the beloved. The gulf between obliteration and enhancement of self can be overcome by the mutual recognition of the two lovers, through which each gains a deeper sense of unity with the other and sense of autonomy of the self. Love (in Hegel's sense) both unifies and differentiates. Thus marriage offers a glimpse of the differentiation and particularity of civil (economic) society and the unity and universality necessary to membership in the state.

Hegel's criticism of the marriage contract goes far beyond the reduction of conjugal relations to a contract of mutual use. If marriage were merely contractual, civil society would be undermined; the necessary, private foundation for public life would be lacking. Or, to make this point in a manner that may seem incongruous in the context of Hegel's theory, the social contract (civil life) depends on the sexual contract (which is displaced onto the marriage contract). The idea of the 'individual' is fundamental to contract, but if ownership is exhaustive of the human personality, then, ironically, the necessary social condition for contract is eliminated. Any example of contract presupposes that contracts must be kept; that is to say, trust and mutual fidelity are presupposed. Individuals understand what 'to contract' means, only because any single contract is part of the wider practice of contracting, and the practice is constituted by the understanding that contracts are binding. The conception of the individual as owner of the property in his person, especially in its most extreme, contractarian form, inevitably generates a problem of keeping faith and 'performing second'. Attempts are made to solve the problem in classic contract theory by strategems such as Leviathan's sword, Kant's postulate of a necessary idea of an original contract which embodies a law that contracts must be sealed, or by building the requisite non-contractual background into the state of nature. Hegel's discussion shows why the idea of the individual as owner undercuts all these stratagems.

The 'individual' at once denies yet presupposes the intersubjective understanding of what it means to enter into a contract. Contract cannot provide a universal basis for social life. Contract must form part of wider non-contractual social institutions. Contracts can be entered into precisely because consciousness is developed and informed within arenas that are non-contractual. If individuals were merely owners they could enter into no contracts at all; strictly, 'contract' would be meaningless to them. Hegel, like Durkheim sometime later, argued that 'a contract supposes something other than itself.'[63] Contract has an appropriate place in social life in the economic sphere – the sphere that Hegel calls 'civil society' – but if contract is extended beyond its own realm, social order is threatened. Contract on its own is an incoherent basis for social life. Hegel, echoing Kant, argues that marriage is an ethical duty; 'marriage, . . . is one of the absolute principles on which the ethical life of a community depends.'[64] Ethical life depends upon marriage because marriage is the origin of the family. In the family, children learn, and adults are continually reminded of, what it means to be a member of a small association based on love and trust; in the private dimension of ethical life they gain experience of a non-contractual association and so are prepared – or, rather, men are prepared – for participation in the universal public sphere of civil society and the state.

In the *Philosophy of Right*, Hegel criticizes Rousseau's social contract theory as well as Kant's marriage contract, but he follows Rousseau closely in his patriarchal understanding of masculinity and femininity, and, therefore, of the public and private. Hegel claims that 'difference in the physical characteristics of the two sexes has a rational basis and consequently acquires an intellectual and ethical significance.'[65] Sexual difference also has patriarchal political significance (rational expression) in Hegel's theory. Woman, Hegel tells us, 'has her substantive destiny in the family, and to be imbued with family piety is her ethical frame of mind'. Hegel goes on to note that, in *Antigone*, family piety, the law of woman, is opposed to public law and, he comments, 'this is the supreme opposition in ethics' – and, we can also add, in politics. Women cannot enter into civil public life because they are naturally lacking in the capacity to submit to 'the demands of universality'. Women, Hegel says, 'are educated – who knows how? – as it were by breathing in ideas, by living rather than by acquiring knowledge'. A man, on the other hand, has 'actual substantive life in the state'. A man acquires the status of manhood only through struggle with himself and struggle in the civil world, through learning and 'much technical exertion'.[66]

Women are what they are by nature; men must create themselves and public life, and they are endowed with the masculine capacity to do so. Women must remain in the natural private sphere of the family. The family is represented in public by the husband, the 'one person' created by the marriage contract. Sexual difference also entails a patriarchal division of labour. The husband has the 'prerogative to go out and work for [the family's] living, to attend to its needs, and to control and administer its capital'.[67] Like Rousseau, Hegel sees women as naturally politically subversive. Women brought about the downfall of the ancient world; in the *Phenomenology* he writes that the ancient community created

> what it suppresses and what is at the same time essential to it an internal enemy – womankind in general. Womankind – the everlasting irony [in the life] of the community – changes by intrigue the universal end of government into a private end, transforms its universal activity into a work of some particular individual, and perverts the universal property of the state into a possession and ornament for the Family.[68]

In the modern world, if 'women hold the helm of government, the state is at once in jeopardy.'[69]

But it is not only if women seize the reins of government that the state is in peril. Women play a substantive part in Hegel's argument. For Hegel, like the classic social contract theorists, marriage and the family provide the natural foundation for civil life, but Hegel goes much further. He also implies that, through their love, husbands and wives play out (in a manner suited to the 'immediate' ethical sphere) the dialectic of mutual acknowledgment that characterizes relations among men as makers of contracts in civil society and as citizens in the state. In contract, men recognize each other as property owners, enjoying an equal standing; as citizens – participants in the social contract – they also recognize their mutual civil equality. Hegel's account of love within marriage suggests that the same process takes place between husband and wife, through the dialectic of autonomy and unity. But one party to the marriage contract is a woman; conjugal relations cannot take the same form as civil relations between men. Sexual difference is political difference, the difference between mastery and subjection; so how can there be mutual acknowledgment by husband and wife as, at one and the same time, particular and universal beings? And if such recognition is impossible, how can marriage and the family constitute a 'moment' of Hegel's social whole of family/civil society/ state?

Some feminist interpretations of Hegel, particularly those drawing on Simone de Beauvoir, have turned to his famous passages in the *Phenomenology*, on the opposition between master and slave, as the model for the relation between husband and wife. The comparison of Hegel's dialectic of mastery and slavery with conjugal relations involves one of the same difficulties as the comparison of husband and wife with employer and worker. The master and slave, like the capitalist and proletarian, are both men. Use of the passages on the master and slave also poses another difficulty. The struggle between these two antagonists is part of Hegel's story of the development of self-consciousness. Indeed, the master and slave appear at the genesis of self-consciousness. Hegel argues that consciousness of self presupposes consciousness of another self; to be self-conscious is to have one's consciousness reflected back from another, who, in turn, has his own consciousness confirmed by you. The mutual acknowledgment and confirmation of self, however, is possible only if the two selves have an equal status. The master cannot see his independence reflected back in the self of the slave; all he finds is servility. Self-consciousness must receive acknowledgment from another self of the same kind, and so the master-slave relation must be transcended. The master and slave can, as it were, move through the 'moments' of Hegel's great story and eventually meet as equals in the civil society of the *Philosophy of Right*. The men's story can be completed once the original pact is sealed and civil society brought into being. In the fraternity of civil society each man can obtain self-confirmation and acknowledgment of his equality in the brotherhood. But this is not quite the end of the story.

The original contract is not merely a social contract; it is a sexual contract which constitutes men's patriarchal right over women. Women are outside the fight to the death between master and slave at the dawn of self-consciousness, but they are part of modern civil society. Hegel's story of the development of universal freedom requires that men recognize each other as equals; the day of the master and slave is past. But men's self-consciousness is not purely the consciousness of free civil equals (the story of the social contract) – it is also the consciousness of patriarchal masters (the story of the sexual contract). The ostensible universalism of Hegel's public world (just like that of the classic contract theorists) gains its meaning when men look from the public world to the private domestic sphere and the subjection of wives. The family (private) and civil society/state (public) are separate and inseparable; civil society is a patriarchal order. As a husband, a man cannot receive acknowledgment as an equal from his wife. But a husband is not engaged in relations with other men, his equals: he is married to a woman, his natural subordinate. Wives do not stand to husbands precisely as slaves do to masters 'in the beginning'. Slaves are not naturally slaves, but a wife cannot be an 'individual' or a citizen, able to participate in the public world. If the family is, simultaneously, to be part of the state and separate from it, constituted through a unique contract, and if patriarchal right is not to be undermined, women's acknowledgment of men cannot be the same as men's acknowledgment of their fellow men. Men cease to be masters and slaves, but Hegel's social order demands a sexually differentiated consciousness (his discussion of ethico-legal love notwithstanding). The recognition that a husband obtains from a wife is precisely what is required in modern patriarchy; recognition as a patriarchal master, which only a woman can provide.

Hegel rejects the social contract, but, in accepting the sexual contract, he embraces the anomalies and contradictions surrounding women, contract and the private and public generated by classic contract theory. Ironically, Hegel's critique of marriage as a contract of sexual use involves the same set of problems as the marriage contract in the hands of the classic contract theorists or Lévi-Strauss. Hegel's argument raises the same question that I have posed of these theorists. Women are held to be natural subordinates lacking the capacities required to enter into contracts; why, then, are women always capable of entering into the marriage contract?

Hegel's argument raises the question in an especially acute form. Why should a theorist who declares that it is shameful to see marriage as merely contractual still insist that marriage originates in a contract? Other forms of non-contractual free agreement exist, to which Hegel could turn; or, more logically, given the patriarchal construction of masculinity and femininity that Hegel shares with the classic contract theorists, the marriage ceremony could provide more than adequate confirmation of the natural subordination of women when they become wives. Of course, Hegel insists that his marriage contract is a unique contract that transcends the standpoint of contract. Hegel has to make this move in order to posit the requisite form of consciousness within the private sphere. From the standpoint of contract, spouses are related only by the mutual advantage of property owners. As owners, their selves are always external to the conjugal relation and so no dialectic of consciousness can take place. Even the bond of mutual use is illusory because it cannot exist over time without the trust and faith which the standpoint of contract eliminates. Hegel's special marriage contract transcends the contractarian standpoint – but it cannot transcend the sexual contract.

The reason why women must enter into the marriage contract is that, although they have no part in the social contract, women must be incorporated into civil society. The major institutional bonds of civil society – citizenship, employment and marriage – are constituted through contract. If the free relations characteristic of civil society are to extend to all social spheres, marriage, too, must originate in a contract. Hegel rejects contract theory, but he retains contract as one essential element of civil freedom. Social life as a whole cannot be constituted through contract, but contract is appropriate in civil society (the economy). Men interact in civil society through the 'particularity' that characterizes makers of contracts, and they can do so because they also interact in the non-contractual state and family. Women, as parties to one of the central contracts in civil society, must share in the attribute of 'particularity'; or, that is to say, they share in the attributes of 'individuals'. Women are incorporated into civil society through the marriage contract, and are incorporated on the same basis as men; parties to contracts enjoy equal standing. Only if women, too, enter into a contract, can Hegel argue that the dialectic of love is a 'moment' in the wider dialectic of family/civil society/state, or the contract theorists write of the mutual exchange of property in the person in marriage. Only if women enter into a contract, can Kant argue that spouses are both property and persons for each other.

Modern civil society is an order of universal freedom and so stands opposed to the old world of status. All inhabitants of civil society enjoy the same standing – and, when marriage is created through a contract, we can be confident that this is the case. The marriage contract, however, also involves a variant of the contradiction of slavery. The social contract story requires that some clear indication is present that women are part of civil society and capable of entering into contracts (slaves must be seen as part of humanity). Women must enter into the marriage contract. But the sexual contract requires that women are incorporated into civil society on a different basis from men. Men create patriarchal civil society and the new social order is structured into two spheres. The private sphere is separated from civil public life; the private sphere both is and is not part of civil society – and women both are and are not part of the civil order. Women are not incorporated as 'individuals' but as women, which, in the story of the original contract, means as natural subordinates (slaves are property). The original contract can be upheld, and men can receive acknowledgment of their patriarchal right, only if women's subjection is secured in civil society.

Hegel's marriage contract that transcends contract replicates the sexual contract just as completely as the marriage contract in classic contract theory. This unique contract is the genesis of a private sphere that throws into relief the masculinity – the fraternity – the freedom and equality of the public world; the family provides the example of (women's) natural subjection on which the meaning of civil society/state as a sphere of freedom depends. Hegel is quite right; the marriage contract is very different from contract in the civil realm. The difference, however, is not quite as Hegel argues. The marriage contract cannot be like, say, the employment contract because *women* are party to the marriage contract. Women have to be incorporated into civil society through a contract because only contract always creates free relations and presupposes the equal standing of the parties, yet, at the same time, because women are involved, the contract must confirm patriarchal right.

The difference between the marriage contract and other contracts has always been indicated plainly enough. Contemporary feminists have paid relatively little attention to the vow of obedience (perhaps because it is not always now included in the speech acts of the marriage ceremony), and when half the story of the original contract is repressed, even an explicit commitment to obey can be overlooked by other critics of contract theory. The employment contract gives an employer right of command over the worker and his labour. Workers must obey directives of employers, but in contracts about property in men's persons, silence is maintained on the matter of obedience. Only the marriage contract – the contract into which women must enter, women who lack the standing of owners – includes the explicit commitment to obey. If the promise of universal freedom heralded by the story of an original contract is not to appear fraudulent from the start, women must take part in contract in the new civil order. If men's civil status as equals and patriarchal masters is to be maintained, the contract into which women enter must be separated from other contracts. A woman agrees to obey her husband when she becomes a wife; what better way of giving public affirmation that men are sexual masters, exercising the law of male sex-right, in their private lives?

Criticism of contract theory rarely takes the sexual contract into account. There is, therefore, a strong temptation for feminists to throw out Hegel's profound insights about the deficiencies of contract along with his patriarchal marriage contract. The conclusion is then all too easy to draw that properly contractual marriage has not yet been tried. Hegel's critique of contract highlights some acute difficulties that arise when feminists embrace contract theory, especially in the extreme form of contractarianism. For example, the classic contract theorists do not tell the story of the primal scene; their stories begin after physical genesis and human development. 'Individuals' appear as fully grown men, equipped with the attributes required to make contracts. At the same time, most of the pictures of the state of nature contain the non-contractual conditions necessary for infants to thrive and grow; love, trust and family life are assumed to be found naturally. Only for Hobbes, as for contemporary contractarians, are all social relationships generated through contract, even that between parent and infant. But would an 'individual' ever enter into a contract to be a parent? A contract for mutual sexual use can accommodate physical genesis without difficulty. The problem arises with the long-term commitment as a parent required for human development. Would the marriage contract for mutual sexual use be extended to include provision to rear an infant?

In chapter 3, I noted that Hobbes' self-interested female individual in the state of nature would have little or no incentive to make a contract to 'breed up' an infant. Of course, without Hobbes' war of all against all the disincentive would be less, since an infant would not endanger personal safety. Nevertheless, from the standpoint of contract, can an infant be seen as anything more than an encumbrance? The question is more pressing when contract demands that, just as soon as the infant is sufficiently grown to make contracts for itself, the parent–child relationship should be placed on an explicitly contractual basis. How can any parents be sure that their trouble will not be wasted and their child will not make a more advantageous contract elsewhere? Again, would anyone want to contract with a child; or would the only contracts open to a small, relatively resourceless contractor be slave contracts? I am concerned with adult heterosexual relations not parent–child relations, so I shall merely raise and not pursue such questions.

There is a closely related point, however, which is directly relevant to my theme. One of Hegel's objections to marriage as a contract is that it leaves the relationship at the mercy of the whims and capricious wills of the contractors. Similarly, Durkheim emphasizes that the bond created by contract is both external and of short duration; it leads to 'transient relations and passing associations'.[70] A contract of mutual advantage and reciprocal use will last only as long as it appears advantageous to either party. A new contract with a different partner will always appear as a possible and enticing alternative. That is to say, exit from the marriage contract becomes as important as entry. Contemporary advocates of marriage contracting stress that one advantage is that the contract can be for a limited term, and run for, say, five years in the first instance. Nor is it accidental that current controversy over slave contracts and paternalism emphasizes the crucial importance of dissoluble contracts. The way in which popular advice-books on marriage and sexual matters present divorce illustrates the influence of a contractual view of marriage; divorce is seen as something that can be 'pre-considered in terms of personal upward mobility, with stress . . . on what lies ahead that may be incorporated into a new and better image'.[71] When the contract is made only for mutual use and advantage, its real point becomes 'to anticipate and provide for divorce'.[72]

To anticipate the termination of the marriage contract in the very act of contracting has become possible only quite recently. In England, for example, there was no divorce before 1700 (a divorce *a mensa et thoro* could be obtained from an ecclesiastical court but it did not permit remarriage) and until 1857 divorce could only be granted through a private Act of Parliament.[73] Not until 1969, when the ground for divorce became the irretrievable breakdown of the marriage, were divorces obtained relatively easily by both wives and husbands and by members of all social classes. Only recently, too, have divorce and divorced persons ceased to be a scandal. Many nineteenth-century feminists who favoured divorce, in particular as the best means for a wife to escape from a brutal husband, steered clear of the subject for fear of compromising their other goals; other feminists were opposed to divorce, fearing that the consequence would be to enable husbands to abandon their wives and children more readily. Divorce is usually seen as the opposite of marriage, but Christine Delphy argues that divorce today is, rather, the transformation of marriage. She argues that, since divorced wives almost always continue to look after the children of the marriage, 'marriage and divorce can be considered as two ways of obtaining a similar result: the collective attribution to women of the care of children and the collective exemption of men from the same responsibility.'[74] However, it is far from clear, from the standpoint of contract, whether such a responsibility would continue to arise.

The logic of contract, and of marriage as nothing more than a contract of mutual sexual use, is that 'marriage' and 'divorce' should be eliminated. The most advantageous arrangement for the individual is an endless series of very short-term contracts to use another's body as and when required. Other services presently provided within marriage would also be contracted for in the market. A universal market in bodies and services would replace marriage. The logic of contract is that marriage would be supplanted by contracts for access to sexual property. Marriage would give way to *universal prostitution*. Moreover, 'individuals', and not 'men' and 'women', would enter these contracts. Contract would then have won the final victory over status (sexual difference). When negotiations about use of sexual property in the person can have no predetermined outcome, and individuals can contract as they see fit to use the property of another, sexual difference would be meaningless.

The Beatles used to sing that 'All You Need is Love.' The objection that contract will never be victorious because love will stand in the way has been anticipated already; love has been reduced to another external relation, or aspect of property in persons, and defined, for example, as a 'particular non-marketable household commodity'.[75] To draw attention to such arguments is not to imply that contract is invincible, but to illustrate the incongruous character of an alliance between feminism and contract. The victory of contract has a considerable appeal for feminists, given the long sway of coverture and the various social and legal means still used to deny women ownership of property in their persons. The conclusion is easy to draw that the denial of civil equality to women means that the feminist aspiration must be to win acknowledgment for women as 'individuals'. Such an aspiration can never be fulfilled. The 'individual' is a patriarchal category. The individual is masculine and his sexuality is understood accordingly (if, indeed, 'sexuality' is a term that can be used of a self that is externally related to the body and sexual property). The patriarchal construction of sexuality, what it means to be a sexual being, is to possess and to have access to sexual property. How access is gained and how the property is used is made clear in the story of the demand of the brothers for equal access to women's bodies. In modern patriarchy, masculinity provides the paradigm for sexuality; and masculinity means sexual mastery. The 'individual' is a man who makes use of a woman's body (sexual property); the converse is much harder to imagine.

The patriarchal construction of sexuality is illustrated in the 'sexual revolution' of the past two decades or so. Initially, emphasis was placed on breaking down the barriers surrounding 'the sex act'. Most of the former social constraints surrounding women's sexual activity outside of marriage have been swept away. Only the individual, according to contract argument, can decide whether and how sexual property should be contracted out. No prior limits can be placed on contract. The argument runs parallel to feminist criticism that parties to the marriage contract are prohibited from deciding from themselves what the content of their contract should be. Marjorie Shultz, for example, raises the following problem; suppose that 'John and Mary decided that she would agree in principle to sex on demand, should such an agreement prevent her from later filing a rape claim against John?' Shultz states that there is a strong argument that private contract should not override the criminal law, but, she writes, 'the idea of enforceable private agreements concerning violent sexual conduct is less offensive than a state declaration that violent sexual conduct is automatically acceptable in marriage.'[76] Such a response begs the question about limitations to and alternatives to contract.

More recently, contract argument has been used to bring other forms of hetero- and homosexual activity within the ambit of the 'sexual revolution'. Hardly coincidentally, when the slave contract is defended by the argument that only the individual can decide in what way to contract out his property, contract doctrine has also been used recently to defend sado-masochism, or what might be called a fantasy slave contract. Some feminists defend sado-masochism on the ground that 'it is a consensual activity. . . . The key word to understanding S/M is *fantasy*. The roles, dialogue, fetish costumes, and sexual activity are part of a drama or ritual . . .

relationships are usually egalitarian.'[77] Feminists who object to sado-masochism have been dismissed as moralistic and as failing to appreciate the element of parody in fetish costumes. Be that as it may, sado-masochism is less a rebellious or revolutionary fantasy than a dramatic exhibition of the logic of contract and of the full implications of the sexuality of the patriarchal masculine 'individual'.

'Individuals' are interchangeable – the difference between men and women disappears – or limitations would still remain on the jurisdiction that individuals exercise over the property in their persons and on the kinds of contracts that they enter. Thus, participants can take any role in sado-masochism depending on their inclination at a particular time.[78] The triumph of contract and the 'individual' over sexual difference was foreshadowed by the Marquis de Sade in the latter part of the eighteenth century. He wrote, 'charming sex, you will be free . . . you are as free as we [men] are and the career of the battles of Venus as open to you as to us' – and de Sade's women fight the battles alongside and in the same way as his men. One of his characters, Noirceuil, enlists another, Juliette, in acting out a fantasy game; Juliette,

> dressed as a woman, must marry a woman dressed as a man at the same ceremony where I, dressed as a woman, become the wife of a man. Next, dressed as a man, you will marry another woman wearing female attire at the same time that I go to the altar to be united in holy wedlock with a catamite disguised as a girl.[79]

The endless permutations of de Sade's characters provide a ghastly parody, and a vivid portrayal, of the consequences of the absolute conquest of status as sexual difference by the individuals of the contractual imagination. From the standpoint of contract, there is nothing surprising in the representation of sexual freedom through the figures of master and slave, through the 'personae of guard and prisoner, cop and suspect, Nazi and Jew, White and Black, straight man and queer, parent and child, priest and penitent, teacher and student, whore and client, etc.'.[80] Civil mastery requires agreement from the subordinate and numerous stories are spun in which slaves and women in chains contract and consent to their subjection. In the famous pornographic story, *The Story of O*, in which O, a woman, is imprisoned and used sexually by her captors, she is always asked before each assault and violation whether or not she consents.[81]

Men exercise their masculine capacity for political creativity by generating political relationships of subordination through contract. How apt it is, in a period when contract and the patriarchal construction of the individual have such widespread appeal, that the end of the movement from status to contract should be proclaimed in feminist defences of fantasy slave contracts.

Contemporary feminists (especially in the United States) often conclude that the only alternative to the patriarchal construction of sexuality is to eliminate sexual difference, to render masculinity and femininity politically irrelevant. At first sight, the complete elimination of status and its replacement by contract appears to signal the final defeat of patriarchy and the law of male sex-right. The realization of the promise of contract as freedom appears to be in sight, and the patriarchal construction of men and women, masculinity and femininity, appears to be breaking down. Feminists have campaigned for, and won, legal reforms that are couched in what are now usually called 'gender neutral' terms. Such reforms can mean that women's civil rights are safeguarded, but this approach to reform can also lead to curious results when, for example, attempts are made to incorporate pregnancy into legislation that applies indifferently to men or women. Odd things happen to women when the assumption is made that the only alternative to the patriarchal construction of sexual difference is the ostensibly sex-neutral 'individual'.

The final victory of contract over status is not the end of patriarchy, but the consolidation of the modern form. The story of the sexual contract tells how contract is the medium through which patriarchal right is created and upheld. For marriage to become merely a contract of sexual use – or, more accurately, for sexual relations to take the form of universal prostitution – would mark the political defeat of women *as women*. When contract and the individual hold full sway under the flag of civil freedom, women are left with no alternative but to (try to) become replicas of men. In the victory of contract, the patriarchal construction of sexual difference as mastery and subjection remains intact but repressed. Only if the construction is intact can the 'individual' have meaning and offer the promise of freedom to both women and men so that they know to what they must aspire. Only if the construction is repressed can women have such an aspiration. Heterosexual relations do not inevitably take the form of mastery and subjection, but free relations are impossible within the patriarchal opposition between contract and status, masculinity and femininity. The feminist dream is continuously subverted by entanglement with contract.

7

What's Wrong with Prostitution?

In modern patriarchy a variety of means are available through which men can uphold the terms of the sexual contract. The marriage contract is still fundamental to patriarchal right, but marriage is now only one of the socially acceptable ways for men to have access to women's bodies. Casual sexual liaisons and 'living together' no longer carry the social sanctions of twenty or thirty years ago, and, in addition to private arrangements, there is a huge, multimillion dollar trade in women's bodies. Prostitution is an integral part of patriarchal capitalism. Wives are no longer put up for public auction (although in Australia, the United States and Britain they can be bought by mail-order from the Philippines), but men can buy sexual access to women's bodies in the capitalist market. Patriarchal right is explicitly embodied in 'freedom of contract'.

Prostitutes are readily available at all levels of the market for any man who can afford one and they are frequently provided as part of business, political and diplomatic transactions. Yet the public character of prostitution is less obvious than it might be. Like other forms of capitalist enterprise, prostitution is seen as private enterprise, and the contract between client and prostitute is seen as a private arrangement between a buyer and a seller. Moreover, prostitution is shrouded in secrecy despite the scale of the industry. In Birmingham, a British city of about one million people, some 800 women work either as street prostitutes, or from their homes or hotels, from 'saunas', 'massage parlours', or 'escort agencies'. Nearly 14,000 men each week buy their services, i.e., about 17 men for each prostitute.[1] A similar level of demand has been recorded in the United States, and the total number of customers each week across the country has been conservatively estimated at 1,500,000 men.[2] One estimate is that $40 million per day is spent on prostitution in the United States.[3] The secrecy exists in part because, where the act of prostitution is not itself illegal, associated activities such as soliciting often are. The criminal character of much of the business of prostitution is not, however, the only reason for secrecy. Not all men wish it generally to be known that they buy this commodity. To be discovered consorting with prostitutes can, for example, still be the downfall of politicians. The empirical evidence also indicates that three-quarters of the clients of prostitutes are married men. Certainly, the prostitutes in Birmingham find that trade slackens during holiday periods when men are away from the city with their wives and children.[4]

The sexual subjection of wives has never lacked defenders, but until very recently an unqualified defence of prostitution has been hard to find. Prostitution was seen, for example, as a necessary evil that protected young women from rape and shielded marriage and the family from the ravages of men's sexual appetites; or as an unfortunate outcome of poverty and the economic constraints facing women who had to support themselves; or prostitution was seen as no worse, and as more honest, than 'legal prostitution', as Mary Wollstonecraft called marriage in 1790.[5] As prostitutes, women openly trade their bodies and, like workers (but unlike a wife), are paid in return. So, for Emma Goldman, 'it is merely a question of degree whether [a woman] sells herself to one man, in or out of marriage, or to many men.'[6] Simone de Beauvoir sees the wife as 'hired for life by one man; the prostitute has several clients who pay her by the piece. The one is protected by one male against all the others; the other is defended by all against the exclusive tyranny of each'.[7] Cicely Hamilton noted in 1909 that although women were prevented from bargaining freely in the only trade, marriage, legitimately open to them, they could exercise this freedom in their illegitimate trade; 'the prostitute class . . . has pushed to its logical conclusion the principle that woman exists by virtue of a wage paid her in return for the possession of her person.'[8]

A radical change has now taken place in arguments about prostitution. Prostitution is unequivocally defended by contractarians. The terms of the defence again illustrate the ease with which some feminist arguments occupy the contractarian terrain. Many recent feminist discussions have argued that prostitution is merely a job of work and the prostitute is a worker, like any other wage labourer.

Prostitutes should, therefore, have trade union rights, and feminists often put forward proposals for workers' control of the industry. To argue in this fashion is not necessarily to defend prostitution – one can argue for trade union rights while calling for the abolition of capitalist wage labour – but, in the absence of argument to the contrary, the implicit suggestion in many feminist discussions is that, if the prostitute is merely one worker among others, the appropriate conclusion must be that there is nothing wrong with prostitution. At the very least, the argument implies that there is nothing wrong with prostitution that is not also wrong with other forms of work.

This conclusion depends on the same assumptions as the contractarian defence of prostitution. Contractarians argue that a prostitute contracts out a certain form of labour power for a given period in exchange for money. There is a free exchange between prostitute and customer, and the prostitution contract is exactly like – or is one example of – the employment contract. From the standpoint of contract, the prostitute is an owner of property in her person who contracts out part of that property in the market. A prostitute does not sell herself, as is commonly alleged, or even sell her sexual parts, but contracts out use of *sexual services*. There is no difference between a prostitute and any other worker or seller of services. The prostitute, like other 'individuals', stands in an external relation to the property in her person. Contract theory thus appears to offer a convincing reply to well-known criticisms of and objections to prostitution. For example, for contractarians, the objection that the prostitute is harmed or degraded by her trade misunderstands the nature of what is traded. The body and the self of the prostitute are not offered in the market; she can contract out use of her services without detriment to herself. Feminists who argue that the prostitute epitomizes women's subjection to men, can now also be told that such a view is a reflection of outmoded attitudes to sex, fostered by men's propaganda and the old world of women's subordination.[9] Contractarians even proclaim that 'people have a human right to engage in commercial sex.'[10]

Defenders of prostitution admit that some reforms are necessary in the industry as it exists at present in order for a properly free market in sexual services to operate. Nevertheless, they insist that 'sound prostitution' is possible (the phrase is Lars Ericcson's).[11] The idea of sound prostitution illustrates the dramatic shift that has taken place in arguments over prostitution. The new, contractarian defence is a universal argument. Prostitution is defended as a trade fit for anyone to enter. Freedom of contract and equality of opportunity require that the prostitution contract should be open to everyone and that any individual should be able to buy or sell services in the market. Anyone who needs a sexual service should have access to the market, whether male or female, young or old, black or white, ugly or beautiful, deformed or handicapped. Prostitution will then come into its own as a form of therapy – 'the role of a prostitute as a kind of therapist is a natural one'[12] – or as a form of social work or nursing (taking care 'of the intimate hygiene of disabled patients').[13] No one will be left out because of inappropriate attitudes to sex. The female hunchback as well as the male hunchback will be able to find a seller of services.[14]

A universal defence of prostitution entails that a prostitute can be of either sex. Women should have the same opportunity as men to buy sexual services in the market. 'The prostitute' is conventionally pictured as a woman, and, in fact, the majority of prostitutes are women. However, for contractarians, this is a merely contingent fact about prostitution; if sound prostitution were established, status, or the sexually ascriptive determination of the two parties (the man as a buyer and the woman as a seller of services), will give way to contract, to a relation between two 'individuals'. A moment's contemplation of the story of the sexual contract suggests that there is a major difficulty in any attempt to universalize prostitution. Reports occasionally appear that, in large cities like Sydney, a few male heterosexual prostitutes operate (the older figure of the gigolo belongs in a very different context), but they are still rare. Male homosexual prostitutes, on the other hand, are not uncommon, and, from the standpoint of contract, they are no different from female prostitutes. The story of the sexual contract reveals that there is good reason why 'the prostitute' is a female figure.

The story is about heterosexual relations – but it also tells of the creation of a fraternity and their contractual relations. Relations between members of the fraternity lie outside the scope of my present discussion, but, as Marilyn Frye has noted, 'there is a sort of "incest taboo" built into standard masculinity.'[15] The taboo is necessary; within the bonds of fraternity there is always a temptation to make the relation more than that of fellowship. But if members of the brotherhood extended their contracts, if they contracted for sexual use of bodies among themselves, the competition could shake the foundations of the original contract. From the standpoint of contract, the prohibition against this particular exercise of the law of male sex-right is purely arbitrary, and the fervour with which it is maintained by men themselves is incomprehensible. The story of the original creation of modern patriarchy helps lessen the incomprehension.

Contractarians who defend an ostensibly sexually neutral, universal, sound prostitution have not, as far as I am aware, taken the logic of their arguments to its conclusion. The final defeat of status and the victory of contract should lead to the elimination of marriage in favour of the economical arrangement of universal prostitution, in which all individuals enter into brief contracts of sexual use when required. The only legitimate restriction upon these contracts is the willingness of another party voluntarily to make services available; the sex of the party is irrelevant. Nor does age provide a determinate limitation, but at least one contractarian draws back from consistent anti-paternalism at this point.[16]

Any discussion of prostitution is replete with difficulties. Although contractarians now deny any political significance to the fact that (most) prostitutes are women, one major difficulty is that, in other discussions, prostitution is invariably seen as a problem about the prostitute, as a problem about *women*. The perception of prostitution as a problem about women is so deep-seated that any criticism of prostitution is likely to provoke the accusation that contemporary contractarians bring against feminists, that criticism of prostitution shows contempt for prostitutes. To argue that there is something wrong with prostitution does not necessarily imply any adverse judgement on the women who engage in the work. When socialists criticize capitalism and the employment contract they do not do so because they are contemptuous of workers, but because they are the workers' champions. Nevertheless, appeals to the idea of false consciousness, popular a few years ago, suggested that the problem about capitalism was a problem about workers. To reduce the question of capitalism to deficiencies in workers' consciousness diverts attention from the capitalist, the other participant in the employment contract. Similarly, the patriarchal assumption that prostitution is a problem about women ensures that the other participant in the prostitution contract escapes scrutiny. Once the story of the sexual contract has been told, prostitution can be seen as a problem about *men*. The problem of prostitution then becomes encapsulated in the question why men demand that women's bodies are sold as commodities in the capitalist market. The story of the sexual contract also supplies the answer; prostitution is part of the exercise of the law of male sex-right, one of the ways in which men are ensured access to women's bodies.

Feminist criticism of prostitution is now sometimes rejected on the grounds that prostitutes exploit or cheat their male clients; men are presented as the injured parties, not women. To be sure, prostitutes are often able to obtain control over the transaction with their customers by various stratagems and tricks of the trade. However, just as arguments about marriage that appeal to the example of benevolent husbands fail to distinguish between the relation of one particular husband and wife and the structure of the institution of marriage, so particular instances of the prostitution contract, in which a prostitute exploits a male customer, should be distinguished from prostitution as a social institution. Within the structure of the institution of prostitution, 'prostitutes' are subject to 'clients', just as 'wives' are subordinate to 'husbands' within the structure of marriage.

There is a huge literature on the subject of prostitution, including many official reports, and a good deal of attention has been devoted to the psychology and psychopathology of the prostitute. In 1969 a pamphlet widely read by probation officers in Britain talked of the 'proof that prostitution is a primitive and regressive manifestation'; and a Home Office report in 1974 stated that the 'way of life of a prostitute is so remarkably a rejection of the normal ways of society as to bear comparison with that of the drug addict'.[17] Much attention is also devoted to the reasons why women become prostitutes. The evidence suggests that there is nothing at all mysterious about why women enter the trade. *In extremis*, women can sell their bodies for food, like the poor unemployed young girl in nineteenth-century England who was asked the question, (by the author of *My Secret Life*), 'what do you let men fuck you for? Sausage-rolls?' She replied that she would comply for 'meat-pies and pastry too'.[18] More generally, prostitution enables women to make more money than they can earn at most other jobs open to women in patriarchal capitalism. In the 1870s and 1880s, the women campaigning against the Contagious Diseases Acts in the Ladies National Association in Britain argued that prostitution was the best-paid industry for poor

women. In 1980, empirical investigation showed that British prostitutes earned much more than most women workers, and were in
the middle- to high-wage band compared to male workers.[19] The
American film *Working Girls* illustrates the attraction of prostitution
for young, middle-class women with college degrees who want to
make relatively large sums of money in a hurry. Prostitutes also
refer to the degree of independence and flexibility that the work
allows, and to the relative ease with which prostitution can be
combined with housework and care of children. Drug addiction is
now also an important reason why women become prostitutes.

The reasons why women become prostitutes are fairly straightforward, but what counts as prostitution is less obvious. Most
discussions take for granted that the meaning of 'prostitution' is self-
evident; 'we seem to know pretty well what we mean by this term.'[20]
To draw the line between amateurs and women engaged in the profession in our society is not always easy, but very different activities
in widely differing cultures and historical periods are also lumped
together. One of the most persistent claims is that prostitution (like
patriarchy) is a universal feature of human social life, a claim
summed up in the cliché, 'the oldest profession'. The cliché is used
to refer to a wide range of cultural phenomena, from ancient times
to the present, all of which are called 'prostitution'. So, for example,
one contractarian defender of prostitution argues that 'commercial
prostitution in the modern sense' developed from ancient temple
prostitution.[21] The same social meaning is attributed to such
disparate activities as, say, temple prostitution in ancient Babylonia,
the sale of their bodies by destitute women for food for themselves
and their children, 'white slavery', the provision of field brothels for
troops, the proffering of women to white explorers, *maisons
d'abattages* or *malaya* prostitution in Nairobi.[22] That all these social
practices have the same significance as the prostitution contract of
patriarchal capitalism is not immediately self-evident. Indeed,
recent studies by feminist historians show that prostitution in the
contemporary sense – the form of prostitution that makes possible
the contractarian defence of 'sound' prostitution – is a distinct
cultural and historical phenomenon, which developed in Britain, the
United States and Australia around the end of the nineteenth and
beginning of the twentieth century.[23]

There is nothing universal about prostitutes as a discrete group of
wage labourers who specialize in a particular line of work, or about

prostitution as a specialized occupation or profession within the patriarchal capitalist division of labour. Until the latter part of the nineteenth century in all three countries, prostitutes were part of the casual labouring poor. Women in this class drifted in and out of prostitution as they drifted in and out of other forms of work. Prostitutes were not seen as a special class of women, nor were they isolated from other workers or working-class communities; there was no specialized 'profession' of prostitution. In Britain, for example, prostitution in the contemporary sense emerged from developments precipitated by the Contagious Diseases Acts (1864, 1866, 1869). Under the Acts, women in military towns could be identified as 'common prostitutes' by plain-clothes policemen, compulsorily subjected to gynaecological examination for venereal disease and, if infected, confined to a lock hospital. An enormous political campaign, in which women were very prominent, was waged for repeal of the Acts.

Rejecting the suggestion that public hygiene required regular inspection of soldiers and sailors, as well as women, for venereal disease, the Report of a Royal Commission into the Acts stated that 'there is no comparison to be made between prostitutes and the men who consort with them. With the one sex the offence is committed as a matter of gain; with the other it is an irregular indulgence of a natural impulse.'[24] Feminist campaigners such as Josephine Butler recognized that much more was at issue than the 'double standard' of sexual morality, the only morality compatible with the sexual contract. She argued that all women were implicated in the Acts, and they should not accept that safety and private respectability for most women depended on a 'slave class' of publicly available prostitutes. Butler wrote later to her sister that 'even if we lack the sympathy which makes us feel that the chains which bind our enslaved sisters are pressing on us also, we cannot escape the fact that we are one womanhood, *solidaire*, and that so long as they are bound, we cannot be wholly and truly free.'[25] For feminists who fought against the Acts, prostitution represented in the starkest form the sexual domination of women by men.

However, feminist questions were submerged in the social purity movement that developed in Britain in the 1880s and helped secure the passage of the Criminal Law Amendment Act in 1885 that gave the police greater summary jurisdiction over poor women. By the time that the Contagious Diseases Acts were repealed in 1886 the character of prostitution was already changing and the trade was being 'professionalized'. Women listed as common prostitutes under the Acts found it hard to have their names removed from the register, or, subsequently, to find other employment. The women had often rented rooms in boarding-house brothels, run by women with families to support who also took in other lodgers in addition to the prostitutes. The 1885 Act gave police powers to close the brothels, which were shut down systematically between 1890 and 1914, and powers against soliciting. The prostitutes turned to pimps for protection. Prostitution shifted from being female-controlled to male-controlled and, as Judith Walkowitz remarks, 'there now existed third parties with a strong interest in prolonging women's stay on the streets.'[26]

In New South Wales, Australia, the elimination of free-lance prostitution took a different path. Unlike many other British colonies, New South Wales did not enact legislation against contagious diseases, nor follow the 1885 Act. Legislation was introduced in 1908 aimed at soliciting, pimping and brothel-keeping and, according to Judith Allen, the aim of policing strategy was the abolition of the most visible aspects of prostitution. The result was that self-employed prostitutes could no longer operate; 'the work of the prostitute became structurally proletarianized.'[27] Prostitutes were forced to turn to organized criminal networks or to pimps employed by the same criminals. A similar consequence ensued from the large campaigns against prostitution in the Progressive Era in the United States. Ruth Rosen summarizes the changes, which included the shift of control of the trade 'from madams and prostitutes themselves to pimps and organized crime syndicates. . . . The prostitute would rarely work henceforth as a free agent. In addition, she faced increased brutality, not only from the police, but also from her new "employers".'[28] Once professionalized, prostitution developed into a major industry within patriarchal capitalism, with the same structure as other capitalist industries; prostitutes work in an occupation that is controlled by men. For example, in Birmingham, most prostitutes have ponces (pimps) and the 'saunas' and other such establishments are usually owned or managed by men. Few prostitutes become managers or 'establish some mutually beneficial business enterprise with other women'.[29]

The claim that prostitution is a universal feature of human society relies not only on the cliché of 'the oldest profession' but also on the widely held assumption that prostitution originates in men's natural sexual urge. There is a universal, natural (masculine) impulse that, it is assumed, requires, and will always require, the outlet provided by prostitution. Now that arguments that extra-marital sex is immoral have lost their social force, defenders of prostitution often present prostitution as one example of 'sex without love', as an example of the satisfaction of natural appetites.[30] The argument, however, is a *non sequitur.* Defenders of sex without love and advocates of what once was called free love, always supposed that the relationship was based on mutual sexual attraction between a man and woman and involved mutual physical satisfaction. Free love and prostitution are poles apart. Prostitution is the use of a woman's body by a man for his own satisfaction. There is no desire or satisfaction on the part of the prostitute. Prostitution is not mutual, pleasurable exchange of the use of bodies, but the unilateral use of a woman's body by a man in exchange for money. That the institution of prostitution can be presented as a natural extension of a human impulse, and that 'sex without love' can be equated with the sale of women's bodies in the capitalist market, is possible only because an important question is begged: why do men demand that satisfaction of a natural appetite must take the form of public access to women's bodies in the capitalist market in exchange for money?

In arguments that prostitution is merely one expression of a natural appetite, the comparison is invariably made between prostitution and the provision of food. To claim that 'we all need food, so food should be available to us. . . . And since our sexual desires are just as basic, natural, and compelling as our appetite for food, this also holds for them', is neither an argument for prostitution nor for any form of sexual relations.[31] Without a minimum of food (or water, or shelter) people die, but to my knowledge no one has ever died for want of an outlet for their sexual appetites. There is also one fundamental difference between the human need for food and the need for sex. Sustenance is sometimes unavailable but everyone has the means to satisfy sexual appetites to hand. There is no natural necessity to engage in sexual *relations* to assuage sexual pangs. Of course, there may be cultural inhibition against use of this means, but what counts as food is also culturally variable. In no society does the form of food production and consumption, or the form of relations between the sexes, follow directly, without cultural mediation, from the natural fact that all humans feel hunger and sexual impulses.

The consequences of sexual inhibitions and prohibitions are likely to be less disastrous than prohibitions on what counts as food.

Another difficulty in discussing prostitution in late twentieth-century patriarchy is that it is also usually assumed to be obvious which activities fall under the heading of 'prostitution'. Prostitution is now part of an international sex industry that includes mass-marketing of pornographic books and films, widespread supply of strip-clubs, peep-shows and the like and marketing of sex-tours for men to poor Third World countries. The general display of women's bodies and sexual parts, either in representation or as live bodies, is central to the sex industry and continually reminds men – and women – that men exercise the law of male sex-right, that they have patriarchal right of access to women's bodies. The story of the original sexual contract helps sort out which of the plethora of activities in the sex industry are appropriately called 'prostitution'. For example, satisfaction of a mere natural appetite does not require a man to have access to a woman's body; what then, is the significance of the fact that 15 to 25 per cent of the customers of the Birmingham prostitutes demand what is known in the trade as 'hand relief'?[32]

The story of the sexual contract suggests that the latter demand is part of the construction of what it means to be a man, part of the contemporary expression of masculine sexuality. The satisfaction of men's natural sexual urges must be achieved through access to a woman, even if her body is not directly used sexually. Whether or nor any man is able and willing to find release in other ways, he can exhibit his masculinity by contracting for use of a woman's body. The prostitution contract is another example of an actual 'original' sexual contract. The exemplary display of masculinity is to engage in 'the sex act'. (Hence, sale of men's bodies for homosexual use does not have the same social meaning.) The institution of prostitution ensures that men can buy 'the sex act' and so exercise their patriarchal right. The activities that, above all else, can appropriately be called prostitution are 'the sex act', and associated activities such as 'hand relief' and oral sex (fellatio), for which there is now a very large demand.[33] Some of the most prevalent confusions in discussions of prostitution might be avoided if other activities were seen as part of the wider sex industry. The market includes a vigorous demand for 'bondage and discipline' or fantasy slave contracts. The mass commercial replication of the most potent relations and symbols of domination is a testament to the power and genius of contract, which proclaims that a contract of subordination is (sexual) freedom.

Since the 1970s prostitutes have been organizing in the United States, Britain and Australia – and the International Committee for Prostitutes' Rights held the second World Whores' Congress in 1986 – to improve their working conditions, to combat hostility and violence and to press for the decriminalization of prostitution. In short, prostitutes are endeavouring to be acknowledged as workers in an occupation that lacks trade union safeguards and protection. The prostitute is a woman and thus shares with all women in paid employment an uncertain status as a 'worker'. But the prostitute is not quite like other women workers; her status is even more uncertain. Prostitution is seen as different from other forms of women's work and, especially at the lower end of the market, prostitutes are set apart from other women workers (almost everyone can picture 'the prostitute' soliciting in the street, with her typical costume, stance and heart of gold). Contractarian defences of prostitution attribute the lack of acceptance of the prostitute as a worker, or purveyor of services, to the hypocrisy and distorted attitudes surrounding sexual activity. To be sure, hypocrisy is rife and irrational attitudes abound around the question of prostitution, as George Bernard Shaw's *Mrs. Warren's Profession* laid bare some time ago. However, reference to hypocrisy hardly seems to capture the emotions with which some men regard prostitutes.

Prostitutes are murdered because they are seen as fonts of pollution and their murderer's names can become household words, like Jack the Ripper. Less dramatically, prostitutes run considerable risk of physical injury every day from their male customers, especially if they work on the streets. Eileen McLeod found that, in Birmingham, 'almost without exception, prostitutes I have had contact with have experienced some form of serious physical violence from their clients.'[34] Prostitutes are not, of course, the only workers who face physical hazards in their work. Little publicity is given to the large numbers of workers killed or injured each year in the workplace through lack of, or inadequate, or unenforced safety precautions, or through genuine accidents. These injuries, though, do not occur because the worker is a *woman*. Contractarians are not alone in denying significance to the fact that prostitutes are women. Apart from some feminist analyses, it is hard to find discussions that acknowledge that prostitution is part of the patriarchal structure of civil society. The Left and Right, as well as some feminists, share the assumption that the prostitute's work is of exactly the same kind as any other paid employment. The prostitute merely works in a different profession and offers a different service (form of labour power) from that of a miner or electrician, secretary or assembler of electronic goods. Not surprisingly, criticism of prostitution is then usually couched in economic terms. For example, the argument that prostitutes are forced by economic necessity to enter the trade has been heard for a very long time. The conditions of entry into the prostitution contract have received as much attention as entry into the employment or marriage contracts, and involuntary entry is often presented as the problem about prostitution. Thus, Alison Jaggar has stated that 'it is the economic coercion underlying prostitution, . . . that provides the basic feminist objection to prostitution.'[35]

Another common argument, now made by the religious Right as well as by the Left, is that what is wrong with prostitution is that, once a woman has entered the trade, she is exploited and degraded like many other workers under capitalism. Once again, the question of subordination is ignored. In arguments about economic coercion and exploitation the comparison is often turned round; instead of prostitutes being seen as exploited workers, workers are held to be in the same position as prostitutes. Marxist critics of prostitution take their lead from Marx's statement that 'prostitution is only a *specific* expression of the *general* prostitution of the *laborer.*' Prostitution then represents the economic coercion, exploitation and alienation of wage labour. As one critic has stated, 'prostitution is the incarnation of the degradation of the modern citizen as producer.'[37] The prostitution contract is not merely one example of the employment contract; rather, the employment contract becomes a contract of prostitution. The figure of the prostitute can, therefore, symbolize everything that is wrong with wage labour.

To see prostitutes as epitomizing exploitation under capitalism, and to represent the worker by the figure of the prostitute, is not without irony. 'The worker' is masculine – yet his degradation is symbolized by a female emblem, and patriarchal capitalism is pictured as a system of universal prostitution. The fact that the prostitute seems to be such an obvious symbol of the degradation of wage labour, raises the suspicion that what she sells is not quite the same as the labour power contracted out by other workers. If prostitution is work in exactly the same sense as any other paid employment, then the present status of the prostitute can only be attributed, as contractarians insist, to legal prohibition, hypocrisy and outdated ideas about sex. The story of the sexual contract provides another explanation for the difference between prostitution and other paid employment in which women predominate. The prostitution contract is a contract with a woman and, therefore, cannot be the same as the employment contract, a contract between men. Even though the prostitution contract is sealed in the capitalist market, it still differs in some significant respects from the employment contract. For example, a worker always enters into an employment contract with a capitalist. If a prostitute were merely another worker the prostitution contract, too, would always involve a capitalist; yet very frequently the man who enters into the contract is a worker.

Supposing, the objection might be raised, that the prostitute works in a 'massage parlour'. She will then be a paid employee and have entered into an employment contract. True; but the prostitution contract is not an employment contract. The prostitution contract is entered into with the male customer, not with an employer. The prostitute may or may not be a paid employee (worker); some prostitutes are 'more adequately described as small-scale private entrepreneurs'.[38] The difference is, however, irrelevant to the question of how prostitution is to be characterized; is it free work and a free exchange, or exploitation, or a specific kind of subordination? Whether the prostitute is a worker or petty entrepreneur she must be seen as contracting out labour power or services if the prostitution contract is also to be seen as an employment contract. From the standpoint of contract, the employment contract is infinitely elastic, stretching from the lifetime of the civil slave to the brief period of the prostitution contract in a brothel for troops or immigrant workers. No matter whether the prostitute is an exploited or free worker or a petty entrepreneur, labour power or services are assumed to be contracted out. As Ericcson asserts, a prostitute must necessarily sell 'not her body or vagina, but sexual *services*. If she actually did sell herself she would no longer be a prostitute but a sexual slave'.[39]

More accurately, she would resemble a slave in something of the same fashion that a worker, a wage slave, resembles a slave. Labour power is a political fiction. The capitalist does not and cannot contract to use the proletarian's services or labour power. The employment contract gives the employer right of command over the use of the worker's labour, that is to say, over the self, person and body of the worker during the period set down in the employment contract. Similarly, the services of the prostitute cannot be provided unless she is present; property in the person, unlike material property, cannot be separated from its owner. The 'john', the 'punter', the man who contracts to use the services of the prostitute, like the employer, gains command over the use of her person and body for the duration of the prostitution contract – but at this point the comparison between the wage slave and the prostitute, the employment contract and the prostitution contract, breaks down.

The capitalist has no intrinsic interest in the body and self of the worker, or, at least, not the same kind of interest as the man who enters into the prostitution contract. The employer is primarily interested in the commodities produced by the worker; that is to say, in profits. The peculiar character of the relation between the owner of labour power and his property means that the employer must organize (embodied) workers, and compel or induce them to labour, in order to produce commodities with his machinery and other means of production. But the employer can and often does replace the worker with machines or, in the 1980s, robots and other computerized machines. Indeed, employers prefer machines to workers because machines are like absolutely faithful slaves; they cannot be insubordinate, resist the employer's commands or combine together in trades unions or revolutionary associations. On the other hand, if the employer replaces all his workers by machines, he becomes merely a proprietor. The employer has an interest in workers as selves in that, without them, he ceases to be a master and loses the enjoyment of command over subordinates.

In contrast to employers, the men who enter into the prostitution contract have only one interest; the prostitute and her body. A market exists for substitutes for women's bodies in the form of inflatable dolls, but, unlike the machines that replace the worker, the dolls are advertised as 'lifelike'. The dolls are a literal substitute for women, not a functional substitute like the machine installed instead of the worker. Even a plastic substitute for a woman can give a man the sensation of being a patriarchal master. In prostitution, the body of the woman, and sexual access to that body, is the subject of the contract. To have bodies for sale in the market, as bodies, looks very like slavery. To symbolize wage slavery by the figure of the prostitute rather than that of the masculine worker is thus not entirely inappropriate. But prostitution differs from wage slavery. No form of labour power can be separated from the body, but only through the prostitution contract does the buyer obtain unilateral right of direct sexual use of a woman's body.

A contractarian might respond at this point that far too much weight is being placed on the body. Even if reference is made to the body rather than (as it should be) to services, moral freedom can be retained when use of the body, or part of the body, is being contracted out. The self or person is not identical to the body, so that the self is not injured if property in the body is used. David Richards has taken issue with Kant, and with Marxists and feminists whom he assumes are following Kant, on this question. Kant condemned prostitution as a *pactum turpe*; to contract out a bodily part for sexual use is to turn oneself into property, a *res*, because of the 'inseparable unity of the members of a Person'. [40] Kant writes that man cannot dispose of himself as he wills:

> He is not his own property; to say that he is would be self-contradictory; for in so far as he is a person he is a Subject in whom the ownership of things can be vested, and if he were his own property, he would be a thing over which he could have ownership . . . it is impossible to be a person and a thing, the proprietor and the property. [41]

Richards argues that Kant's condemnation of prostitution is inconsistent with his general view of autonomy. I shall not attempt to ascertain whether it is more inconsistent than his view of wage labour or, in particular, the marriage contract, since Richards fails to mention that Kant upholds patriarchal right and so has to deny that women are persons and, hence, autonomous. Kant's inconsistency is that he wants to confine fulfillment of the terms of the sexual contract to conjugal relations; women's bodies may be used as property by men as husbands, but women must not sell this commodity in the market and be paid for sexual use. Richards claims that to argue against prostitution is arbitrarily to limit sexual freedom. The embodiment of the self places no constraints on an individual's moral autonomy. Richards' argument is based on a version of the disembodied, rational entities who inhabit (one aspect of) Kant's contract theory and Rawls' original position. Autonomy is merely 'persons' self-critical capacities to assess their present wants and lives. . . . Autonomy occurs in a certain body, occasioning a person self-critically to take into account that body and its capacities in deciding on the form of his or her life'.[42] In short, freedom is the unconstrained capacity of an owner (rational entity), externally related to property in its person (body), to judge how to contract out that property.

Human beings certainly possess the capacity for critical self-reflection – and that capacity can be understood as if it encompassed nothing more than individual rational calculation of how property can be used to the maximum advantage. If a complex, multifaceted capacity could not be reduced to this bleak, culturally and historically specific achievement, patriarchal civil society could not have developed. Richards' 'autonomy' was summed up more economically in Richard Lovelace's lines:

Stone walls do not a prison make,
Nor iron bars a cage.

Nor is this very partial and socially tangential (though in some circumstances, heroic) notion of moral – or spiritual – freedom at issue in prostitution or other forms of civil subordination. Civil subordination is a *political* problem not a matter of morality, although moral issues are involved. To try to answer the question of what is wrong with prostitution is to engage in argument about political right in the form of patriarchal right, or the law of male sex-right. Subordinates of all kinds exercise their capacity for critical self-reflection every day – that is why masters are thwarted, frustrated and, sometimes, overthrown. But unless masters are overthrown, unless subordinates engage in political action, no amount of critical reflection will end their subjection and bring them freedom.

To grant that human embodiment is of more than merely contingent or incidental significance for freedom and subordination, may not seem sufficient to distinguish the profession of prostitution from some other forms of work, or sufficient to establish that there is something wrong with prostitution that is not also wrong with wage labour. A prostitute's body is for sale in the market, but there are also other professions in which bodies are up for sale and in which employers have an intrinsic interest in their workers' bodies. For example, now that sport is part of patriarchal capitalism, the bodies of professional sportsmen and sportswomen are also available to be contracted out. Orlando Patterson discusses the case of baseball in the United States where, until 1975, players could be bought and sold like any material property at the will and for the profit of the owners of their teams. Patterson emphasizes that the baseball players were not and are not slaves, they are juridically free citizens, and they now have some voice in their disposition – but their bodies are still bought and sold. Patterson comments that employers do not now demand that workers

> stand naked on an auction block being prodded and inspected by the employers and their physicians. But when an employer requires a medical certificate from a worker or professional athlete before hiring him, he is not only soliciting the same kind of information as a slavemaster inspecting his latest cargo of bodies, he is betraying the inherent absurdity of the distinction between 'raw bodies' and the services produced by such bodies. [43]

However, there is a difference in the uses to which bodies are put when they are sold. Owners of baseball teams have command over the use of their players' bodies, but the bodies are not directly used sexually by those who have contracted for them.

There is an integral relationship between the body and self. The body and the self are not identical, but selves are inseparable from bodies. The idea of property in the person has the merit of drawing attention to the importance of the body in social relations. Civil mastery, like the mastery of the slave-owner, is not exercised over mere biological entities that can be used like material (animal) property, nor exercised over purely rational entities. Masters are not interested in the disembodied fiction of labour power or services. They contract for the use of human embodied selves. Precisely because subordinates are embodied selves they can perform the required labour, be subject to discipline, give the recognition and offer the faithful service that makes a man a master. Human bodies and selves are also sexually differentiated, the self is a masculine or feminine self. One illustration of the integral connection between the body and the self is the widespread use of vulgar terms for women's sexual organs to refer to women themselves, or the use of a slang term for the penis to make disparaging reference to men.

Masculinity and femininity are sexual identities; the self is not completely subsumed in its sexuality, but identity is inseparable from the sexual construction of the self. In modern patriarchy, sale of women's bodies in the capitalist market involves sale of a self in a different manner, and in a more profound sense, than sale of the body of a male baseball player or sale of command over the use of the labour (body) of a wage slave. The story of the sexual contract reveals that the patriarchal construction of the difference between masculinity and femininity is the political difference between freedom and subjection, and that sexual mastery is the major means through which men affirm their manhood. When a man enters into the prostitution contract he is not interested in sexually indifferent, disembodied services; he contracts to buy sexual use of a *woman* for a given period. Why else are men willing to enter the market and pay for 'hand relief'? Of course, men can also affirm their masculinity in other ways, but, in relations between the sexes, unequivocal affirmation is obtained by engaging in 'the sex act'. Womanhood, too, is confirmed in sexual activity, and when a prostitute contracts out use of her body she is thus selling *herself* in a very real sense. Women's selves are involved in prostitution in a different manner from the involvement of the self in other occupations. Workers of all kinds may be more or less 'bound up in their work', but the integral connection between sexuality and sense of the self means that, for self-protection, a prostitute must distance herself from her sexual use.

Women engaged in the trade have developed a variety of distancing strategies, or a professional approach, in dealing with their clients. Such distancing creates a problem for men, a problem that can be seen as another variant on the contradiction of mastery and slavery. The prostitution contract enables men to constitute themselves as civil masters for a time, and, like other masters, they wish to obtain acknowledgment of their status. Eileen McLeod talked to clients as well as prostitutes in Birmingham and, noting that her findings are in keeping with similar investigations in Britain and the United States, she states that 'nearly all the men I interviewed complained about the emotional coldness and mercenary approach of many prostitutes they had had contact with.'[44] A master requires a service, but he also requires that the service is delivered by a person, a self, not merely a piece of (disembodied) property. John Stuart Mill remarked of the subordination of wives that, 'their masters require something more from them than actual service. Men do not want solely the obedience of women, they want their sentiments. All men, except the most brutish, desire to have, not a forced slave but a willing one, not a slave merely, but a favourite.'[45]

An employer or a husband can more easily obtain faithful service and acknowledgment of his mastery than a man who enters into the prostitution contract. The civil slave contract and employment and marriage contracts create long-term relationships of subordination. The prostitution contract is of short duration and the client is not concerned with daily problems of the extraction of labour power. The prostitution contract is, one might say, a contract of specific performance, rather than open-ended like the employment contract and, in some of its aspects, the marriage contract. There are also other differences between the employment and prostitution contracts. For example, the prostitute is always at a singular disadvantage in the 'exchange'. The client makes direct use of the prostitute's body and there are no 'objective' criteria through which to judge whether the service has been satisfactorily performed. Trades unions bargain over pay and conditions for workers, and the products of their labours are 'quality controlled'. Prostitutes, in contrast, can always be refused payment by men who claim (and who can gainsay their subjective assessment?) that their demands have not been met.[46]

The character of the employment contract also provides scope for mastery to be recognized in numerous subtle ways as well as in an open, direct fashion. The worker is masculine, and men must mutually acknowledge their civil equality and fraternity (or the social contract cannot be upheld) at the same time as they create relations of subordination. The brief duration of the prostitution contract gives less room for subtlety; but, then, perhaps it is not so necessary. There need be no such ambiguities in relations between men and women, least of all when a man has bought a woman's body for his use as if it were like any other commodity. In such a context, 'the sex act' itself provides acknowledgment of patriarchal right. When women's bodies are on sale as commodities in the capitalist market, the terms of the original contract cannot be forgotten; the law of male sex-right is publicly affirmed, and men gain public acknowledgment as women's sexual masters – that is what is wrong with prostitution.

Another difference between the prostitution contract and the other contracts with which I am concerned is also worth noting. I have argued that contracts about property in persons take the form of an exchange of obedience for protection. A civil slave and wives (in principle) receive lifelong protection, the family wage includes protection and the organizational complexities of extracting labour power for use in capitalist production have led to provision of protection over and above the wage. But where is the protection in the prostitution contract? The pimp stands outside the contract between client and prostitute, just as the state stands outside, but regulates and enforces, the marriage and employment contracts. The short-term prostitution contract cannot include the protection available in long-term relations. In this respect, the prostitution contract mirrors the contractarian ideal. The individual as owner will never commit himself far into the future; to do so is to give himself up as hostage to the self-interest of other individuals. The individual will make simultaneous exchanges, an impossible exchange if use is to be made of property in persons. The exchange of money for use of a woman's body comes as close as is feasible in actual contracts to a simultaneous exchange. For Marx, prostitution was a metaphor for wage labour. The more appropriate analogy is also more amusing. The contractarian idea of universal sale of property (services), is a vision of unimpeded mutual use or universal prostitution.

The feminist argument that prostitutes are workers in exactly the same sense as other wage labourers, and the contractarian defence of prostitution, both depend on the assumption that women are 'individuals', with full ownership of the property in their persons. Women are still prohibited from contracting out their property in their sexual parts in some legal jurisdictions in the three countries with which I am concerned. Nevertheless, while I was completing this chapter, a judge in New Jersey, in the leading case of Baby M, ruled that women could contract out another piece of property, their wombs, and that they must be held to this contract. This contract of so-called surrogate motherhood is new, and it provides a dramatic example of the contradictions surrounding women and contract. The surrogacy contract also indicates that a further transformation of modern patriarchy may be underway. Father-right is reappearing in a new, contractual form.

My argument, as I have emphasized, is not about women as mothers, but the significantly named 'surrogate' motherhood has little to do with motherhood as generally understood. The political implications of the surrogacy contract can only be appreciated when surrogacy is seen as another provision in the sexual contract, as a new form of access to and use of women's bodies by men. A 'surrogate' mother contracts to be artificially inseminated with the sperm of a man (usually the sperm belongs to a husband whose wife is infertile), to bear a child, and to relinquish the child to the genetic father. In exchange for use of her services the 'surrogate' receives monetary payment; the market rate at present appears to be US$10,000.

Artificial insemination is far from new – the first human pregnancy was achieved by this means in 1799 – but 'surrogate' motherhood is frequently and confusingly discussed together with a range of developments, such as *in vitro* fertilization, which have resulted from new technologies. [47] (*In vitro* fertilization is now sold on the capitalist market; in the United States the market is estimated at $30–40 million per year, even though the success rate of the technology is very low). New technology also makes other forms of 'surrogacy' possible. For instance, the ovum and sperm of a married couple may be joined and grown *in vitro*, and the embryo then inserted into the uterus of a 'surrogate'. In this case, the baby is the genetic offspring of husband and wife and such a surrogacy contract differs significantly from a contract involving artificial insemination. I shall concentrate on the latter to draw out a point about paternity and patriarchy, but technological developments and *in vitro* surrogacy also raise some general, profoundly important issues about contract and use of women's bodies.

In mid-1987, there is no legal consensus about the legitimacy or status of surrogacy contracts. In the United States, the judgement in the case of Baby M – which arose from a dispute over a contract when the 'surrogate' mother refused to relinquish the baby – unequivocally confirmed the binding legal status of such contracts (the case is currently under appeal to the New Jersey Supreme Court). Long before this, however, surrogacy agencies had been set up and press reports state that some 600 contracts have been made, at least one woman having entered and fulfilled two contracts. The agencies are profitable; one is reported to have made $600,000 gross in 1986. In Australia, only Victoria has legislated on the question and has prohibited commercial surrogacy and denied legal enforcement to informal arrangements. In Britain, the 1985 Surrogacy Arrangements Act has effectively prohibited commercial surrogacy contracts. For third parties to benefit from a surrogacy contract is a criminal offence, and to pay a 'surrogate' mother or for her to receive payment may be an offence under the Adoption Act. Non-commercial surrogacy arrangements are not illegal.[48]

At this point, the old argument about prostitution and legal prostitution (marriage) immediately presents itself. Is not a contract in which money is exchanged for services more honest about the position of the woman involved than marriage or informal surrogacy? The Report of the Waller Committee which led to the Victorian legislation (and which considered 'surrogate' motherhood in the context of *in vitro* fertilization) recommended that neither commercial nor non-commercial surrogacy should form part of *in vitro* programmes.[49] But is a *gift* of the 'surrogate's' services more acceptable than an exchange of her services for money? The British legislation clearly implies that this is the case. To see surrogacy as a gift relation is, however, to beg the question of to whom it is that the service is rendered. Is surrogacy an example of one woman donating a service to another woman, or is it an example of a woman being inseminated with the sperm of a man to bear his child in exchange for money? Prostitution is often defended as a type of social work or therapy, and, similarly, 'surrogate' motherhood is defended as a service offered in the market from compassion for the plight of infertile women. To ask questions about the surrogacy contract is not to deny that women who enter the surrogacy contract may feel compassion for infertile women, nor to deny that women can be made miserable by infertility (although in current debates it is frequently forgotten, or even implicitly ruled out, that infertile women, and their husbands, can come to terms with the condition and lead satisfying lives). As in so many discussions of prostitution, the argument from compassion assumes that any problem about 'surrogate' motherhood is a problem about women, and about the supply of a service. The character of men's participation in the surrogacy contract and the character of the demand for this service is treated as unproblematic.

In the controversy over 'surrogate' motherhood, the comparison with prostitution is often made. As the eminent historian, Lawrence Stone, commented about the case of Baby M, 'contracts should be fulfilled. This is a rather bizarre contract, I agree. You're renting out your body. But one expects a prostitute to fulfill a contract'.[50] Most of the arguments used to defend or condemn prostitution have reappeared in the controversy over 'surrogate' motherhood. Obviously, surrogacy contracts raise questions about the conditions of entry into the contract and economic coercion. The sexual division of labour in patriarchal capitalism and the 'feminization of poverty' ensure that a surrogacy contract will appear financially attractive to working-class women, although the payment is very meagre for the time involved and nature of the service. Class questions are also clearly raised. In the Baby M case, for instance, the 'surrogate' mother dropped out of high school and was married aged sixteen to a man who is now a sanitation worker earning $28,000 per year. The income of the man who entered into the contract, together with that of his wife, both professionals with doctoral degrees, is about $91,500 per year.[51] However, emphasis on class inequality and economic coercion to enter the contract, draws attention away from the question of what exactly is being contracted for and how the surrogacy contract resembles or differs from other contracts about property in the person.

In Victoria, 'surrogate' motherhood was rejected on the grounds that 'arrangements where fees are paid are, in reality, agreements for the purchase of a child, and should not be countenanced. . . The buying and selling of children has been condemned and proscribed for generations. It should not be allowed to reappear.'[52] Adoption is strictly regulated to avoid poor women – or, at least, poor white women – being offered incentives to sell their babies. The problem with this line of argument is not that common sense is a poor guide here, but that references to baby-selling completely fail to meet the defence of surrogacy contracts derived from contract theory. From the standpoint of contract, talk of baby-selling reveals that surrogacy is misunderstood in exactly the same way that prostitution is misunderstood. A prostitute does not sell her body, she sells sexual services. In the surrogacy contract there is no question of a baby being sold, merely a service.

The qualifier 'surrogate' indicates that the point of the contract is to render motherhood irrelevant and to deny that the 'surrogate' is a mother. A woman who enters a surrogacy contract is not being paid for (bearing) a child; to make a contract of that kind *would* be tantamount to baby-selling. The 'surrogate' mother is receiving payment in return for entering into a contract which enables a man to make use of her services. In this case the contract is for use of the property a woman owns in her uterus.

From the standpoint of contract, the fact that provision of a service involves motherhood is purely incidental. The womb has no special status as property. A woman could just as well contract out use of a different piece of property in her person. Furthermore, the fact that disposition of a baby is at issue is of no special significance. Contracts for the use of other forms of service, notably that provided through the employment contract, also result in property over which one party alone has jurisdiction. The worker has no claim to the commodities produced through use of his labour; they belong to the capitalist. In a similar fashion, the baby that is produced through use of a 'surrogate' mother's services is the property of the man who contracts to use the service. The judge in the case of Baby M made this point very clearly. In his decision he stated that:

> the money to be paid to the surrogate is not being paid for the surrender of the child to the father. . . . The biological father pays the surrogate for her willingness to be impregnated and carry his child to term. At birth, the father does not purchase the child. It is his own biologically genetically related child. He cannot purchase what is already his.[53]

Appeal is often made in discussions of 'surrogate' motherhood to two biblical precedents in the book of *Genesis*. In the first story, Sarai, unable to have a child, says to her husband Abram, 'I pray thee, go in unto my maid; it may be that I obtain children by her.' Then Sarai 'took Hagar her maid the Egyptian, . . . and gave her to her husband Abram to be his wife'. In the second story, Rachel, another infertile wife, gives Jacob 'Bilhah her handmaid to wife: and Jacob went in unto her'.[54] In the biblical stories, the 'surrogate' mother is a maid, a servant, a subordinate – and she is the *wife*'s servant. The stories will thus seem to reinforce an objection that will be made to my characterization of 'surrogate' motherhood as a contract in which the services of the 'surrogate' mother are used by a man. On the contrary, the objection will be pressed, the biblical stories show that the surrogacy contract has been misrepresented; the service is used by women. The contract is made by a husband and a wife for use of the 'surrogate's' services. The man's infertile wife, not the man himself, is the true user of the service. She is the mother for whom the 'surrogate's' services are contracted. A woman enters a surrogacy contract with another woman (although male sperm is needed for insemination).

Ironies never cease in the matter of women and contract. After the long history of exclusion of women from contract, the surrogacy contract is presented as a woman's contract; women are now seen as the parties to the contract. The question of men's demand for the service is thus obscured, together with the character of the 'exchange' that takes place. The question of who exactly uses the services of a 'surrogate' mother is confused by the strong social pressures in Britain, Australia and the United States to restrict surrogacy contracts (and access to the new reproductive technologies) to married couples. But there is no need at all for a wife to be involved. The comparison with prostitution is revealing here (though not quite in the way that is always intended). From the standpoint of contract, the demand for use of prostitutes is sexually indifferent, and so is the demand for 'surrogate' motherhood; men can contract for the use of a 'surrogate' without the mediation of another woman. All that is taking place is that one individual is contracting to use another's property. A wife is superfluous to the contract (though, socially, her presence legitimizes the transaction). A wife may be a formal party to the surrogacy contract but the substance of her position is quite different from that of her husband. A wife contributes no property to the contract; she merely awaits its outcome.

The exchange in the surrogacy contract is between part of the property of a man, namely his sperm or seed, and part of the property of the 'surrogate', her uterus. A surrogacy contract differs from a prostitution contract in that a man does not make direct sexual use of a woman's body; rather, his use is indirect via artificial insemination. The man's seed, to use Locke's language, is mixed with the woman's uterus, and, if she performs her service faithfully, he can claim the property thereby produced as his own. Locke's language brings out the way in which contract is now taking a new turn. Contract transformed classic into modern patriarchy, but, with the invention of the surrogacy contract, one aspect of classic patriarchy has returned. If a woman's uterus is nothing more than a piece of property to which she is externally related, she is analogous to Sir Robert Filmer's empty vessel. But now the empty vessel can be contracted out for use by a man who fills it with his seed and, in another example of masculine creativity, thereby creates a new piece of property. Perhaps the man who enters into the surrogacy contract might be compared to the employer who, in contract doctrine, is the creative principle who transforms labour power into commodities. But he can now also do much more; in a spectacular twist of the patriarchal screw, the surrogacy contract enables a man to present his wife with the ultimate gift – a child.

Labour power is a political fiction, but the service performed by the 'surrogate' mother is a greater fiction. The worker contracts out right of command over the use of his body, and the prostitute contracts out right of direct sexual use of her body. The selves of the worker and the prostitute are, in their different ways, both put out for hire. The self of the 'surrogate' mother is at stake in a more profound sense still. The 'surrogate' mother contracts out right over the unique physiological, emotional and creative capacity of her body, that is to say, of herself as a woman. For nine months she has the most intimate possible relation with another developing being; the being is part of herself. The baby, once born, is a separate being, but the mother's relation to her infant is qualitatively different from that of workers to the other products that ensue from contracts about the property in their persons. The example of a smoothly completed surrogacy contract and an unconcerned 'surrogate' mother, like examples of husbands who have renounced patriarchal right or prostitutes who exploit clients, reveals little about the *institution* of marriage, prostitution, or 'surrogate' motherhood. The surrogacy contract is another medium through which patriarchal subordination is secured. In one respect, a surrogacy contract is rather like an employment contract. The employer obtains right of command over the use of the bodies of workers in order, unilaterally, to have power over the process through which his commodities are produced. There is no reason why a surrogacy contract should not enable a man to ensure that the service for which he has contracted is faithfully performed by restricting the use to which the 'surrogate' may put her body until the service is fulfilled.

That women are willing to be parties to contracts that constitute other women as patriarchal subordinates is not surprising. Women are still treated as less than women if we do not have children. Contract doctrine entails that there are no limits to the uses that may legitimately be made of property in persons, providing only that access to use is established through contract. Why, then, in a period when contract holds sway, should childless women not take advantage of this new contract? Using the services of a 'surrogate' mother to provide an infertile married couple with a child is often compared to adoption, previously their only legitimate recourse if they were not prepared to accept their condition, but there is a crucial difference between the two practices. An adopting couple are not, except in rare circumstances, genetically related to the child. But the child of the 'surrogate' is also the child of the husband. The wife is more accurately called the surrogate mother, just as, in cases of adoption, the couple are surrogate mother and father. The wife will, of course, like adopting parents, bring up the child 'as if it were her own' but, irrespective of the happiness of the marriage and how well the child flourishes and *is* their own, in the last analysis, the child is the father's.

The story of the original contract tells of the political defeat of the father and how his sons, the brothers, establish a specifically modern non-paternal form of patriarchy. The emergence of 'surrogate' motherhood suggests that contract is helping to bring about another transformation. Men are now beginning to exert patriarchal right as paternal right again, but in new forms. The logic of contract as exhibited in 'surrogate' motherhood shows very starkly how extension of the standing of 'individual' to women can reinforce and transform patriarchy as well as challenge patriarchal institutions. To extend to women the masculine conception of the individual as owner, and the conception of freedom as the capacity to do what you will with your own, is to sweep away any intrinsic relation between the female owner, her body and reproductive capacities. She stands to her property in exactly the same external relation as the male owner stands to his labour power or sperm; there is nothing distinctive about womanhood.

From the standpoint of contract, not only is sexual difference irrelevant to sexual relations, but sexual difference becomes irelevant to physical reproduction. The former status of 'mother' and 'father' is thus rendered inoperative by contract and must be replaced by the (ostensibly sex-neutral) 'parent'. At least in the case of the surrogacy contract, the term 'parent' is far from sexually indifferent. The shade of Sir Robert Filmer hangs over 'surrogate' motherhood. In classic patriarchalism, the father is *the* parent. When the property of the 'surrogate' mother, her empty vessel, is filled with the seed of the man who has contracted with her, he, too, becomes the parent, the creative force that brings new life (property) into the world. Men have denied significance to women's unique bodily capacity, have appropriated it and transmuted it into masculine political genesis. The story of the social contract is the greatest story of men giving political birth, but, with the surrogacy contract, modern patriarchy has taken a new turn. Thanks to the power of the creative political medium of contract, men can appropriate physical genesis too. The creative force of the male seed turns the empty property contracted out by an 'individual' into new human life. Patriarchy in its literal meaning has returned in a new guise.

Until the present, womanhood has been seen as inseparable from, even subsumed in, maternity. For at least three centuries, feminists have spent enormous efforts endeavouring to show that women, like men, have a range of capacities that could be exercised in addition to their unique capacity to create physical life. Now motherhood has been separated from womanhood – and the separation expands patriarchal right. Here is another variant of the contradiction of slavery. A woman can be a 'surrogate' mother only because her womanhood is deemed irrelevant and she is declared an 'individual' performing a service. At the same time, she can be a 'surrogate' mother only because she is a *woman*. Similarly, the relevant property of the man in the surrogacy contract can only be that of a *man*; it is the property that can make him a father. Appropriately, sperm is the only example of property in the person that is not a political fiction. Unlike labour power, sexual parts, the uterus, or any other property that is contracted out for use by another, sperm *can* be separated from the body. Indeed, sperm can be used in artificial insemination, and the sperm of men deemed genetically superior can be stored away until a suitable woman is located, only because it can be separated from the person.

Until the surrogacy contract was invented, this peculiarity of the male seed rendered genetic paternity inherently problematic; paternity always hinged on a woman's testimony. Maternity, however, was always certain and, according to Hobbes, in the natural condition the mother was the lord, with political right over her child; a man had to contract with a mother to obtain mastery as a father. Thanks to the power of contract, genetic paternity can now be made secure and brought together with masculine political creativity. Through contract, men can at last be certain of paternity. A momentous change has thus occurred in (one aspect of) the meaning of 'fatherhood' and the power of fatherhood – or patriarchy in the traditional sense.

It is far too soon to say exactly how important 'surrogate' motherhood will be in the future development of patriarchal domination. In 1979, when (with Teresa Brennan) I published my first examination of social contract theory from a feminist perspective, the term was unknown to us. There are other straws in the wind that point in the same direction as 'surrogate' motherhood – for instance, men have taken legal action as fathers in Britain, Australia and the United States to try to prevent women obtaining abortions and to keep women's bodies artificially alive in order to sustain a foetus. Fathers are also fighting for custody of children. In recent years, in a reversal of the practice in the mid-nineteenth century, the mother has usually been awarded custody of any children if a marriage breaks down. Indeed, the practice of awarding custody to mothers led Christine Delphy to argue that divorce is merely an extension of marriage in which men, once again, are exempted from responsibility for children. Now that feminists have succeeded in winning some much-needed legal reforms, and now that, in many matters, women and men are being placed on the same civil footing, mothers can no longer assume that they will attain custody. Nor can unmarried mothers be sure that the father will not be awarded access to and rights over the child. Some winds, though, blow in a different direction. For example, artificial insemination enables women to become mothers without sexual relations with men.

The contractual subjection of women is full of contradictions, paradoxes and ironies. Perhaps the greatest irony of all is yet to come. Contract is conventionally believed to have defeated the old patriarchal order, but, in eliminating the final remnants of the old world of status, contract may yet usher in a new form of paternal right.

8

The End of the Story?

An old anarchist slogan states that 'no man is good enough to be another man's master'. The sentiment is admirable, but the slogan is silent on one crucial issue. In modern civil society all men are deemed good enough to be women's masters; civil freedom depends on patriarchal right. The failure to see patriarchal right as central to the political problem of freedom, mastery and subordination is so deep-seated that even the anarchists, so acutely aware of subjection among men, have had few quarrels with their fellow socialists about sexual domination. From the beginning of the modern era, when Mary Astell asked why, if all men were born free, all women were born slaves, feminists have persistently challenged masculine right; but, despite all the social changes and legal and political reforms over the past three hundred years, the question of women's subordination is still not seen as a matter of major importance, either in the academic study of politics or in political practice. Controversy about freedom revolves round the law of the state and the law of capitalist production: silence is maintained about the law of male sex-right.

The original contract is merely a story, a political fiction, but the invention of the story was also a momentous intervention into the political world; the spell exerted by stories of political origins has to be broken if the fiction is to be rendered ineffective. The continuing fascination with origins is well illustrated by the conjectural histories of the origins of patriarchy produced by the contemporary feminist movement. Many feminists believe that to tell a story of matriarchy 'in the beginning' provides a precedent to show that the 'world historical defeat of the female sex' will not have been final and absolute for all time, but preoccupation with mother-right and father-right merely perpetuates patriarchal structures of thought.

No doubt the fact that *the* human beginning – or even if there was one – is a mystery, helps explain the allure of stories of political genesis, but there is also another reason for their popularity. The stories express the specifically masculine creative power, the capacity to generate, to give birth to, new forms of political life.

To begin to understand modern patriarchy the whole story of the original contract must be reconstructed, but to change modern patriarchy, to begin to create a free society in which women are autonomous citizens, the story must be cast aside. Indeed, fully to understand modern patriarchy requires a very different undertaking from the task I have attempted here. The political fiction of an original contract is part of the history of modern patriarchy, but modern patriarchy did not begin with a dramatic act of contract; there is no origin, in that sense, from which to begin an historical investigation. One might plausibly argue that modern patriarchy began in the seventeenth century when the contractual institutions familiar today first began to develop, but the 'beginning' was not clear cut. Historians often say that a particular event, whether a battle, an Act of Parliament, a popular uprising or a natural disaster, was a turning-point, a beginning, but a great deal has always gone before, other events can be cited and such origins are always open to continual reinterpretation.

Talk of founding has been in vogue in recent years among political theorists, especially in the United States, but how should the real historical 'foundings' of two of the countries with which I am concerned be interpreted? When the First Fleet arrived in Australia in 1788, the men unloaded the ships and built shelters, then, five days later, the female convicts were allowed ashore and into the men's hands. By 1809, the colony was being described as 'little better than an extensive brothel'. As more women convicts were transported, 'the inhabitants of the colony each [selected] one at his pleasure, not only as servants but as avowed objects of intercourse'.[1] Exactly which conjectural history of origins could appropriately be told about these events? The bicentennial of the founding is being celebrated in 1988, but the indigenous people of Australia, like their counterparts in the United States in 1976, see nothing to celebrate. Examples of acts that resemble contractual beginnings can be found in the first white settlements in America, but the 'founding' of white America and Australia took protracted campaigns of conquest and forcible seizure of vast areas of land from indigenous inhabitants.

In order to bring out as sharply as possible something of what is at stake in alternative readings of the original contract, I have exaggerated and described the sexual contract as half the story. The story of political genesis needs to be told again from yet another perspective. The men who (are said to) make the original contract are *white* men, and their fraternal pact has three aspects; the social contract, the sexual contract and the slave contract that legitimizes the rule of white over black. I have touched on the slave contract only where germane to the retrieval of the story of the sexual contract.

The political fiction of the original contract tells not only of a beginning, an act of political generation, but also of an end, the defeat of (the classic form of) patriarchy. Moreover, the story is not merely about ends and beginnings, but is used by political theorists and, in more popular versions, by politicians, to represent social and political institutions to contemporary citizens and to represent citizens to themselves. Through the mirror of the original contract, citizens can see themselves as members of a society constituted by free relations. The political fiction reflects our political selves back to us – but who are 'we'? Only men – who can create political life – can take part in the original pact, yet the political fiction speaks to women, too, through the language of the 'individual'. A curious message is sent to women, who represent everything that the individual is not, but the message must continually be conveyed because the meaning of the individual and the social contract depend on women and the sexual contract. Women must acknowledge the political fiction and speak the language even as the terms of the original pact exclude them from the fraternal conversation.

The standard readings of the classic texts (readings that underwrite contract argument that makes no explicit reference to the classics) fail to show in what kind of enterprise the classic theorists were engaged. Instead of interrogating the texts to see how it came about that a certain conception of free political relations became established, the standard interpretations take their departure from the assumption that sexual difference, relations between the sexes and the private sphere are paradigmatically non-political. The classics are thus read in the light of the construction of modern civil society in the texts themselves! The manner in which the classic theorists set about their tasks and the multitude of problems, contradictions and paradoxes about women and contract that they bequeathed never come to the surface. No hint is ever given that, although men and women associate with each other in many different ways, the classic theorists have left a legacy within which the complex, varied dealings and relations between the sexes are ruled outside of critical inquiry. Chapters and passages in the texts dealing with marriage and relations between men and women typically are passed over altogether or merely presented as a matter peripheral to political theory, of interest only because great men thought such questions worth discussing.

The familiar readings of the texts neither acknowledge, nor can answer, the question of how the classic contract theorists began from premises that rendered illegitimate any claim to political right that appealed to nature, and then went on to construct the difference between men and women as the difference between natural freedom and natural subjection. The argument that the subjection of women to men has a foundation in nature, and Hobbes' rejection of any such masculine right, are both tacitly accepted without examination. To retrieve the story of the sexual contract is not, therefore, merely to add something to the standard accounts, to add a chapter to the story of the social contract. The sexual contract is part of the original contract, and to tell the whole story is to transform the reading of the texts, which can no longer be interpreted from within the patriarchal confines established by the classic contract theorists themselves. And if the texts are reinterpreted, so, too, must the contractual relations of civil society be reexamined.

Feminists have not always appreciated the full extent of the paradox and contradiction involved in women's incorporation into civil society. If women had been merely excluded from civil life, like slaves, or wives when coverture held sway, the character of the problem would have been self-evident. But women have been incorporated into a civil order in which their freedom is apparently guaranteed, a guarantee renewed with each telling of the story of the social contract in the language of the individual. Freedom is enjoyed by all 'individuals', a category that, potentially, pertains to everyone, men and women, white and black alike. In the fullness of time, any historical, accidental exceptions to the principle of freedom will be removed. Women's capacity eventually to take their rightful place is demonstrated by the fact that they are parties to the marriage contract. Women, too, are participants in the act – contract – that constitutes freedom. Feminists seized on the

apparently unambiguous guarantee of emancipation offered by
contract; thus, in 1791, Olympe de Gouges included a 'Form for a
Social Contract Between Man and Woman', which set out the
conditions of their marital union, in her *Declaration of the Rights of
Woman and the Female Citizen*. The guarantee seems all the firmer now
that the feminist movement has succeeded in removing most of the
formal juridical barriers to women's civil equality.

The appeal of contract as the enemy of patriarchy, striking the
death-blow against sexual domination, is strengthened by contractarianism and the idea of the individual as owner, an individual who
is so like all others as to be interchangeable. Critics have remarked
that this individual is disembodied and so, they argue, has no
identity; a self with an identity is, necessarily, an embodied self. The
criticism is valid, but the critics miss the same point as feminists
attracted by contract. The individual as owner is separated from a
body that is of one sex or the other. A human body, except through
misfortunes of birth, is not male and female at the same time, no
matter how the body is dressed or positioned in the social structure,
although now it can be stripped of both male and female characteristics; if dissatisfied with their 'gender orientation', men can become
'transsexuals' and turn themselves into simulacra of women. The
'individual' is constructed from a male body so that his identity is
always masculine. The individual is also a unitary figure; a being of
the other sex can only be a modification of the individual, not a
distinctive being, or his unity and masculine identity is endangered.
In effect, as Rawls' version of the state of nature shows, there is only
one individual, duplicated endlessly. How the duplication takes
place is a mystery.

Critics of the individual as owner do not consider his genesis (the
story of the primal scene and the creation of the private sphere are
absent from the tales of fathers, sons and original pacts); their
attention is directed to the finished product of the classic contract
theorists, the individual in his civil world. Rousseau asked how the
new men required for a free social order were to be created in
advance of a new society, and, ever since, men have puzzled over
this central political question. But the new men always look
remarkably like the old men – their civil freedom does not disturb
patriarchal right. A free society is still held to stand apart from
sexual relations and have no connection with sexual identity, to
manhood and womanhood. Movements for free work, for example,

for industrial democracy, workers' control or self-management, have taken for granted the masculinity of the 'worker' and the existence of a (house)wife rendering him domestic service. The long history of socialist attempts to restore or recreate the community, solidarity or fraternity that is lost when the individual is stripped bare of social relations have uncovered his masculinity plainly enough – yet the sex of the individual is still not noticed because 'fraternity' is interpreted as (universal) community. And even socialist criticism is now muted; the individual as owner has made a spectacular entry into socialist argument with the development of rational choice or analytical Marxism.

An exploration of contracts about property in the person to which women must be a party – the marriage contract, the prostitution contract and the surrogacy contract – show that the body of a *woman* is precisely what is at issue in the contract. Furthermore, when women are a party to the men's contract, the employment contract, their bodies are never forgotten. Women can attain the formal standing of civil individuals but as embodied feminine beings we can never be 'individuals' in the same sense as men. To take embodied identity seriously demands the abandonment of the masculine, unitary individual to open up space for two figures; one masculine, one feminine.

The body, sex and sexual difference are inseparable from civil subordination, but the body and sex must be separated from the individual if civil subordination is to be created and called freedom. The general assumption is that sex and subordination stand at opposite poles. Sex is consensual; after all, is not rape – enforced sexual submission – a criminal offence (at least outside of marriage)? Some feminists have argued that rape is not sex but violence, but this approach serves to reinforce the separation of sex from subordination; where there is no consent there is only violence, not sex. Sex may be conjured away, but the question remains why such difficulty is encountered in distinguishing women's consent from enforced submission, and why men demand to buy women's sexual submission in the capitalist market. An answer is unlikely to be forthcoming all the time that sex is divided up into discrete, watertight areas of discussion – and never discussed as sex. Rape, discussed here, is about violence; prostitution, discussed there, is about free access to employment; pornography is about freedom of expression; and sado-masochism is about consent and equality. The stories of the sexual contract and the primal scene allow questions to be asked about the meaning of sex in late twentieth-century patriarchy and allow the fragmented structure of sexual subordination to be put back together. An answer to the question whether sex means men's mastery is writ large from all sides in the books, magazines, films, videos, peep-shows and other commodities of the sex industry. One of the more remarkable features of contemporary political relations is that the answer is so seldom connected to the question.

Sex is central to the original contract. The brothers make the agreement to secure their natural liberty, part of which consists in the patriarchal right of men, the right of one sex. Only one sex has the capacity to enjoy civil freedom. Civil freedom includes right of sexual access to women and, more broadly, the enjoyment of mastery as a sex – not a gender. The term 'gender' is now ubiquitous but frequently lies idle, used merely as an often not very apt synonym for 'women'. 'Gender' was introduced as a crucial weapon in the struggle against patriarchy. The patriarchal claim is that women are naturally subject to men, subject, that is, because of their biology, their sex. To refer to gender instead of sex indicates that women's position is not dictated by nature, by biology or sex, but is a matter of social and political contrivance. True; what men and women are, and how relations between them are structured, depends on a good deal more than their natural physiology and biology. It is also true, however, that the meaning of men's and women's natures, even the depiction of male and female skeletons and physiology, has depended on the political significance accorded to manhood and womanhood. To use the language of gender reinforces the language of the civil, the public and the individual, language that depends on the repression of the sexual contract.

The meaning of the 'individual' remains intact only so long as the dichotomies (internal to civil society) between natural/civil, private/public, women/individual – and sex/gender – remain intact. Women's inclusion into civil society as members of a gender, as individuals, is also their inclusion as members of a sex, as women. The new surrogacy contract illustrates the mutual dependence of sex and the individual/gender in the most dramatic fashion. Two sexually indifferent individuals (owners, representatives of the genders) must be party to the contract or the contract will be illegitimate, nothing more than a case of baby-selling. On the other hand, the surrogacy contract is only possible at all because one party is a woman; only a woman has the requisite capacity (property) to provide the service demanded, a capacity integral to (natural to) her sex.

For feminists to argue for the elimination of nature, biology, sex in favour of the 'individual' is to play the modern patriarchal game and to join in a much wider onslaught on nature within and beyond the boundaries of civil societies. Nature is represented not only by women, but also, for example, by land, indigenous peoples, the descendants of the slaves whom the Reverend Seabury imagined to have contracted with their masters, and animals (and the latter may become property in a new fashion; the Patent and Trademark Office in the United States will now take applications for patents for genetically altered animals, which are being given the same status as any other human invention). To suppose that the patriarchal appeal to nature and natural, sexual difference implies that patriarchal theories and institutions follow directly from what is given by nature (from physiology, from biology, from sex) is to remain locked within patriarchal confines. The classic contract theorists are instructive here; they did not simply take their pictures of the state of nature and the natural inhabitants of the original condition from nature. Nothing about political relations can be read directly from the two natural bodies of humankind that must inhabit the body politic. The state of nature is drawn by each theorist in a manner that enables him to reach 'the desired solution' – the political solution he has already formulated. Sexual difference in the classic contract theories is, and can only be, a political construct.

To ask whether sexual difference is politically significant is to ask the wrong question; the question is always how the difference is to be expressed. One reason why the wrong question is so often posed is that a good deal of contemporary feminist argument assumes that a choice has to be made between femininity as subordination and the ostensibly sex-neuter 'individual'. In modern patriarchy, as a (re)reading of the texts of classic contract theory makes clear, these are *not alternatives*; to choose one is to choose the other too. The classic theorists, unlike some patriarchal extremists in the nineteenth century, did not have any doubts about women's humanity. They did not, for example, suggest that women were at a lower stage of evolution than men. They argued that sexual difference was the difference between subordination and freedom, but, at the same time, the classic theorists had to grant that women possessed the capacities of naturally free beings, the capacities of individuals.

If the claim that civil society was an order of universal freedom was to be plausible, women had to be incorporated through contract, the act that, at one and the same time, signifies freedom and constitutes patriarchal right. The perception of women (subordination, sex) and the individual (freedom, gender) as alternatives rather than the two inseparable spheres of civil society, underlies a significant historical shift in feminist argument. The juridical equality and legal reform so central to contract doctrine (and which, contrary to the impression cultivated on all sides, has not yet been completely achieved) is invariably seen today as a matter of women acting like men. The suffrage, and more recent reforms such as the participation of women on juries, equal-pay and anti-discrimination legislation, reform of marriage and rape law, decriminalization of prostitution, are all seen as allowing women to become citizens like men and owners of property in their persons like men. Historically, this form of argument is unusual; until recently, most feminists demanded civil equality in the expectation that they would give their equal standing a distinctive expression as women.

Contemporary feminists often treat such a presumption as no more than an illustration of their predecessors' inability to see beyond their own immersion in the private sphere and as a sign that feminists in the past merely accepted the patriarchal appeal to natural sexual difference. To be sure, for feminists to demand a re-evaluation of the (private) tasks undertaken by women when, in modern patriarchy, what counts as 'citizenship' and 'work' takes place in the civil masculine world, is to ask for something that cannot be granted. Nevertheless, when feminists in the past demanded juridical equality and recognition *as women*, and proclaimed that what they did as women in the private sphere was part of their citizenship, they grappled with the political problem of expressing sexual difference; they did not attempt to deny political significance to womanhood. They may have had a different view of the relation between private and public from feminists today, but the perception of the division between private and public (civil) as a *political* problem is a recent development, possible, perhaps, only after a considerable measure of civil equality had been won.

After a century or more of legal reform women are near juridical equality with men and all but a few reminders of coverture have been swept away, but men still enjoy extensive power as a sex and have gained some new advantages, for example, as fathers. The

series of 'gender neutral' reforms over the past decade or so highlight the problem. The reforms enable women to enjoy equality of
opportunity, to enter all areas of paid employment, to engage in
freedom of contract, contracting out any of the property in their
persons, and to wage 'the battle of Venus' alongside men. But, at
the same time, 'sexual harassment' has been discovered in the workplace and the patriarchal division of labour has not been greatly
upset, except where men use anti-discrimination legislation to enter
the few high-status jobs once reserved for women; women's economic
circumstances still place them at a disadvantage in the termination
of the marriage contract; sexuality and sexual freedom have been
subsumed under 'the sex act' and encompassed within capitalism in
the sex industry, which provides men with new forms of access to
women's bodies.

Men are, once again, also being seen as the 'principal agents' in
human generation. Ironically, one of the central tenes of classic
patriarchalism is being summoned up in the onward march of the
individual and freedom of contract. No one could doubt until a few
years ago that if the human species was to reproduce women had to
become pregnant and give birth. Technological developments have
now cast doubt on this seemingly natural necessity of human existence. If there is indeed the prospect that reproduction could take
place outside the human body (or inside men's bodies), women's
natural capacity would no longer be needed – and nor would
women. The latter possibility may be no more than a figment of
sensational imaginations, but I raise it because nature, biology and
sex place limits on contract. Contract theory both rejects and
requires those very limits. In a social order constituted by nothing
but contract, all the way down, freedom is limitless. There can be no
limitation on the jurisdiction of the individual over the property in
his person, no restriction on freedom of contract. All the old limits of
nature, status, ascription or paternalism must be abandoned. That
is to say, in the movement from the old world of status to the new
world of contract, the freedom of the individual consists in *emancipation* from the old bonds and constraints, whether those of
absolutism, the *patria potestas*, the state – or sexual difference.

From the perspective of the opposition between the old world of
status and the new civil world, or the opposition between the state of
nature and civil society – the perspective of contract theory (save for
Rousseau's arguments) – the problem of freedom is solved, or will

be solved when the movement to contract is complete. The individual is emancipated from old restrictions or the endemic insecurity of the natural condition. Freedom is exhibited and expressed through contract, an 'original' act that can always be performed anew, and which is limited only by the legitimate constraint of the jurisdiction of the individual. Freedom is an act . . . an act that establishes new bonds even as the old limitations are overthrown. Freedom is limitless but the act that signifies the end of the old constraints also creates the new civil limits of mastery and obedience. In the new world, the act of emancipation creates civil subordination and patriarchal right.

The premise of natural individual freedom and equality is necessary to create the civil world, and as an abstract universal principle, individual freedom can be appealed to by everyone. Abolitionists and defenders of the slave contract alike could talk of natural freedom; the premise could generate Hobbes' Leviathan, Rousseau's participatory order and the early feminist attack on marital despotism. The idea of individual freedom can be used so promiscuously because of the inherent ambiguity of the meaning of 'civil' society. The ambiguity obscures the fact that critics of contract theory adopt a different perspective from the theorists they criticize and understand freedom differently. The critics argue from a vantage point within civil society. They do not look back to the old world but at the bifurcation of civil society into private and public spheres, albeit that they typically concentrate on the class division between the spheres. The critics are concerned with freedom as *autonomy*, with a structure of free social relations among political equals, but their criticism, like Rousseau's attack on his fellow contract theorists, is fatally compromised. Their argument remains caught within the dichotomies that are under attack, bouncing back and forth within the boundaries established by the story of the original contract. Socialist critics of contract, followed by many feminists, focus on the inadequacy of juridical equality in a context of social inequality. There is no doubt about the inadequacy, or the cogency of their criticisms, but the combination of public equality and private inequality, as the story of the sexual contract shows, is not a contradiction of modern patriarchy. Juridical equality and social inequality – public/private, civil/natural, men/women – form a coherent social structure. If the complicity of feminists and socialists with contract is to end, attention must turn to subordination and the contradiction of slavery.

Contract theory is haunted by the contradiction of slavery in a variety of guises, and the critics of contract have failed to exorcize the spectre. The contradiction of slavery lies at the heart of the construction of civil society in the classic contract theorists' simultaneous denial and affirmation of women's freedom, and continually reappears because freedom as autonomy is still coupled to sexual mastery. The embrace of the sexual contract by the critics of contract is readily apparent in the legacy that Rousseau and Hegel gave to socialism. Rousseau rejected wage slavery and advocated a non-statist, participatory political order, but his apparently thoroughgoing alternative to the 'individual' and the social contract (couched in contractual language) depended on the natural foundation of women's subjection. Similarly, Hegel's famous dialectic of the master and slave overcomes slavery only to replace slave-masters by (free) sexual masters, who gain recognition of their freedom from the brotherhood and recognition of their patriarchal right from wives. Contractarianism claims to have overcome the contradiction of slavery. The unlimited freedom of the individual as owner to contract out property in his person (his labour power or services) entails that he can rightfully contract himself into civil slavery, an exemplification of freedom. The contradiction disappears – a civil slave is juridically free – then immediately reappears. Property in the person is a political fiction. A civil slave provides a service merely; but what use is a disembodied service to a master? The delights of mastery, including civil mastery, can be obtained only from jurisdiction over a living man or woman.

The marriage and prostitution contracts, contracts to which women are necessarily a party, have always been tainted by the odour of slavery, and provide an embarrassing reminder of 'brutal origins'. The reminder is shrugged off as politically irrelevant, and the analogy with slavery is not taken really seriously. Feminist criticism of the two contracts usually proceeds along the lines of socialist criticism of the employment contract – but without the assistance of the idea of wage slavery. Feminists are thus in the curious position of presupposing that the worker stands in the same position as a wife or prostitute, but failing to ask how the subordination of the worker comes about. The ground is thus conceded to contract doctrine on a vital point; the political fiction of labour power, property in the person, is tacitly accepted, and the paradoxes of women and contract and the contradiction of slavery then continue to be played out.

Civil subordination depends upon the capacity of human beings to act *as if* they could contract out labour power or services rather than, as they must, contract out themselves and their labour to be used by another. If contract is not to be a vain endeavour, the means must be available to ensure that the service contracted for is faithfully performed. The party who demands the service (the employer, the husband, the client) must have the right to command that a body is put to use, or access to the body is made available, in the requisite manner. Contracts about property in the person must always create obedience and constitute a man as a civil master. Exactly what form subordination takes, to what use the body is put or what kind of access is granted, depends on whether a man or a woman is constituted as a subordinate. The buyer is never indifferent to the sex of the owner of property in the person. He contracts for jurisdiction over a masculine or feminine body and forms of subjection differ according to the sex of the body.

A brilliant piece of political inventiveness has given the name of freedom to civil subordination and repressed the interdependence of civil freedom and patriarchal right. If the spectre of slavery is ever, finally, to be laid to rest, political theory and practice has to move outside the structure of oppositions established through the story of the original contract. The move would not diminish the importance of juridical freedom as advocates of contract doctrine often assert. On the contrary, the achievement of juridical freedom and equality is a necessary step towards women's autonomy and necessary to safeguard our bodily integrity. The achievement will, with one important caveat, help in the task of creating the social conditions for the development of an autonomous femininity; the caveat is that women's equal standing must be accepted as an expression of the freedom of women *as women*, and not treated as an indication that women can be just like men. Much feminist energy over the past three centuries has gone into the attempt to show that women have the same capacities as men and so are entitled to the same freedom. In one sense, of course, the efforts were all too necessary; women had to fight against, and must continue to fight against, coverture and the multitude of legal and social supports for masculine right, and continue to fight for access to the social resources required to gain their livelihood and to exercise their citizenship. In another sense, the need to wage this battle helps repress the fact that there is no need to try to show that women are (have the capacities of) free beings. Modern contractual patriarchy both denies and *presupposes women's freedom* and could not operate without this presupposition. The retrieval of the story of the sexual contract allows access to this profoundly important insight.

Political argument must leave behind stories of origins and original contracts and move from the terrain of contract and the individual as owner. To look to an 'original' act of contract is systematically to blur the distinction between freedom and subjection. A free social order cannot be a contractual order. There are other forms of free agreement through which women and men can constitute political relations, although in a period when socialists are busy stealing the clothes of contract little political creativity is directed towards developing the necessary new forms. If political relations are to lose all resemblance to slavery, free women and men must willingly agree to uphold the social conditions of their autonomy. That is to say, they must agree to uphold limits. Freedom requires order and order requires limits. In modern civil society individual freedom is unconstrained – and order is maintained through mastery and obedience. If men's mastery is to be replaced by the mutual autonomy of women and men, individual freedom must be limited by the structure of social relations in which freedom inheres.

A great deal has been heard about freedom from the governments of the Right in Britain and the United States in the 1980s. The rhetoric of private enterprise and freedom from the constricting paternalistic embrace of the state dominates official political debate and the same refrain is now being heard from the Labor Government in Australia. At the same time, the old dream of the anarchists and Marx that the state will 'wither away' is no longer fashionable. Yet the sexual contract and the social contract, the 'individual' and the state, stand and fall together. Perhaps the dream has faded for good reason; despite the prevailing rhetoric of rolling back the state and diminishing state power, the military and surveillance capacity of the state has increased very rapidly in recent years. The figure of the individual is now all too often dressed in combat uniform and brandishing weapons. The conjuncture of the rhetoric of individual freedom and a vast increase in state power is not unexpected at a time when the influence of contract doctrine is extending into the last, most intimate nooks and crannies of social life. Taken to a conclusion, contract undermines the conditions of its own existence. Hobbes showed long ago that contract – all the way down – requires absolutism and the sword to keep war at bay. If the fiction of the original contract is not to come to an end from which there can be no beginning, or if force instead of will is not to be the principle of the post-modern era, a new story about freedom is urgently needed.

To retrieve the story of the sexual contract does not, in itself, provide a political programme or offer any short cuts in the hard task of deciding what, in any given circumstances, are the best courses of action and policies for feminists to follow, or when and how feminists should form alliances with other political movements. Once the story has been told, however, a new perspective is available from which to assess political possibilities and to judge whether this path or that will aid or hinder (or both) the creation of a free society and the creation of sexual difference as diverse expressions of freedom. When the repressed story of political genesis is brought to the surface the political landscape can never look the same again. Nature, sex, masculinity and femininity, the private, marriage and prostitution become political problems; so, therefore, does the familiar, patri- archal understanding of work and citizenship. New anti-patriarchal roads must be mapped out to lead to democracy, socialism and freedom.

In any case, the political landscape has changed substantially over the past two decades. The story of the original contract must now be told in a less hospitable political context. Patriarchal structures and divisions are no longer as solid as they were between, say, the 1867 Reform Act and the turmoil of 1968. The old manufacturing indus- tries and other arenas in which the worker, his unions and his class solidarity and fraternity flourished are disappearing and the idea of the 'employment society' now looks utopian; 'the family' – the breadwinner, dependent wife and children – now forms a small minority of households in the United States, Australia and Britain; the separation/integration of private and public has been raised as a political problem; and long-standing political allegiances are crumbling and new social movements raise some similar questions to feminism, but from different vantage-points. Men have a vested interest in maintaining the silence about the law of male sex-right, but the opportunity exists for political argument and action to move outside the dichotomies of patriarchal civil society, and for the creation of free relations in which manhood is reflected back from autonomous femininity.

Baudelaire once wrote that 'there is a world of difference between a "completed" subject and a "finished" subject and that in general what is "completed" is not "finished".'[2] I have completed what I have to say about the sexual contract, but the story is far from finished. The political fiction is still showing vital signs and political theory is insufficient to undermine the life-supports.

Notes

1 Contracting In

1　A. Rich, 'Compulsory Heterosexuality and Lesbian Existence', *Signs*, 5, 4 (1980), p. 645.

2　G. D. H. Cole, *Self-Government in Industry* (London, G. Bell and Sons, 1919), p. 34.

3　Sir H. Maine, *Ancient Law*, (London, J. M. Dent and Sons, 1917 [1861]), p. 100.

4　P. S. Atiyah, *The Rise and Fall of Freedom of Contract* (Oxford, Clarendon Press, 1979), p. 716. Atiyah and some other legal writers also discuss the question whether promising is paradigmatic of obligation and contract. I have explored some of these matters elsewhere and will not deal with this aspect of contract in this study; see my *The Problem of Political Obligation*, 2nd edn (Cambridge, Polity Press; Berkeley and Los Angeles, University of California Press, 1985).

5　For example, M. Carnoy, D. Shearer and R. Rumberger, *A New Social Contract: The Economy and Government After Reagan* (New York, Harper and Row, 1983); D. L. Bawden (ed.), *The Social Contract Revisited* (Baltimore, The Urban Institute Press, 1984).

6　J. Locke, *Two Treatises of Government*, ed. P. Laslett, 2nd edn (Cambridge, Cambridge University Press, 1967), II, §27.

7　G. W. F. Hegel, *Philosophy of Right*, tr. T. M. Knox (Oxford, Clarendon Press, 1952), §163.

8　M. Foucault, *The History of Sexuality* (New York, Vintage Books, 1980), vol. I: *An Introduction*, p. 85.

9　Ibid., p. 89.

2 Patriarchal Confusions

1　F. Engels, *The Origin of the Family, Private Property and the State* (New York, International Publishers, 1942), p. 50.

2 V. Beechey, 'On Patriarchy', *Feminist Review*, (1979), p. 66. Another discussion claims that 'the contemporary analysis' goes back to Wollstonecraft, de Sade and Mill; R. W. Connell, *Which Way Is Up?: Essays on Sex, Class and Culture* (Sydney, George Allen and Unwin, 1983), p. 51.

3 G. J. Schochet, *Patriarchalism in Political Thought: The Authoritarian Family and Political Speculation and Attitudes Especially in Seventeenth-Century England* (Oxford, Basil Blackwell, 1975), p. 273.

4 M. A. Butler, 'Early Liberal Roots of Feminism: John Locke and the Attack on Patriarchy', *American Political Science Review*, 72, 1 (1978), p. 149.

5 L. J. Nicholson, *Gender and History: The Limits of Social Theory in the Age of the Family* (New York, Columbia University Press, 1986), p. 161.

6 J. B. Elshtain, *Public Man, Private Woman: Women in Social and Political Thought* (Princeton, Princeton University Press, 1981), pp. 215, 128.

7 Z. R. Eisenstein, *The Radical Future of Liberal Feminism* (New York, Longman, 1981), pp. 41, 49.

8 Cited in Schochet, *Patriarchalism in Political Thought*, p. 80.

9 Ibid., p. 276.

10 Ibid., p. 193.

11 Ibid., p. 16.

12 S. Rothblatt, *Tradition and Change in English Liberal Education* (London, Faber and Faber, 1976), p. 18.

13 R. Williams, *Keywords: A Vocabulary of Culture and Society*, rev. edn (New York, Oxford University Press, 1985), p. 58. (I am grateful to Ross Poole for drawing my attention to 'civilization' and for these references.)

14 R. Coward, *Patriarchal Precedents: Sexuality and Social Relations* (London, Routledge and Kegan Paul, 1983), pp. 12, 26.

15 Ibid., p. 18.

16 Sir H. Maine, *Ancient Law* (London, J. M. Dent and Sons, 1917 [1861]), p. 76.

17 Ibid., p. 78.

18 Ibid., p. 99.

19 Coward, *Patriarchal Precedents*, pp. 47-8.

20 Ibid., p. 73.

21 Ibid., p. 53.

22 G. Lerner, *The Creation of Patriarchy* (New York, Oxford University Press, 1986), p. 10.

23 Ibid., p. 30.

24 For instance, Simone de Beauvoir stated that women 'have no past, no history, no religion of their own' (cited by Lerner, *Creation of Patriarchy*, p. 221). More recently, Andrea Dworkin has stated that 'I think that the situation of women is basically ahistorical'; E. Wilson, 'Interview with Andrea Dworkin', *Feminist Review*, 11 (1982), p. 27.

25 M. Barrett, *Women's Oppression Today: Problems in Marxist Feminist Analysis* (London, Verso Books, 1980), p. 14.

26 S. Rowbotham, 'The Trouble with "Patriarchy"', *New Statesman*, (21–8 December 1979), p. 970.

27 J. Mitchell, *Psychoanalysis and Feminism* (Harmondsworth, Penguin Books, 1975), p. 409.

28 G. Rubin, 'The Traffic in Women', in *Toward an Anthropology of Women*, ed. R. Reiter (New York, Monthly Review Press, 1975), p. 168.

29 Barrett, *Women's Oppression Today*, p. 250.

30 Lerner, *Creation of Patriarchy*, pp. 191–2.

31 Ibid., pp. 217–18.

32 Schochet, *Patriarchalism in Political Thought*, pp. 81–2.

33 T. H. Marshall, 'Citizenship and Social Class', reprinted in *States and Societies*, ed. D. Held et. al. (New York and London, New York University Press, 1983), p. 258.

34 N. Chodorow, *The Reproduction of Mothering: Psychoanalysis and the Sociology of Gender* (Berkeley, University of California Press, 1978), pp. 9–10.

35 I. Balbus, *Marxism and Domination: A Neo-Hegelian, Feminist, Psychoanalytic Theory of Sexual, Political, and Technological Liberation* (Princeton, Princeton University Press, 1982), pp. 311–12, 324. Such an interpretation draws on psychoanalytic theory that stresses the pre-Oedipal period of infancy, and the mother who appears all-powerful, devouring and engulfing (see also Hanna Pitkin's new interpretation of Machiavelli, *Fortune is a Woman*). The conjectural histories of origins that are found in psychoanalytic theory come from the theory that stresses the Oedipus complex itself; like social contract theory, they tell of the (wish for the) death of the father at the hands of the sons.

36 C. Delaney, 'The Meaning of Paternity and the Virgin Birth Debate', *Man*, 21, 3 (1986), p. 495. (I am grateful to Albert Hirschman for drawing my attention to Delaney's argument.)

37 J-J. Rousseau, *Emile or On Education*, tr. A. Bloom (New York, Basic Books, 1979), p. 361.

38 M. O'Brien, *The Politics of Reproduction* (London, Routledge and Kegan Paul, 1981), p. 56.

39 Delaney, 'The Meaning of Paternity', p. 495 (my emphasis); also pp. 500–2.

40 Reported in *The New York Times*, (15 March 1987).

41 J. S. Mill, 'Principles of Political Economy', in *Collected Works*, ed. J. M. Robson, (Toronto, University of Toronto Press, 1965), vol. II, bk II, ch. ii, §3.

42 J. Benjamin, 'Authority and the Family Revisited: or, A World without Fathers?', *New German Critique*, 4, 3 (1978), p. 35.

43 K. Tribe, *Land, Labour and Economic Discourse* (London, Routledge and Kegan Paul, 1978), ch. 3.

44 For example, C. Brown, 'Mothers, Fathers and Children: From Private to Public Patriarchy', in *Women and Revolution: A Discussion of the Unhappy Marriage of Marxism and Feminism*, ed. L. Sargent (Boston, South End Press, 1981).

45 H. Hartmann, 'The Unhappy Marriage of Marxism and Feminism: Towards a More Progressive Union', in Sargent (ed.), *Women and Revolution*, pp. 19, 3.

46 See especially I. Young, 'Beyond the Unhappy Marriage: A Critique of the Dual Systems Theory', in Sargent (ed.), *Women and Revolution*.

47 Eisenstein, *Radical Future of Liberal Feminism*, p. 20.

3 Contract, the Individual and Slavery

1 J. Rawls, *A Theory of Justice* (Cambridge, MA, Harvard University Press, 1971), p. 141.

2 I. Kant, *Political Writings*, ed. H. Reiss (Cambridge, Cambridge University Press, 1970), p. 79.

3 J. Rawls, 'Justice as Fairness: Political not Metaphysical', *Philosophy and Public Affairs*, 14, 3 (1985), pp. 225, 238.

4 Rawls, *Theory of Justice*, pp. 137–8.

5 Rawls, 'Justice as Fairness', pp. 241, 236.

6 M. Sandel, *Liberalism and the Limits of Justice* (Cambridge, Cambridge University Press, 1982), p. 131.

7 Rawls, *Theory of Justice*, p. 139.

8 Ibid., p. 128.

9 T. Hobbes, *Leviathan*, in *The English Works of Thomas Hobbes of Malmesbury* (hereafter *EW*) (Germany, Scientia Verlag Aalen, 1966), vol. III, ch. XX, p. 186.

10 T. Hobbes, *Philosophical Rudiments Concerning Government and Society* (the English version of *De Cive*), *EW*, vol. II, ch. IX, p. 116.

11 Ibid., ch. IX, p. 116.

12 Hobbes, *Leviathan*, ch. XX, p. 188.

13 Ibid., p. 187.

14 R. W. K. Hinton, 'Husbands, Fathers and Conquerors', *Political Studies*, XVI, 1 (1968), pp. 62, 57.

15 Hobbes, *Leviathan*, ch. XVII, p. 154.

16 T. Hobbes, *De Corpore Politico, or The Elements of Law*, *EW*, vol. IV, ch. IV, pp. 158–9.

17 Hobbes, *Philosophical Rudiments*, ch. IX, p. 122.

18 Hobbes, *Leviathan*, ch. XV, p. 133.

19 Ibid., ch. XX, p. 191.

20   Hobbes, *Philosophical Rudiments*, ch. IX, p. 121.
21   Hobbes, *De Corpore Politico*, ch. IV, p. 158.
22   Hobbes, *Leviathan*, ch. XX, p. 189.
23   Hobbes, *De Corpore Politico*, ch. III, pp. 149–50.
24   T. Brennan and C. Pateman, ' "Mere Auxiliaries to the Common-wealth": Women and the Origins of Liberalism', *Political Studies* XXVII, 2 (1979), pp. 189–90. I was prompted to look at this again by J. Zvesper, 'Hobbes' Individualistic Analysis of the Family', *Politics* (UK), 5, 2 (1985), pp. 28–33; Zvesper, though, sees Hobbes' 'family' in the state of nature as like a 'family' in civil society, despite the absence of 'matrimonial laws'.
25   Hobbes, *Leviathan*, ch. XV, p. 187.
26   Hobbes, *Philosophical Rudiments*, ch. IX, p. 118.
27   Hobbes, *De Corpore Politico*, ch. IV, pp. 157–58.
28   Hobbes, *Philosophical Rudiments*, ch. IX, p. 121.
29   S. Pufendorf, *On the Law of Nature and Nations*, tr. C. H. and W. A. Oldfather (Oxford, The Clarendon Press, 1934), bk VI, ch. I, §9, p. 853.
30   Ibid., p. 854.
31   Ibid., §10, p. 855.
32   Ibid., §9, p. 853.
33   Ibid., §11, p. 860.
34   Ibid., pp. 859–60.
35   Ibid., §12, p. 861.
36   Hinton, 'Husband, Fathers and Conquerors', p. 66; and M. A. Butler, 'Early Liberal Roots of Feminism: John Locke and the Attack on Patriarchy', *American Political Science Review*, 72, 1 (1978), pp. 135–50.
37   J. Locke, *Two Treatises of Government*, 2nd edn, ed. P. Laslett (Cambridge, Cambridge University Press, 1967), II, §183, II, §81–82.
38   Ibid., I, §47.
39   Ibid., II, §82.
40   Ibid.
41   Ibid., §4.
42   Ibid., I, §48.
43   J-J. Rousseau, *Emile or on Education*, tr. A. Bloom (New York, Basic Books, 1979), pp. 370, 404. In *The Problem of Political Obligation*, I argued that the form of Rousseau's original pact meant that it was not a 'contract'. Rousseau is, however, the leading theorist of the original sexual contract, which certainly is a contract. So, without implying that I have changed my mind about my previous interpretation (which is not the case), I shall refer to Rousseau here as a 'classic contract theorist'.
44   Locke, *Two Treatises*, II, §27.

45 G. W. F. Hegel, *Philosophy of Right*, tr. T. M. Knox (Oxford, The Clarendon Press, 1952), §71.

46 I. Kant, *The Philosophy of Law*, tr. W. Hastie (Edinburgh, T. and T. Clark, 1887), part first, second section, §19, pp. 102–3.

47 Hobbes, *Leviathan*, ch. XIV, p. 123.

48 R. H. Coase, 'The Nature of the Firm', *Economica*, IV, 16 (1937), pp. 387, 391. In a world of transnational enterprises, talk of a contract with an entrepreneur reaches into only a small part of the organization of capitalist economic production. However, contract theory deals, above all, with political fictions. I cannot discuss transnationals in the scope of this study: I will merely counterpose the contractarian ideal of 'contracts all the way down' to the reality that in 1982 the sales income of Exxon was $97.172 billion (few countries have a GNP that size); figure from M. Kidron and R. Segal, *The New State of the World Atlas* (New York, Simon and Schuster, 1984), section 30.

49 C. Lévi-Strauss, *The Elementary Structures of Kinship*, rev. edn (Boston, Beacon Press, 1969), p. 483.

50 Ibid., p. 61.

51 J. M. Buchanan, *The Limits of Liberty: Between Anarchy and Leviathan* (Chicago, University of Chicago Press, 1975), p. 54.

52 Ibid., p. 59.

53 The section, from which the rest of the quotations are taken, is on pp. 59–60.

54 A. Baier, 'Trust and Antitrust', *Ethics* 96 (1986), p. 247.

55 See O. Patterson, *Slavery and Social Death: A Comparative Study* (Cambridge, MA, Harvard University Press, 1982), pp. 130–1.

56 S. Engerman, 'Some Considerations Relating to Property Rights in Man', *The Journal of Economic History*, XXXIII, 1 (1973), p. 44, note 2.

57 T. Jefferson, *Democracy*, ed. S. K. Padover (New York, Greenwood Press, 1969), p. 24.

58 D. B. Davis, *The Problem of Slavery in Western Culture* (Ithaca, Cornell University Press, 1966), p. 31.

59 Patterson, *Slavery and Social Death*, pp. 4, 10.

60 Ibid., p. 5.

61 Ibid., p. 3.

62 Davis, *Problem of Slavery*, p. 9.

63 The list is from Patterson, *Slavery and Social Death*, p. 8.

64 M. I. Finley, *Ancient Slavery and Modern Ideology* (London, Chatto and Windus, 1980), p. 118.

65 F. Nietzsche, 'Thus Spoke Zarathustra', in *The Portable Nietzsche*, ed. W. Kaufman (London, Chatto and Windus, 1971), p. 179.

66 G. Lerner, *The Creation of Patriarchy* (New York, Oxford University Press, 1986), p. 70.

67 Ibid., ch. 4.

68 Cited in Ibid., p. 87.
69 See Ibid., p. 78.
70 Fitzhugh's use of Filmer is discussed in C. Vann Woodward, 'George Fitzhugh: *Sui Generis*', the introduction to G. Fitzhugh, *Cannibals All!: or Slaves without Masters* (Cambridge, MA, Harvard University Press, 1960), pp. xxxiv–xxxviii.
71 Cited in Vann Woodward, 'George Fitzhugh', p. xxxiv.
72 Fitzhugh, *Cannibals All!*, p. 29.
73 S. Seabury, *American Slavery Distinguished from the Slavery of English Theorists and Justified by the Law of Nature* (New York, Mason Bros., 1861), p. 201.
74 Ibid., pp. 201, 202.
75 Cited in D. B. Davis, *The Problem of Slavery in the Age of Revolution, 1770–1823* (Ithaca and London, Cornell University Press, 1975), pp. 486–7, note 30.
76 I have argued the case in detail for this reading of Hobbes in *The Problem of Political Obligation* 2nd edn (Cambridge, Polity Press; Berkeley, University of California Press, 1985), ch. 3.
77 Hobbes, *Leviathan*, pt II, ch. XX, p. 189.
78 Ibid., p. 190.
79 H. Grotius, *The Law of War and Peace*, tr. F. W. Kelsey (New York, Bobbs-Merrill, 1925), bk I, ch. II, §VII, p. 103.
80 Ibid., bk II, ch. V, §XXVII, p. 255; §XXX, p. 258.
81 Ibid., bk II, ch. V, §XXVII, p. 255.
82 S. Pufendorf, *On the Duty of Man and Citizen According to the Natural Law*, tr. F. G. Moore (New York, Oxford University Press, 1927), vol. II, p. 90.
83 Ibid., p. 101.
84 Pufendorf, *On the Law of Nature*, bk VI, ch. 3, p. 936.
85 Cited in Patterson, *Slavery and Social Death*, p. 9.
86 Pufendorf, *On the Law of Nature*, bk VI, ch. 3, p. 939. Pufendorf also notes that the master has a more extensive right of sexual use over female slaves; 'the body of a female slave belongs to her master'; *On the Law of Nature*, bk VI, ch. 3, p. 942.
87 Locke, *Two Treatises*, II, §172.
88 Ibid., §24.
89 Ibid., §85.
90 R. Nozick, *Anarchy, State and Utopia* (New York, Basic Books, 1974), p. 331.
91 J. Philmore, 'The Libertarian Case for Slavery', *The Philosophical Forum*, XIV (1982), p. 48 (my emphasis).
92 Ibid., p. 55.
93 Ibid., p. 49.
94 Finley, *Ancient Slavery and Modern Ideology*, pp. 99–100.

95　Davis, *Problem of Slavery in the Age of Revolution*, p. 492 (I have drawn on pp. 488–93).

96　Philmore, 'Libertarian Case for Slavery', p. 55.

97　J. Kleinig, 'John Stuart Mill and Voluntary Slavery Contracts', *Politics*, 18, 2 (1983), p. 82.

98　J. C. Callahan, 'Enforcing Slave Contracts: A Liberal View', *The Philosophical Forum*, XVI, 3 (1985), pp. 223–36. R. M. Hare 'What is Wrong with Slavery', *Philosophy and Public Affairs*, 8, 2 [1979], pp. 103–21) presents a utilitarian case against slavery. He argues that slavery has effects, namely human misery, which make it wrong, and that they always occur because human property (unlike other kinds) can be subjected to terror. But slavery does not have to exist for such misery to be inflicted, so that the argument does not show that slavery is wrong in a way different from other relationships of domination and subjection.

99　J. S. Mill, *On Liberty* (New York, J. W. Lovell Co., n.d.), pp. 171–2.

100　J-J. Rousseau, *The Social Contract*, tr. M. Cranston, (Harmondsworth, Penguin Books, 1968), bk I, ch. 4, p. 58.

101　Ibid., p. 55.

102　Kant, *Philosophy of Law*, part first, third section, §30, p. 119.

4 Genesis, Fathers and the Political Liberty of Sons

1　Cited in G. J. Schochet, *Patriarchalism in Political Thought* (Oxford, Basil Blackwell, 1975), p. 202.

2　W. C. McWilliams, *The Idea of Fraternity in America* (Berkeley, University of California Press, 1973), p. 2.

3　N. O. Brown, *Love's Body* (New York, Vintage Books, 1966), p. 5.

4　A. Esheté, 'Fraternity', *Review of Metaphysics*, 35 (1981), p. 27, pp. 32–3.

5　S. de Beauvoir , *The Second Sex*, tr. H. M. Parshley (New York, Knopf, 1953), pp. 716, 732.

6　G. F. Gaus, *The Modern Liberal Theory of Man* (London, Croom Helm, 1983), pp. 90–4.

7　B. Crick, *In Defence of Politics*, 2nd edn (Harmondsworth, Penguin Books, 1982), p. 228.

8　P. Abbott, *Furious Fancies: American Political Thought in the Post-Liberal Era* (Westport, Greenwood Press, 1980), p. 185.

9　J. F. Stephen, *Liberty, Equality, Fraternity* (Cambridge, Cambridge University Press, 1967), pp. 52, 241.

10　E. Hobsbawm, 'The Idea of Fraternity', cited in M. Taylor, *Community, Anarchy and Liberty* (Cambridge, Cambridge University Press, 1982), p. 31.

11　Crick, *In Defence of Politics*, p. 233.

12 J. Dunn, *Rethinking Modern Political Theory: Essays 1979–83* (Cambridge, Cambridge University Press, 1985), p. 137.

13 McWilliams, *Idea of Fraternity*, pp. 12–13.

14 Ibid., p. 14.

15 Ibid., p. 25.

16 Ibid., p. 29.

17 Ibid., p. 64.

18 S. Freud, *Civilization and Its Discontents*, tr. J. Strachey (New York, W. W. Norton and Co., 1961), p. 54.

19 My colleague Patricia Springborg is undertaking some detailed research on the importance of *phratries* to the *polis*. She has also pointed out to me that the term for members of brotherhood, *phrateres*, was distinct from that for a brother (kin, *adelphoi*).

20 An excellent feminist discussion of early modern and nineteenth-century fraternal orders can be found in M. A. Clawson, 'Early Modern Fraternalism and the Patriarchal Family', *Feminist Studies*, 6, 2 (1980), pp. 368–91; and M. A. Clawson, 'Nineteenth-Century Women's Auxiliaries and Fraternal Orders', *Signs*, 12, 1 (1986), pp. 40–61. On contemporary socialist fraternity see A. Phillips, 'Fraternity', in *Fabian Essays in Socialist Thought*, ed. B. Pimlott (London, Heinemann, 1984).

21 B. Crick, *Socialist Values and Time*, Fabian Tract 495 (London, The Fabian Society, 1984), pp. 24–5.

22 Crick, *In Defence of Politics*, p. 230. A small illustration of the magnitude of this task is provided by a comment on Crick's argument about fraternity which ignores Crick's recognition of the masculinity of 'fraternity': see N. Ellison, 'Equality, Fraternity – and Bernard Crick', *Politics* (UK), 5, 2 (1985), pp. 45–9.

23 J-J. Rousseau, *The Social Contract* (Harmondsworth, Penguin Books, 1968), bk 1, ch. 4, p. 53.

24 Schochet, *Patriarchalism in Political Thought*, p. 35.

25 Ibid., p. 104.

26 Sir R. Filmer, *Patriarcha or, the Natural Powers of the Kings of England Asserted and Other Political Works*, ed. P. Laslett (Oxford, Basil Blackwell, 1949), p. 54.

27 Ibid., p. 211.

28 Ibid., p. 287.

29 Ibid.

30 S. Pufendorf, *Of the Law of Nature and Nations*, tr. C. H. and W. A. Oldfather (Oxford, Clarendon Press, 1934), bk VI, ch. 2, §IV, pp. 914–15.

31 J. Locke, *Two Treatises of Government*, 2nd edn, ed. P. Laslett (Cambridge, Cambridge University Press, 1967), II, §61. Compare Rousseau, *The Social Contract*, bk I, ch. 2, p. 50.

32 R. W. K. Hinton, 'Husbands, Fathers and Conquerors', *Political Studies*, XV, 3 (1967), p. 294.

33 Locke, *Two Treatises*, II, §71.

34 J-J. Rousseau, 'Discourse on Political Economy', in *On the Social Contract and Discourses*, ed. D. A. Cress (Indianapolis, Hackett Publishing Co., 1983), p. 165. (The text has 'Sir [Richard] Filmer'.)

35 Filmer, *Patriarcha*, p. 71.

36 Ibid., p. 188.

37 Ibid., pp. 57, 71, 194.

38 Ibid., p. 96.

39 Locke, *Two Treatises*, I, §9.

40 Laslett, 'Introduction', in Filmer, *Patriarcha*, p. 28.

41 Filmer, *Patriarcha*, p. 256.

42 Ibid., pp. 241, 283. *Genesis*, too, can be interpreted in more than one way, and equality of men and women in the sight of God is not incompatible with male supremacy in human affairs; e.g. Calvin argued from both the perspective of *cognitio dei* (the eternal, Divine perspective in which all things are equal) and the perspective of *cognitio hominis* (the worldly perspective in which humans are hierarchically ordered). See M. Potter, 'Gender Equality and Gender Hierarchy in Calvin's Theology', *Signs* 11, 4 (1986), pp. 725–39.

43 Locke, *Two Treatises*, II, §110.

44 Filmer, *Patriarcha*, p. 245.

45 N. C. M. Hartsock, *Money, Sex and Power: Toward a Feminist Historical Materialism* (New York, Longman, 1983), ch. 8.

46 J. B. Elshtain, *Public Man, Private Woman: Women in Social and Political Thought* (Princeton, Princeton University Press, 1981), p. 39.

47 Cited in O'Brien, *Politics of Reproduction*, pp. 130–1.

48 M. Daly, *Pure Lust: Elemental Feminist Philosophy*, (Boston, Beacon Press, 1984), p. 93.

49 H. F. Pitkin, *Fortune Is a Woman: Gender and Politics in the Thought of Niccolo Machiavelli* (Berkeley, University of California Press, 1984), p. 54.

50 Ibid., pp. 237, 241. According to Pitkin, 'the Founder is a fantasy of the impotent' (p. 104). On the contrary the Founder, like Filmer's father, is anything but impotent; rather he is barren. The figures of the Founder and Filmer's father are fantasies, not of the impotent, but of those who are naturally incapable of giving physical birth and who then spin stories of purely masculine political origins. They must, however, be potent to become 'fathers'.

51 M. Astell, *Some Reflections Upon Marriage* (New York, Source Book Press, 1970; from the 4th edn of 1730), p. 107.

52 See M. L. Shanley, 'Marriage Contract and Social Contract in Seventeenth-Century English Political Thought', *Western Political Quarterly*, XXXII, 1 (1979), pp. 79–91.

53 Sir W. Blackstone, *Commentaries on the Laws of England*, 4th edn, ed. J. DeWitt Andrews (Chicago, Callaghan and Co., 1899) bk I, ch. 15, §111, p. 442.

54 Locke, *Two Treatises*, II, §74–6.

55 Ibid., II, §77–8.

56 For this aspect of Locke's conjectural history, see my *The Problem of Political Obligation*, ch. 4.

57 Astell, *Reflections Upon Marriage*, p. 86.

58 William Thompson, *Appeal of One Half of the Human Race, Women, Against the Pretensions of the Other Half, Men, to Retain them in Political, and Thence in Civil and Domestic, Slavery* (New York, Source Book Press, 1970; originally published 1825), p. 120.

59 Reprinted in A. Goreau, *The Whole Duty of a Woman; Female Writers in Seventeenth-Century England* (New York, The Dial Press, 1985), p. 290.

60 Rousseau, *Social Contract*, bk I, ch. 2, p. 50.

61 J-J. Rousseau, 'Discourse on the Origin and Foundations of Inequality among Men', in *The First and Second Discourses*, tr. and ed. V. Gourevitch (New York, Harper and Row, 1986), pp. 153, 162, 164.

62 Rousseau, *First and Second Discourses*, pp. 173–4.

63 J-J. Rousseau, *Emile or on Education*, tr. A. Bloom (New York, Basic Books, 1979), p. 360.

64 Ibid., pp. 358–9.

65 Ibid., p. 370; also pp. 364, 396.

66 Ibid., p. 445.

67 Ibid., p. 404.

68 Ibid., p. 382; and *Discourse on Political Economy*, p. 164.

69 Ibid., p. 363; see also p. 448.

70 Ibid., p. 408.

71 J-J. Rousseau, *Politics and the Arts: A Letter to M. d'Alembert on the Theatre*, tr. A. Bloom (Ithaca, Cornell University Press, 1968), p. 109.

72 Cited in J. Schwartz, *The Sexual Politics of Jean-Jacques Rousseau* (Chicago, University of Chicago Press, 1984), p. 125.

73 Freud, *Civilization and Its Discontents*, p. 51.

74 Ibid., pp. 54–6.

75 S. Freud, 'Female Sexuality', in *On Sexuality*, ed. A. Richards, (Harmondsworth, Penguin Books, 1977), Pelican Freud Library, vol. 7, p. 377.

76 S. Freud, 'Some Psychological Consequences of the Anatomical Distinction between the Sexes', in *Collected Papers* ed. J. Strachey (London, Hogarth Press, 1953) vol. 5, pp. 196–7.

77 Rousseau, *Social Contract*, bk I, ch. 8, p. 64.

78 J. Mitchell, *Psychoanalysis and Feminism* (Harmondsworth, Penguin Books, 1975), p. 405.

79   Rousseau, *Emile*, p. 409.
80   I. Kant, *Anthropology from a Pragmatic Point of View*, tr. M. J. Gregor (The Hague, Martin Nijhoff, 1974), p. 171.
81   Pitkin, *Fortune is a Woman*, p. 236.
82   P. Rieff, *Freud: The Mind of the Moralist* (London, Methuen, 1965), ch. VII.
83   Brown, *Love's Body*, p. 4. I am grateful to Peter Breiner for drawing my attention to Brown's interpretation in *Love's Body*. A similar point is made, though its implications for patriarchy are not pursued, by M. Hulliung, 'Patriarchalism and its Early Enemies', *Political Theory*, 2 (1974), pp. 410–19. Hulliung (p. 416) notes that there is no reason why the parricide 'cannot just as well be turned into a morality play on behalf of . . . democratic ideals', and that 'the assassins are "brothers" toward each other, and brothers are equal.'
84   S. Freud, *Moses and Monotheism*, tr. K. Jones (New York, Vintage Books, n.d.), p. 104.
85   Ibid., pp. 107–9.
86   S. Freud, *Totem and Taboo*, tr. A. A. Brill (New York, Vintage Books, n.d.), p. 184.
87   Freud, *Moses and Monotheism*, p. 103.
88   Locke, *Two Treatises*, II, §90.
89   Freud, *Totem and Taboo*, p. 183.
90   Freud, *Civilization and Its Discontents*, p. 53.
91   Ibid.; *Moses and Monotheism*, p. 153.
92   Freud, *Totem and Taboo*, p. 206.
93   S. Freud, 'From the History of an Infantile Neurosis', in *Case Histories II*, (Harmondsworth, Penguin Books, 1979), Pelican Freud Library, vol. 9, p. 277, note 2. I was alerted to the importance of the primal scene by M. Ramas, 'Freud's Dora, Dora's Hysteria; the Negation of a Woman's Rebellion', *Feminist Studies*, 6, 3 (1980), especially pp. 482–5.
94   Freud's analysis of the case of the Wolf Man offers three alternatives: the child actually saw his parents' act of sexual intercourse; he displaced his observation of animals' copulation onto his parents; the scene is a phylogenetic inheritance. Freud's use of phylogenetic argument is discussed by R. Coward, *Patriarchal Precedents* (London, Routledge and Kegan Paul, 1983), ch. 7.
95   See my 'Women and Consent', *Political Theory*, 8, 2 (1980), pp. 149–68; also, for example, S. Estrich, *Real Rape* (Cambridge, MA, Harvard University Press, 1987).
96   Report in *The New York Times* (5 September 1986).
97   G. Zilboorg, 'Masculine and Feminine: Some Biological and Cultural Aspects', *Psychiatry*, 7 (1944), p. 282.

98 Ibid., pp. 266, 268.

99 Zilboorg takes the term 'gynaecocentric period' and the basis for his conjectural history from the sociologist, Lester Ward.

100 Zilboorg, 'Masculine and Feminine', pp. 282–3. Zilboorg (pp. 288–90) argues that 'the primordial male' was hostile to children; 'man does not want the woman to be a mother, but a convenient sexual servant or instrument.' Yet man was also envious of woman's capacity to give birth to children who then loved her 'without stint', and who never loved him. Zilboorg explains the *couvade* as an outcome of this hostile masculine identification with the woman and as the origin of psychological fatherhood – but the story could also be used to explain why men have appropriated women's unique capacity and turned it into the ability to give political birth.

101 Ibid., pp. 285, 287.

102 Freud, *Moses and Monotheism*, p. 153.

103 Freud, *Totem and Taboo*, p. 186.

104 C. Lévi-Strauss, *The Elementary Structures of Kinship*, rev. edn, ed. R. Needham (Boston, Beacon Press, 1969), p. 42.

105 Ibid., pp. 29, 481.

106 Ibid., p. 62.

107 Ibid., p. 115.

108 McWilliams, *Idea of Fraternity in America*, p. 16.

5 Wives, Slaves and Wage Slaves

1 J. Schouler, *A Treatise on the Law of the Domestic Relations*, 2nd edn (Boston, Little, Brown and Co., 1874), pt VI, ch. 1, p. 599.

2 M. Eichler, *The Double Standard* (London, Croom Helm, 1980), pp. 106–7.

3 P. Corrigan, 'Feudal Relics or Capitalist Monuments: Notes on the Sociology of Unfree Labour', *Sociology*, 11, 3, (1977), pp. 438, 449. See also R. K. Aufhauser, 'Slavery and Scientific Management', *Journal of Economic History*, 33, 4 (1973), pp. 811–24.

4 Cited in R. Scruton, *Sexual Desire: A Moral Philosophy of the Erotic* (New York, The Free Press, 1986), p. 186.

5 W. Thompson, *Appeal of One Half the Human Race, Women, Against the Pretensions of the Other Half, Men, to Retain Them in Political, and Thence in Civil And Domestic, Slavery* (New York, Source Book Press, 1970), pp. 54–5.

6 J. S. Mill, 'The Subjection of Women', in *Essays on Sex Equality*, ed. A. S. Rossi (Chicago, University of Chicago Press, 1970), p. 130.

7 See N. Basch, 'Invisible Women: The Legal Fiction of Marital Unity in Nineteenth-Century America', *Feminist Studies*, 5, 2 (1979), pp. 346–66.

8 Sir H. Maine, *Ancient Law* (London, J. M. Dent and Sons, 1972), pp. 93–4.

9 D. Defoe, *Roxana* (Harmondsworth, Penguin Books, 1982), p. 187.

10 Mill, 'Subjection of Women', p. 217.

11 L. C. Bullard, 'The Slave-Women of America', in W. L. O'Neill, *The Woman Movement: Feminism in the United States and England* (London, George Allen and Unwin, 1969), pp. 119, 121.

12 Cited in E. Griffith, *In Her Own Right: The Life of Elizabeth Cady Stanton* (New York and Oxford, Oxford University Press, 1984), p. xx.

13 S. P. Menefee, *Wives for Sale: An Ethnographic Study of British Popular Divorce* (Oxford, Basil Blackwell, 1981), p. 160, table 3; and p. 167, table 5; cases of wife-selling are listed in the Appendix.

14 Ibid., p. 88.

15 Ibid., pp. 209–10.

16 Ibid., p. 66.

17 Report in *New Statesman* (2 May 1980).

18 Cited by E. D. Genovese, *Roll, Jordan, Roll: The World the Slaves Made* (New York, Vintage Books, 1976), p. 427. See also A. Rich, 'Disloyal to Civilization', in *On Lies, Secrets, and Silence* (London, Virago Press, 1980).

19 Genovese, *Roll, Jordan, Roll*, p. 483.

20 See F. M. Brodie, *Thomas Jefferson: An Intimate History* (New York, W. W. Norton and Co., 1974), p. 358. I have followed Brodie's (controversial) argument about Jefferson's 'black family'.

21 Genovese, *Roll, Jordan, Roll*, p. 483.

22 Reprinted in S. G. Bell and K. Offen (eds.), *Women, the Family and Freedom: The Debate in Documents*, (Stanford, Stanford University Press, 1983), vol. I, p. 487; see also Mill, 'Subjection of Women', p. 163. Cobbe's article appeared in *The Contemporary Review* in 1878.

23 Sir M. Hale, *The History of the Pleas of the Crown* (London, Sollom Emlyn, 1778), vol. I, ch. LVIII, p. 628.

24 J-J. Rousseau, *Emile or on Education*, tr. A. Bloom (New York, Basic Books, 1979), pp. 478–9.

25 Thompson, *Appeal*, p. 65.

26 Mill, 'Subjection of Women', pp. 159–60.

27 Cited in Griffith, *In Her Own Right*, p. 140.

28 S. Cronan, 'Marriage', in *Radical Feminism*, eds. A. Koedt, E. Levine, A. Rapone (New York, Quadrangle, 1973), p. 217.

29 M. Astell, *Some Reflections Upon Marriage* (New York, Source Book Press, 1970), p. 88.

30 Lady Chudleigh, 'To the Ladies', in *The Whole Duty of a Woman: Female Writers in Seventeenth-Century England*, ed. A. Goreau (New York, The Dial Press, 1985), p. 273.

31   D. Defoe, *Conjugal Lewdness; or, Matrimonial Whoredom. A Treatise concerning the Use and Abuse of the Marriage Bed* (Gainesville, Florida, Scholars' Facsimilies and Reprints, 1967 [originally published 1727]), p. 26.

32   M. Wollstonecraft, *A Vindication of the Rights of Woman*, ed. C. Poston (New York, W. W. Norton and Co., 1975 [1792]), p. 40.

33   T. Veblen, *The Theory of the Leisure Class* (New York, The Modern Library, 1934), p. 182.

34   Genovese, *Roll, Jordan, Roll*, esp. pp. 70–86; 123–49.

35   Cited in P. Hollis, *Women in Public 1850–1900: Documents of the Victorian Women's Movement* (London, George Allen and Unwin, 1979), p. 12.

36   L. Davidoff, 'Mastered for Life: Servant and Wife in Victorian and Edwardian England', *Journal of Social History*, 7 (1974), pp. 410–11; 420.

37   L. J. Weitzman, *The Marriage Contract: Spouses, Lovers, and the Law* (New York, The Free Press, 1981), p. 60.

38   Report in *Sydney Morning Herald* (15 March 1982).

39   Cited in Corrigan, 'Feudal Relics', p. 454, note 19.

40   See F. E. Dudden, *Serving Women: Household Service in Nineteenth Century America* (Middleton, CT, Wesleyan University Press, 1983), intro.

41   See B. Kingston, *My Wife, My Daughter, and Poor Mary Ann: Women and Work in Australia* (Melbourne, Nelson, 1975), ch. 3.

42   For Cullwick's account see L. Stanley (ed.), *The Diaries of Hannah Cullwick: Victorian Maidservant* (London, Virago Press, 1984). Also, L. Davidoff, 'Class and Gender in Victorian England: The Diaries of Arthur J. Munby and Hannah Cullwick', *Feminist Studies*, 5, 1 (1979), pp. 86–141. Hannah Cullwick offered a remarkable contrast to the (cross-class) ideal of womanhood centered on the wife as a dependent in the home. A physically very strong, vigorous working-class woman, she would threaten 'over-familiar males with her fists' (and other working women were observed intimidating passing men). She wrote in her diary in May 1871 of Arthur Munby, that 'I can heave my Master easy & carry him as if he was a child nearly, & he's 11 stone 7 lbs' (Stanley, *The Diaries*, pp. 2, 167).

43   Davidoff, 'Mastered for Life', pp. 409–10.

44   A. Oakley, *The Sociology of Housework* (London, Martin Robertson, 1974), p. 49.

45   J. Finch, *Married to the Job: Wives' Incorporation in Men's Work* (London, George Allen and Unwin, 1983). Finch (pp. 132–3) provides eight rules for women to follow who wish to marry but to avoid incorporation in their husbands' work.

46   C. Delphy, *Close to Home: A Materialist Analysis of Women's Oppression*, tr. D. Leonard (Amherst, University of Massachusetts Press, 1984), pp. 87–9.

47 H. Hartmann, 'The Family as the Locus of Gender, Class, and Political Struggle: The Example of Housework', *Signs*, 6, 3 (1981), pp. 388–9; see also A. Oakley, *Housewife* (Harmondsworth, Penguin Books, 1976), p. 7, table A.

48 Oakley, *Housewife*, p. 6; *Sociology of Housework*, pp. 92–3.

49 S. F. Berk, *The Gender Factory: The Apportionment of Work in American Households* (New York, Plenum Press, 1985), p. 161.

50 Hartmann, 'Family as Locus', pp. 378–9; 382–3.

51 Davidoff, 'Mastered for Life', p. 419.

52 Delphy, *Close to Home*, p. 70.

53 For a feminist critique of Orwell, see D. Patai, *The Orwell Mystique: A Study in Male Ideology* (Amherst, University of Massachusetts Press, 1984), esp. ch. 3. Beatrix Campbell has retrodden the road to Wigan Pier; see *Wigan Pier Revisited: Poverty and Politics in the 80s* (London, Virago Press, 1984).

54 This aspect of housework was the most highly valued by Oakley's respondents; over half the sample referred to being 'your own boss'; Oakley, *Sociology of Housework*, pp. 42, 182; and *Housewife*, ch. 6.

55 Figure from H. Land, 'The Family Wage', *Feminist Review*, 6 (1980), p. 61.

56 G. A. Cohen, 'The Structure of Proletarian Unfreedom', *Philosophy and Public Affairs*, 12, 1 (1983), p. 12.

57 Thompson, *Appeal*, p. 57.

58 C. Hamilton, *Marriage as a Trade* (London, The Women's Press, 1981), p. 27.

59 In Britain, for example, in 1901, 88 per cent of women worked in occupations dominated by women; in 1971, 84 per cent did so. In the United States today 80 per cent of women's jobs are located in only 20 of the 420 occupations listed by the Department of Labor, and in Australia in 1986, in only 69 out of 267 occupational categories did the proportion of women reach a third or more.

60 Cited in W. Leach, *True Love and Perfect Union: The Feminist Reform of Sex and Society* (New York, Basic Books, 1980), p. 192.

61 P. Rothenberg, 'The Political Nature of Relations between the Sexes', in *Beyond Domination: New Perspectives on Women and Philosophy*, ed. C. C. Gould (Totowa, NJ, Rowman and Allanheld, 1984), p. 213.

62 H. Hartmann, 'The Unhappy Marriage of Marxism and Feminism: Towards a More Progressive Union', in *Women and Revolution*, ed. L. Sargent (Boston, South End Press, 1981), p. 15.

63 C. Delphy, *Close to Home*, pp. 94, 95.

64 F. Engels, *The Origin of the Family, Private Property and the State* (New York, International Publishers, 1942), pp. 58, 65–6.

65 The domestic labour debate can be followed in E. Malos (ed.), *The Politics of Housework* (London, Alison and Busby, 1980).

66 See B. Taylor, *Eve and the New Jerusalem* (London, Virago Press, 1983), esp. ch. VIII.

67 I have taken the term 'employment society' from J. Keane and J. Owens, *After Full Employment* (London, Hutchinson, 1986). I have explored the link between work, masculinity and citizenship in 'The Patriarchal Welfare State', in *Democracy and the Welfare State*, ed. A. Gutmann (Princeton, Princeton University Press, 1987).

68 Cited in Cohen, 'The Structure of Proletarian Unfreedom', p. 13. (From Brecht's 'Song of the United Front').

69 See D. Deacon, 'Political Arithmetic: The Nineteenth-Century Australian Census and the Construction of the Dependent Woman', *Signs*, 11, 1 (1985); the quotation is from p. 34.

70 M. Barrett and M. McIntosh, 'The "Family Wage": Some Problems for Socialists and Feminists', *Capital and Class*, 11 (1980), p. 51.

71 I owe this point to J. W. Scott, ' "L'Ouvrièr! Mot impie, sordide . . .": Women Workers in the Discourse of French Political Economy (1840–1860)', in *The Historical Meanings of Work*, ed. P. Joyce (Cambridge, Cambridge University Press, forthcoming).

72 A. Hacker, ' "Welfare": The Future of an Illusion', *New York Review of Books* (28 February 1985), p. 41.

73 Campbell, *Wigan Pier Revisited*, p. 101.

74 Cited in Land, 'The Family Wage', p. 58.

75 Cited in S. Okin, *Women in Western Political Thought* (Princeton, Princeton University Press, 1979), p. 258; and A. C. Hill, 'Protection of Women Workers and the Courts; A Legal Case History', *Feminist Studies*, 5, 2 (1979), p. 253.

76 M. Porter, *Home, Work and Class Consciousness* (Manchester, Manchester University Press, 1983), p. 123. Forty-two per cent of the male workers interviewed in a Queensland mining town regarded it as the husband's prerogative to decide if a wife should work, only 28 per cent of wives agreed; C. Williams, *Open Cut: The Working Class in an Australian Mining Town* (Sydney, George Allen and Unwin, 1981), p. 149. On outwork, see S. Allen and C. Wolkowitz, 'The Control of Women's Labour: The Case of Homeworking', *Feminist Review*, 22 (1986), esp. p. 41. Recent feminist investigations of outwork and the 'informal' economy suggest that the number of full-time housewives in the past has been overestimated.

77 J. Smith, 'The Paradox of Women's Poverty: Wage-Earning Women and Economic Transformation', *Signs*, 10, 2 (1984), p. 304.

78 Hartmann, 'Family as Locus', p. 379. In the Old South, married women (slave) field-hands also worked longer than their husbands, undertaking household tasks when they left the field; Genovese, *Roll, Jordan, Roll*, p. 495.

79 Porter, *Home, Work and Class Consciousness*, p. 128.

80 C. Cockburn, *Brothers: Male Dominance and Technological Change* (London, Pluto Press, 1983), p. 17; on skill, see pp. 112–22.

81 A. Pollert, *Girls, Wives and Factory Lives* (London, Macmillan, 1981), p. 111.

82 Porter, *Home, Work and Class Consciousness*, p. 124.

83 J. Wajcman, *Women in Control: Dilemmas of a Workers' Cooperative* (New York, St Martin's Press, 1983), pp. 149, 154, 137.

84 Cockburn, *Brothers*, p. 134.

85 Pollert, *Girls, Wives and Factory Lives*, p. 140.

86 Cited in J. Walvin, *Black and White: The Negro and English Society 1555–1945* (London, Allen Lane The Penguin Press, 1973), p. 50.

87 Cited in Walvin, p. 39. Walvin discusses the number of slaves on pp. 46–50.

88 Cited in Walvin, pp. 111, 112.

89 Cited in Davis, *The Problem of Slavery in the Age of Revolution, 1770–1823* (Ithaca and London, Cornell University Press, 1975), p. 488.

90 The case for Blackstone's tergiversation is made in F. O. Shyllon, *Black Slaves in Britain* (London, Oxford University Press, for the Institute of Race Relations, 1974), ch. 5. Shyllon provides details of textual changes and dates of publication of the various editions.

91 Sir W. Blackstone, *Commentaries on the Laws of England*, 4th edn, ed. J. DeWitt Andrews (Chicago, Callaghan and Company, 1899), vol. I, bk I, ch. 14, pp. 424–5.

92 J. Feinberg, 'Legal Paternalism', *Canadian Journal of Philosophy*, 1, 1 (1971), p. 121.

93 G. W. F. Hegel, *Philosophy of Right*, tr. T. M. Knox (Oxford, Oxford University Press, 1952), §67.

94 Williams, *Open Cut*, p. 116.

95 R. Edwards, *Contested Terrain: The Transformation of the Workplace in the Twentieth Century* (New York, Basic Books, 1979), pp. 139–41.

96 K. Marx, *Grundrisse: Foundations of the Critique of Political Economy*, tr. M. Nicolaus, London, Allen Lane, 1973), pp. 274–5.

97 H. Benyon, *Working for Ford* (Harmondsworth, Penguin Books, 1973), p. 253.

98 A Fox, *Beyond Contract: Work, Power and Trust Relations* (London, Faber and Faber, 1974), p. 183.

99 K. Marx, 'Critique of the Gotha Program', in *The Marx-Engels Reader*. 2nd edn, ed. R. C. Tucker (New York, W. W. Norton and Co., 1978), p. 535 [my emphasis].

100 C. Arthur, 'Personality and the Dialectic of Labour and Property – Locke, Hegel, Marx', *Radical Philosophy*, 26 (1980), p. 14.

101 T. H. Green, 'Lecture on "Liberal Legislation and Freedom of Contract"', in *Lectures on the Principle of Political Obligation and Other*

Writings, ed. P. Harris and J. Morrow (Cambridge, Cambridge University Press, 1986), pp. 201, 204–5.

102 H. Gintis and S. Bowles, 'Structure and Practice in the Labor Theory of Value', *The Review of Radical Political Economics*, 12, 4 (1981), pp. 14–15.

103 A. A. Alchian and H. Demsetz, 'Production, Information Costs, and Economic Organization', *The American Economic Review*, 62 (1972), pp. 794–5, 782–3.

6 Feminism and the Marriage Contract

1 Cited in E. Griffith, *In Her Own Right: The Life of Elizabeth Cady Stanton* (New York, Oxford University Press, 1984), p. 104.

2 M. McMurtry, 'Monogamy: A Critique', in *Philosophy and Sex*, ed. R. Baker and F. Elliston, (Buffalo, Prometheus Books, 1975), p. 173.

3 M. M. Shultz, 'Contractual Ordering of Marriage: A New Model for State Policy', *California Law Review*, 70, 2 (1982), p. 311. (I am grateful to Herma Hill Kay for drawing this article to my attention.)

4 Sir W. Blackstone, *Commentaries on the Laws of England*, 4th edn, ed. J. Dewitt Andrews (Chicago, Callaghan and Company, 1899), vol. I, bk I, ch. XV, p. 433.

5 The terms 'intimate contract' and 'marriage contracting' are used by, respectively, L. J. Weitzman, *The Marriage Contract: Spouses, Lovers, and the Law* (New York, Free Press, 1981); and Shultz, 'Contractual Ordering of Marriage'.

6 J. Shouler, *A Treatise on the Law of the Domestic Relations*, 2nd edn (Boston, Little Brown and Comany, 1874), pt II, ch. 1, p. 23.

7 Cited in Shultz, 'Contractual Ordering of Marriage', p. 226, note 45.

8 P. Atiyah, *The Rise and Fall of Freedom of Contract* (Oxford, Clarendon Press, 1979), p. 759.

9 Blackstone, *Commentaries*, bk I, ch. 15, p. 442.

10 W. Thompson, *Appeal of One Half the Human Race, Women, Against the Pretensions of the Other Half, Men, to Retain them in Political, and Thence in Civil and Domestic, Slavery* (New York, Source Book Press, 1970), p. 172.

11 Ibid., p. 201.

12 Ibid., p. 60.

13 Ibid., pp. 55–6.

14 C. Delphy, *Close to Home: A Materialist Analysis of Women's Oppression* (Amherst, University of Massachusetts Press, 1984), p. 116.

15 Thompson, *Appeal*, pp. 79, 84. Compare one of Clarissa's objections to marriage, S. Richardson, *Clarissa* (Harmondsworth, Penguin Books, 1985 [1747–8]) letter 32, p. 149.

16 Thompson, *Appeal*, p. 89.
17 Ibid., p. 65–6.
18 Ibid., pp. 104–5.
19 Ibid., p. 62.
20 T. Ball, 'Utilitarianism, Feminism, and the Franchise: James Mill and His Critics', *History of Political Thought*, 1, 1 (1980), p. 115.
21 Trilling is cited by Alice Rossi in her 'Introduction' to J. S. Mill and H. Taylor Mill, *Essays on Sex Equality* (Chicago, University of Chicago Press, 1970), p. 35; and G. Himmelfarb, *On Liberty and Liberalism* (New York, Alfred A. Knopf, 1974), chs 9, 10.
22 Thompson, *Appeal*, p. vii.
23 Cited by Rossi in Mill and Taylor Mill, *Essays on Sex Equality*, pp. 45–6.
24 J. S. Mill, 'The Subjection of Women', in *Essays on Sex Equality*, p. 158.
25 Ibid., pp. 168–70.
26 Ibid., pp. 178–9.
27 H. Taylor Mill, 'The Enfranchisement of Women', in *Essays on Sex Equality*, pp. 104–5.
28 For examples of feminist argument, in addition to Weitzman, *Marriage Contract*; and Shultz, 'Contractual Ordering of Marriage'; see S. A. Ketchum, 'Liberalism and Marriage Law', in *Feminism and Philosophy* ed. M. Vetterling-Braggin, F. A. Elliston and J. English (Totowa, NJ, Littlefield, Adams, 1977); and D. L. Barker, 'The Regulation of Marriage: Repressive Benevolence', in *Power and the State*, ed. G. Littlejohn, B. Smart, J. Wakeford and N. Yuval-Davis (London, Croom Helm, 1978). For a discussion of the empirical evidence on the deleterious effects of marriage for women, see J. Bernard, *The Future of Marriage* (New York, Bantam Books, 1974).
29 See Weitzman, *Marriage Contract*, p. xvii.
30 I. Kant, *The Philosophy of Law*, tr. W. Hastie (Edinburgh, T. and T. Clark, 1887), chapter second, §27, p. 113.
31 Weitzman, *Marriage Contract*, p. 338.
32 Barker, 'Regulation of Marriage', p. 242.
33 Mill, 'Subjection of Women', pp. 217, 146, 142–3.
34 M. L. Shanley, 'Marriage Contract and Social Contract in Seventeenth-Century English Political Thought, *Western Political Quarterly*, 32, 1 (1979), p. 79.
35 Barker, 'Regulation of Marriage', p. 254.
36 Weitzman, *Marriage Contract*, p. xix.
37 Shultz, 'Contractual Ordering of Marriage', pp. 303–4, and p. 248, footnote 373.
38 Kant, *Philosophy of Law*, §24, p. 110.
39 J. Locke, *Two Treatises of Government*, ed. P. Laslett (Cambridge, Cambridge University Press, 1967), II, §78.

40 I. Kant, 'Observations on the Feeling of the Beautiful and Sublime', in *Woman in Western Thought*, ed. M. L. Osborne, (New York, Random House, 1979), p. 157.

41 H. Williams, *Kant's Political Philosophy* (Oxford, Basil Blackwell, 1983), p. 121.

42 I. Kant, *Political Writings*, ed. H. Reiss (Cambridge, Cambridge University Press, 1970), p. 78. This edition of Kant's writings is very widely used, and the book provides interesting confirmation that conjugal right is still seen as outside the 'public' matters properly discussed by political theorists – sections dealing with 'private right', including marriage, are omitted from the extracts from *The Metaphysics of Morals* (*The Philosophy of Law*), whereas sections on 'public right' are included.

43 Ibid., p. 139.

44 Ibid., p. 76.

45 Kant, *Philosophy of Law*, chapter second, third section, §22, p. 108.

46 Ibid., §23, p. 109.

47 I. Kant, *Lectures on Ethics*, tr. L. Infield (New York, Harper and Row, 1963), p. 164.

48 Kant, *Philosophy of Law*, §25, p. 111.

49 Kant, *Lectures on Ethics*, pp. 166–7.

50 Kant, *Philosophy of Law*, §24, p. 110.

51 Kant, *Lectures on Ethics*, p. 167.

52 Kant, *Philosophy of Law*, p. 239.

53 Ibid., §26, pp. 111–12.

54 Ibid., §25, pp. 111.

55 Ibid., 'Supplementary Explanations of the Principles of Right', p. 238, footnote 1.

56 G. W. F. Hegel, *Philosophy of Right*, tr. T. M. Knox (Oxford, Clarendon Press, 1952), §75, and addition to §161.

57 Ibid., §75.

58 Ibid., §163.

59 Ibid., §162.

60 Ibid., §163.

61 Ibid., addition to §161.

62 Ibid., addition to §158.

63 E. Durkheim, *The Division of Labor in Society* (New York, Free Press, 1964), p. 381.

64 Hegel, *Philosophy of Right*, §167.

65 Ibid., §165.

66 Ibid., §166 and addition.

67 Ibid., §171.

68 G. W. F. Hegel, *Phenomenology of Spirit*, tr. A. V. Miller (Oxford, Oxford University Press, 1977), §475, p. 288.

69 Hegel, *Philosophy of Right*, addition to §166.
70 Durkheim, *Division of Labor*, p. 204.
71 Cited in B. Ehrenreich and D. English, *For Her Own Good: 150 Years of the Experts' Advice to Women* (New York, Anchor Press, 1978), p. 276. On the advice manuals see E. Ross, ' "The Love Crisis": Couples Advice Books of Late 1970s', *Signs*, 6, 1, (1980) pp. 109–22.
72 B. Barber, *Liberating Feminism* (New York, The Seabury Press, 1975), pp. 62–3.
73 For a fascinating study of the divorces obtained under private Acts (applicants included clergymen, who were conspicuous among adulterers), see S. Wolfram, 'Divorce in England 1700–1857', *Oxford Journal of Legal Studies*, 5, 2, (1985), pp. 155–86.
74 Delphy, *Close to Home*, p. 102.
75 G. S. Becker, 'A Theory of Marriage: Part II', *Journal of Political Economy*, 82, 2, pt II, (1974), p. 12.
76 Shultz, 'Contractual Ordering of Marriage', p. 280.
77 P. Califia, 'Feminism and Sadomasochism', *Heresies*, 12 (1981), p. 31. For further discussion and references see 'Forum: The Feminist Sexuality Debates', *Signs*, 10, 1 (1984), pp. 106–35.
78 Califia, 'Feminism and Sadomasochism', p. 32.
79 Passages cited in A. Carter, *The Sadeian Woman and the Ideology of Pornography* (New York, Harper and Row, 1980), pp. 119, 98.
80 Califia, 'Feminism and Sadomasochism', p. 32.
81 The point is emphasized by J. Benjamin, 'The Bonds of Love: Rational Violence and Erotic Domination', *Feminist Studies*, 6, 1 (1980), p. 157.

7 What's Wrong with Prostitution?

1 E. McLeod, *Women Working: Prostitution Now* (London and Canberra, Croom Helm, 1982), pp. 12–13; table 1.1.
2 Figure cited in M. A. Jennings, 'The Victim as Criminal: A Consideration of California's Prostitution Law', *California Law Review*, 64, 5 (1976), p. 1251.
3 Cited in *San Francisco Examiner* (3 February 1985).
4 McLeod, *Women Working*, p. 43.
5 M. Wollstonecraft, 'A Vindication of the Rights of Men' in *A Mary Wollstonecraft Reader*, ed. B. H. Solomon and P. S. Berggren (New York, New American Library, 1983), p. 247. She also uses the phrase in *A Vindication of the Rights of Woman* (New York, W. W. Norton and Co., 1975) [1792]), p. 148. According to her biographer Clair Tomalin, Wollstonecraft was the first to use the phrase 'legal prostitution' to refer to marriage.

6   E. Goldman, 'The Traffic in Women', in *Anarchism and Other Essays* (New York, Dover Publications, 1969), p. 179.

7   S. de Beauvoir, *The Second Sex*, tr. H. M. Parshley, (New York, Vintage Books, 1974), p. 619.

8   C. Hamilton, *Marriage as a Trade* (London, The Women's Press, 1981), p. 37.

9   They are so instructed by J. Radcliffe Richards, *The Sceptical Feminist: A Philosophical Enquiry* (Harmondsworth, Penguin Books, 1980), p. 246.

10 D. A. J. Richards, *Sex, Drugs, Death, and the Law: An Essay on Human Rights and Decriminalization*, (Totowa, NJ, Rowman and Littlefield, 1982), p. 121.

11 The term is used by L. Ericcson, 'Charges Against Prostitution: An Attempt at a Philosophical Assessment', *Ethics*, 90 (1980), pp. 335–66.

12 D. A. J. Richards, *Sex, Drugs, Death, and the Law*, p. 115; also p. 108.

13 Ericcson, 'Charges Against Prostitution', p. 342.

14 The example comes from M. McIntosh, 'Who Needs Prostitutes? The Ideology of Male Sexual Needs', in *Women, Sexuality and Social Control*, ed. C. Smart and B. Smart (London, Routledge and Kegan Paul, 1978), p. 54.

15 M. Frye, *The Politics of Reality: Essays in Feminist Theory* (Trumansburg, NY, The Crossing Press, 1983), p. 143. Where men are confined together and prevented from obtaining access to women (as in prison) the 'taboo' is not observed; masculinity is then exhibited by using other men, usually young men, as if they were women.

16 Ericcson, 'Charges Against Prostitution', p. 363, argues (unconvincingly) that 'paternalism' does not conflict with his contractual defence of sound adult prostitution and that prostitution by minors should be prevented. He poses the problem as one of the causes (the supply) of child prostitutes, but fails to mention the problem of the *demand*. Why do men demand to have sexual relations with (sometimes very young) children? Why do resorts like Pagsanjan in the Philippines exist to cater for this demand? This question falls outside my concerns here, but a recent survey of investigations of 'incest' (father–daughter is the most common form) notes that in conjugal relations, 'many men are accustomed to the experience of sex with a weaker and unwilling partner': W. Breines and L. Gordon, 'The New Scholarship on Family Violence', *Signs*, 8, 3 (1983), p. 527.

17 Cited E. McLeod, 'Man-Made Laws for Men? The Street Prostitutes' Campaign Against Control', in *Controlling Women: The Normal and the Deviant*, ed. B. Hutter and G. Williams (London, Croom Helm, 1981), p. 63.

18 Cited in E. M. Sigsworth and T. J. Wyke, 'A Study of Victorian Prostitution and Venereal Disease', in *Suffer and Be Still: Women in the Victorian Age*, ed. M. Vicinus, (Bloomington, Indiana University

Press, 1972), p. 181. Contemporary prostitutes may still receive food from 'regulars' if, for example, he is a baker, see McLeod, *Women Working*, p. 6.

19 McLeod, *Women Working*, pp. 17, 20; tables 1.2(a), 1.2(b), 1.3.

20 Ericcson, 'Charges Against Prostitution', p. 348.

21 D. A. J. Richards, *Sex, Drugs, Death, and the Law*, p. 88. For a different view of temple prostitution, see G. Lerner, *The Creation of Patriarchy*, (New York, Oxford, Oxford University Press, 1986), chapter 6.

22 On *maisons d'abbatages* see K. Barry, *Female Sexual Slavery* (Englewood Cliffs, Prentice Hall, 1979), pp. 3–4; 80–3. The *malaya* form flourished in Nairobi before the Second World War, and is discussed by L.White, 'Prostitution, Identity and Class Consciousness in Nairobi during World War II', *Signs*, II, 2 (1986), pp. 255–73. Working men in Nairobi could not support their wives if they left their farms to come to the city to join their husbands, and the colonial administration did not supply sufficient accommodation for labourers. The men visited *malaya* prostitutes who 'provided bed space – cleaning, cooking, bath water, companionship, hot meals, cold meals, and tea, and . . . men who spent the night . . . received breakfast' (p. 256). How should these services be categorized; as an enlarged prostitution contract or a truncated marriage contract?

23 On Britain, see J. R. Walkowitz, *Prostitution and Victorian Society: Women, Class and the State*, (Cambridge, Cambridge University Press, 1980); on the United States, see R. Rosen, *The Lost Sisterhood: Prostitution in America, 1900–1918*, (Baltimore and London. The Johns Hopkins University Press, 1982); on New South Wales, see J. Allen, 'The Making of a Prostitute Proletariat in Early Twentieth-Century New South Wales', in *So Much Hard Work: Women and Prostitution in Australian History*, ed. K. Daniels (Sydney, Fontana Books, 1984).

24 Cited in M. Trustram, 'Distasteful and Derogatory? Examining Victorian Soldiers for Venereal Disease', in *The Sexual Dynamics of History*, ed. The London Feminist History Group, (London, Pluto Press, 1983,) pp. 62–3. At present AIDS is provoking a similar response; for example a Bill has been presented to the Nevada legislature to allow murder charges to be brought against prostitutes who have the disease and continued to work. No mention is made of their male customers in the report that I read in *Washington Post* (24 April 1987).

25 J. E. Butler, *An Autobiographical Memoir*, 3rd edn (London, J. W. Arrowsmith, 1928), p. 215.

26 Walkowitz, *Prostitution and Victorian Society*, p. 212.

27 Allen, 'The Making of a Prostitute Proletariat', p. 213.

28 Rosen, *Lost Sisterhood*, p. xii. Rosen (p. 172) also notes new hazards

facing American prostitutes today, such as being used by the CIA to extract information or in experiments with drugs.

29 McLeod, *Women Working*, p. 51.

30 For this use of the phrase, see, e.g., J. R. Richards, *The Sceptical Feminist*, p. 244.

31 Ericcson, 'Charges Against Prostitution', p. 341. Compare D. A. J. Richards, *Sex, Drugs, Death, and the Law*, p. 49.

32 McLeod, *Women Working*, p. 69. The men give a variety of reasons, all of which beg the question of the capitalist virtue of self-help.

33 In the 1930s in the United States, only 10 per cent of customers demanded oral sex; by the 1960s nearly 90 per cent did so, either instead of or in addition to intercourse (figures cited by R. Rosen, *The Lost Sisterhood*), p. 97. Could it be conjectured that men's current widespread demand to buy women's bodies to penetrate their mouths is connected to the revitalization of the feminist movement and women's demand to speak?

34 McLeod, *Women Working*, p. 53.

35 A. Jaggar, 'Prostitution', in *The Philosophy of Sex: Contemporary Readings*, ed. A. Soble (Totowa, NJ, Rowman and Littlefield, 1980), p. 360.

36 K. Marx, *Economic and Philosophic Manuscripts of 1844*, ed. D. J. Struik (New York, International Publishers, 1964), p. 133, footnote.

37 J. H. Reiman, 'Prostitution, Addiction and the Ideology of Liberalism', *Contemporary Crises*, 3 (1979), p. 66.

38 Ericcson, 'Charges Against Prostitution', p. 351.

39 Ibid., p. 341.

40 I. Kant, *The Philosophy of Law*, tr. W. Hastie (Edinburgh, T. and T. Clark, 1887), third section, §26, p. 112; cf. I. Kant, *Lectures on Ethics*, tr. L. Infield, (New York, Harper and Row, 1963), p. 166.

41 Kant, *Lectures on Ethics*, p. 165.

42 D. A. J. Richards, *Sex, Drugs, Death, and the Law*, p. 109.

43 O. Patterson, *Slavery and Social Death: A Comparative Study* (Cambridge, MA and London, Harvard University Press, 1982), p. 25.

44 McLeod, *Women Working*, p. 84.

45 J. S. Mill, 'The Subjection of Women', in *Essays on Sex Equality*, ed. A. S. Rossi (Chicago and London, University of Chicago Press, 1970), p. 141.

46 I owe thanks to Mary Douglas for drawing my attention to this point.

47 See V. Stolcke, 'Old Values, New Technologies: Who Is the Father?', paper presented to the Kolloquium am Wissenschaftskolleg zu Berlin, March 1987, p. 6. (My thanks to Verena Stolcke for sending me a copy of the paper.)

48 Information from D. Brahams, 'The Hasty British Ban on Commercial Surrogacy', *Hastings Center Report*, February 1987,

pp. 16–19. (Lionel Gossman kindly supplied me with a copy of this paper.)

49 The Committee to Consider the Social, Ethical and Legal Issues Arising from In Vitro Fertilization, *Report on the Disposition of Embryos Produced by In Vitro Fertilization*, (Victoria, August 1984), §4.17. (I am grateful to Rebecca Albury for sending me a copy of the relevant part of the *Report.*)

50 *The New York Times* (5 April 1987).

51 Information from *The New York Times* (12 January 1987).

52 Committee to Consider In Vitro Fertilization, *Report on the Disposition of Embryos*, §4.6; §4.11.

53 Cited in excerpts from the decision by Judge Harvey R. Sorkow, printed in *The New York Times* (1 April 1987).

54 *Genesis* 16:2, 3; *Genesis* 30:4.

8 The End of the Story?

1 In a letter from a settler to Colonel Macquarie in London; cited in A. Summers, *Damned Whores and God's Police: The Colonization of Women in Australia* (Harmondsworth, Penguin Books, 1975), p. 269.

2 Cited in R. Hayman, *Nietzsche: A Critical Life* (Harmondsworth, Penguin Books, 1982), p. 360.

Index